THE URBANA FREE LIBRARY

3 1230 00834 5643

The Urbana Free Library

To renew: call 217-367-4057
or go to "*urbanafreelibrary.org*"
and select "Renew/Request Items"

THE FOCUS ON THE FAMILY® GUIDE TO
TALKING WITH YOUR KIDS ABOUT SEX

DISCARDED BY THE
URBANA FREE LIBRARY

THE FOCUS ON THE FAMILY® GUIDE

to Talking with Your Kids about Sex

HONEST ANSWERS *for* EVERY AGE

THE PHYSICIANS RESOURCE COUNCIL

J. THOMAS FITCH, MD,
AND DAVID DAVIS, EDITORS

Revell

a division of Baker Publishing Group
Grand Rapids, Michigan

© 2005, 2013 by the Medical Institute for Sexual Health

Portions of this book originally appeared in *Questions Kids Ask About Sex*, published by Fleming H. Revell.

Published by Revell
a division of Baker Publishing Group
P.O. Box 6287, Grand Rapids, MI 49516–6287
www.revellbooks.com

Printed in the United States of America

All rights reserved. No part of this publication may be reproduced, stored in a retrieval system, or transmitted in any form or by any means—for example, electronic, photocopy, recording—without the prior written permission of the publisher. The only exception is brief quotations in printed reviews.

Library of Congress Cataloging-in-Publication Data
Questions kids ask about sex.
    The Focus on the family guide to talking with your kids about sex : honest answers for every age / The Physicians Resource Council, J. Thomas Fitch, MD and David Davis, editors.—Revised edition.
        pages cm
    "Portions of this book originally appeared in Questions Kids Ask About Sex, published by Fleming H. Revell."
    Includes bibliographical references and index.
    Summary: "This candid resource is full of the latest information, practical insights, and age-appropriate answers to the questions kids ask about sex"— Provided by publisher.
    ISBN 978-0-8007-2228-9 (pbk. : alk. paper)
    1. Sex instruction for children. 2. Sex instruction for youth. 3. Sex instruction. I. Fitch, J. Thomas. II. Physicians Resource Council. III. Title.
HQ57.Q47 2013
649'.65—dc23   2013023241

All Scripture quotations are taken from the HOLY BIBLE, NEW INTERNATIONAL VERSION®. Copyright © 1973, 1978, 1984 Biblica. Used by permission of Zondervan. All rights reserved.

The information in this book is intended solely as an educational resource, not a tool to be used for medical diagnosis or treatment. The information presented is in no way a substitute for consultation with a personal health care professional. Readers should consult their personal health care professional before adopting any of the suggestions in this book or drawing inferences from the text. The author(s) and publisher specifically disclaim all responsibility for any liability, loss, or risk, personal or otherwise, which is incurred as a consequence, directly or indirectly, of the use of and/or application of any of the contents of this book.

In keeping with biblical principles of creation stewardship, Baker Publishing Group advocates the responsible use of our natural resources. As a member of the Green Press Initiative, our company uses recycled paper when possible. The text paper of this book is composed in part of post-consumer waste.

13 14 15 16 17 18 19   7 6 5 4 3 2 1

CONTENTS

Contents

ACKNOWLEDGMENTS

This book would not have been possible without the tireless efforts of all the individuals involved. Thanks to the Medical Institute for Sexual Health, along with the following individuals for their contribution and passion to help motivate parents to talk with their children about sex.

Medical Institute Writing Team

Melissa R. Cox, Highlands Ranch, Colorado

J. Thomas Fitch, MD, Pediatrics, San Antonio, Texas

Patricia Francis, MD, Pediatrics, Moraga, California

Wilson Wayne Grant, MD, Pediatrics, San Antonio, Texas

Marilyn A. Maxwell, MD, Internal Medicine/Pediatrics, St. Louis, Missouri

Joe S. McIlhaney Jr., MD, Obstetrics/Gynecology, Austin, Texas

Margaret J. Meeker, MD, Pediatrics, Traverse City, Michigan

Paul A. Warren, MD, Behavioral Pediatrics, Plano, Texas

Focus on the Family Writing and Editorial Team

David Davis, Colorado Springs, Colorado

John Duckworth, Colorado Springs, Colorado

Jim Ware, Colorado Springs, Colorado

Contributors

W. David Hager, MD, Obstetrics/Gynecology, Lexington, Kentucky
Joneen Krauth Mackenzie, RN, BSN, WAIT Training, Denver, Colorado
Lynn Lutz, PhD, Dallas, Texas
Mary Anne Nelson, MD, Cedar Rapids, Iowa
Curtis C. Stine, MD, Tallahassee, Florida

Research Editor

Anjum Khurshid, MBBS, MPAFF, MA, the Medical Institute, Austin, Texas

Reviewers

Lisa Beck, Colorado Springs, Colorado
Reed Bell, MD, Pensacola, Florida
Steven Brown, MD, Midland, Texas
Christina Browning, LCSW, Colorado Springs, Colorado
Byron Calhoun, MD, Charleston, West Virginia
Joann Condie, RN, LPC, Colorado Springs, Colorado
Cynthia Barlow Dervaes, LPC, Colorado Springs, Colorado
Freda McKissic Bush, MD, Jackson, Mississippi
Kate Hendricks, MD, MPH, Austin, Texas
Beverly Henry, LCSW, Colorado Springs, Colorado
Leanna Hollis, MD, Blue Springs, Mississippi
Daniel Huerta, MSW, LCSW, Colorado Springs, Colorado
Jeff Johnston, Colorado Springs, Colorado
Gaylen M. Kelton, MD, Indianapolis, Indiana
Grace Ogbeche, MBBS, MPH, Austin, Texas
David Roper, San Antonio, Texas
Brooke Spencer, San Antonio, Texas
Lynne Tingle, PhD, Charlotte, North Carolina

About the Medical Institute
for Sexual Health

This book is a resource from Focus on the Family, which is responsible for its content. We have relied heavily, however, on input from the Medical Institute for Sexual Health (MI), especially regarding medical, scientific, and statistical information.

MI is a nonprofit organization that promotes healthy sexuality (physically, emotionally, socially, and psychologically) for all ages—rooted in credible science, in an attempt to combat the damaging effects of the casual-sex culture that has infected our society.

MI identifies, evaluates, and communicates scientific data in understandable, practical, dynamic formats to promote healthy sexual decisions and behavior. It distributes almost one hundred thousand pieces of material each year to individuals and organizations across the United States and throughout the world, and maintains a national advisory board of medical doctors, counselors, psychologists, educators, and parents.

Leaders at the Centers for Disease Control, the US Health and Human Services Department, the White House, and state-level government offices, as well as educators and parents across the nation, have sought advice from the Medical Institute about sexual issues affecting our nation's teens. You can reach MI at 1101 S. Capital of Texas Highway, Building B, Suite 100, Austin, TX 78746. To order resources, contact www.medinstitute.org or call 512–328–6268 weekdays, 8 a.m. to 5 p.m. (central time). You can also reach the Medical Institute by email at medinstitute@medinstitute.org or on the web at www.medinstitute.org/contact/contact.htm.

Editor

Melissa Cox is vice-president of Cox Creative, Inc., a full-service marketing and advertising firm in Denver. Previously she served the Medical Institute for Sexual Health as director of marketing and public relations. She also was editor of Focus on the Family's *Physician* magazine and managing editor of the bestselling *Complete Book of Baby and Child Care* (Focus on the Family/Tyndale, 1997).

Medical Institute Writing Team

J. Thomas Fitch, MD, is a retired pediatrician in San Antonio, Texas, who practiced for over forty years. He's especially interested in helping parents of adolescents understand how they can help their children avoid risk-taking behaviors like alcohol and drug use as well as nonmarital sexual activity. He's become a national authority on condom effectiveness and was an expert member of the National Institutes of Health Condom Effectiveness Panel. As past president of the Texas Pediatric Society, he's given numerous professional presentations to colleagues and has been published in a variety of periodicals. Dr. Fitch previously served as a clinical professor in the department of pediatrics at the University of Texas Health Sciences Center in San Antonio, Texas. A content editor for *Complete Book of Baby and Child Care* and member of Focus on the Family's Physician Resource Council, he has served as the chairman of the Medical Institute's board of directors.

Patricia Francis, MD, a pediatrician in Lafayette, California, has been in private practice since 1985. As the mother of two daughters, she's focused on issues affecting young women, including eating disorders and making healthy decisions about sex. Dr. Francis volunteers for a number of organizations in the Bay Area and in developing countries. She's a member of a variety of professional medical organizations and was a content editor for Focus on the Family's *Complete Book of Baby and Child Care*. She previously served as a member of the Medical Institute's national advisory board and the Physicians Resource Council of Focus on the Family.

Wilson Wayne Grant, MD, a pediatrician with one of the busiest private practices in San Antonio, Texas, works with children from at-risk populations. He's a child development specialist with more than thirty years of experience and a unique ability to communicate with his patients at their level—plus a special interest in helping teens make wise choices. He's written many books, including *From Parent to Child about Sex, Growing Parents Growing Children, The Caring Father,* and *Strategies for Success—How to Help Your Child with Attention Deficit Disorder*. He's a member of a variety of professional medical organizations, and has served as medical director of the South Texas Children's Habilitation Center and on the clinical faculty of the University of Texas at San Antonio Medical School. He is also a member of the Medical Institute's national advisory board.

Marilyn A. Maxwell, MD, is professor of internal medicine and pediatrics and director of the internal medicine-pediatrics residency program at St. Louis University. Previously she was medical director of People's Health Centers, Inc., a large, federally funded community health center where she established an adolescent clinic. Many of her patients were unwed mothers or teens with sexually transmitted infections. A member of numerous professional organizations, she was a content editor for Focus on the Family's *Complete Book of Baby and Child Care*. She also serves on the Physicians Resource Council of Focus on the Family.

Joe S. McIlhaney Jr., MD, an obstetrician gynecologist in Austin, Texas, established the Medical Institute for Sexual Health in 1992. He left his private practice of twenty-eight years in 1995 to join the Medical Institute full time. During his tenure as an ob-gyn, he was on the medical staff of St. David's Community Hospital and focused on reproductive technologies, contraceptive techniques, sexuality education, sexually transmitted diseases, and social behavior education. During his time in practice, he wrote five books with an emphasis on the problem of STDs. He speaks and writes about the twin epidemics of sexually transmitted diseases and nonmarital pregnancy, as well as the problems that can result from premarital sexual activity, and the benefits of limiting sexual involvement to marriage. He's the author of six books, including *1,001 Health-Care Questions Women Ask* and *Sex: What You Don't Know Can Kill You*. Dr. McIlhaney has also coauthored, with Dr. Freda M. Bush, *Hooked: New Science on How Casual Sex Is Affecting Our Children*, and *Girls Uncovered: New Research on What America's Sexual Culture Does to Young Women*. He has been an advisor to President George W. Bush on issues related to STDs and nonmarital pregnancy, and has served on the Presidential Advisory Council on HIV/AIDS, the advisory committee to the director of the Centers for Disease Control, and the research task force at the National Campaign to Prevent Teen Pregnancy.

Meg Meeker, MD, is a pediatrician and author of six books, including the bestselling *Strong Fathers, Strong Daughters: Ten Secrets Every Father Should Know*. She has appeared on numerous television and radio shows, speaks nationally on parenting issues, and is an associate clinical professor of medicine at the Michigan State College of Human Medicine.

Paul A. Warren, MD, contributed to this book before his untimely death in 2006. Dr. Warren was a behavioral pediatrician in private practice in Dallas, Texas. He specialized in working with children with developmental and behavioral problems and served as a consultant for special-education services to multiple school districts. He wrote three books and coauthored nine, with an emphasis on the emotional issues that prevent children from thriving. Dr. Warren served as a guest lecturer for many organizations and was featured on numerous national radio programs. He was a member of Focus on the Family's Physicians Resource Council and was a member of the Medical Institute's national advisory board.

INTRODUCTION

This book was developed to help parents like you navigate the often-challenging task of talking with their children about sex. You probably picked it up because you know you need to start the conversation, but you're just not sure how to go about it. You're not alone.

The medical doctors, educators, and parents associated with the Medical Institute for Sexual Health compiled more than four hundred questions from teachers, physicians, and parents across the United States. They combed the Internet to find out what kids are eager to know. This book is a result of those efforts, and we're grateful that they've shared their work with Focus on the Family. We don't regard the questions and answers in this book as the be-all and end-all, but rather as a starting place for your journey of helping your kids achieve a future full of health, hope, and happiness.

For some parents, talking with their kids about sex is very embarrassing. For others, it's not such a big deal. No matter where you are on that spectrum, we hope the answers offered here will enhance your parenting experience by providing practical, accurate tools that foster deeper discussions and more meaningful relationships with your kids.

These discussions and relationships are especially important for Christian families. To the believer, sex isn't just a physical or medical issue. It has profound spiritual and moral implications. In the first place, sexuality matters to God; in some deep, mysterious way, the distinction between genders is rooted in and reflects the divine nature: "So God created man in His own image; in the image of God He created him; male and female He created them" (Gen. 1:27). In the second place, the Bible tells us in many passages and in many different ways that there's a right way and a wrong way to approach sexuality.

Scripture makes it clear that sex is meant exclusively for marriage and that marriage is heterosexual by definition. Contrary to the popular wisdom of contemporary culture, sex is not just a matter of personal preference or style. Anyone who wants to follow Christ needs to take this idea seriously. We can't expect to walk with God and experience the abundant life that Jesus came to bring if we aren't willing to cooperate with His design for human sexuality.

We'll explore this side of the subject more thoroughly in the first part of the book (chapters 1–6), which was developed to help you establish a basic spiritual, moral, and philosophical context in which to frame your discussions with your children.

The second part of the book (chapters 7–13) is divided into age-oriented sections, with answers to questions parents ask listed first, followed by answers to questions kids wonder about. The answers for younger kids are written so that you can use them line-for-line or rephrase them in your own words. For adolescents, questions were written in such a way that you can simply hand the book to your adolescent and go over the response together, or create your own response based on the information provided.

We wanted this book to be one you can pick up repeatedly over the years as your children mature. That's why you'll see some topics addressed more than once, but in distinctively age-appropriate ways.

Two short appendixes introduce you to the topics of sexually transmitted infections and contraceptive options. These sections are intended to help you and your child understand the medical risks associated with nonmarital sexual activity.

Overall, our goal is to empower you to talk with your kids about sex more freely, confidently, and effectively. If you make this investment, we believe it will pay rich dividends in the future. Among other benefits, you'll enable your children to experience a healthy, satisfying, and spiritually meaningful sex life in the context of marriage—a sex life more likely to be free of guilt, pain, and disease because it's consistent with God's plan.

Remember, sex is not a four-letter word. And research shows that your kids want to hear about it from *you*.

Part 1

KNOWING WHAT YOU'RE DOING

1

·············

WHERE'S THE PARTY?

The Need for Parental Guidance

No doubt about it: People of all ages are keenly interested in sex. That's especially true of preteens and teens who are just becoming sexually aware. They want to know more about this strange, wonderful, and exciting side of life.

There's good reason for this. The Creator has hard-wired sexual curiosity and sexual longings into the very essence of our humanity. He's designed people to function as sexual creatures and blessed them with the gift of sex as a way of addressing some of their most fundamental needs: procreation, companionship, and interpersonal connection on the physical, emotional, mental, and spiritual levels.

For the Christian, sex is a mystery, a sacred symbol, and a great joy. A biblical understanding of the nature and purpose of sex begins with God's observation that "it is not good for the man to be alone" (Gen. 2:18). It receives further definition in His declaration that "a man will leave his father and mother and be united to his wife, and they will become one flesh" (Gen. 2:24). It reaches its peak in the amazing statement that this "one flesh" bond is in some sense a picture of "Christ and the church" (Eph. 5:32). In the end, it leaves us with the distinct impression that sex was designed to be a very good and very holy thing.

No wonder the designer of human beings laid down some rules and guidelines to govern the sexual aspect of life. He didn't do this because He hates pleasure. Instead, His purpose was to maximize our joy and fulfillment and protect us from the painful consequences of abusing the gift. Sex experienced within the boundaries He's established—between one man and one woman, within a committed marriage relationship—is safe and pleasurable as well as holy and good.

Unfortunately, we live in a culture that's not only sex-saturated, but saturated with a view of sex that directly counters this biblical understanding. And this twisted culture can exert a huge influence on your child.

Sex sells—and believe it or not, kids are in the target audience. Young people are constantly bombarded with sexual messages—on television, in music, on the Internet, on billboards, and even at clothing stores in the mall. Beer commercials mesmerize viewers with beautiful bodies and seductive music. MTV lures viewers with hours of spring-break reporting showing girls and guys dressed in nothing but whipped cream. A myriad of "reality dating shows" encourages young people to abandon all restrictions and reservations—even encouraging involvement with multiple partners of both genders in just about every type of sexual act.

Is it any wonder that children (and even many adults) are confused about sexuality? Misinformation permeates the airwaves. Sexual innuendo creates unrealistic fantasies about what sex "should" be. Advertisers make illicit sexual activity look like a big party, tantalizing adolescents with dazzling images of exciting encounters with multiple partners. Many kids swallow the deception whole, believing that promiscuity is the doorway to happiness. But they end up sadly disillusioned when the reality leaves them empty and cold.

How can we help them avoid this painful trap? How can we show them that sex is not a self-centered party, but part of God's plan for a full and rewarding life?

Impossible Standards

Advertisers promote pleasure—sexual pleasure in particular—as the goal of existence and the pinnacle of personal fulfillment. Whether the product is an exotic cruise or frozen food, the basic message is always the same: Indulgence is the name of the game, and feeling good is the only thing that counts. Happy people are physically beautiful people. They're the kind of people who engage in lots of sexual activity (with no negative consequences). Is it any wonder young people are so consumed with sex?

So is it the media's fault that kids are having oral sex in seventh grade and babies in ninth grade? Are entertainers and advertisers responsible when adolescents reenact porn flicks at home? Has showbiz directly inspired same-sex experimentation among young teens? Or is Hollywood simply cashing in on preexisting social trends?

In a way, it doesn't matter. Some experts believe the media merely represent the world around us. Others feel that entertainment profoundly influences and directs our culture and has contributed significantly to the increased interest in sexual pleasure and sensuality. Either way, the *practical* challenge facing Christian parents and kids is the same: If we want to live by the standards God has established for human sexuality, we have to make up our minds to go against the flow of culture.

Nowhere is this more evident than in our young people's world. Promiscuous sex has become all too common on high school and college campuses. As a result, sexually transmitted infection (STI) rates among teens are skyrocketing. Of the almost nineteen million new STI cases each year in the US alone, over 50 percent occur in people under the age of twenty-five.[1]

If you're a parent of young children, you may react to these statistics with disbelief. If you have older kids, you may feel overwhelmed by despair. But this isn't the time to give up hope! If you want your kids to embrace a healthy, godly, biblical understanding of sexuality, all you have to do is open your eyes and make up your mind to act.

Your child doesn't have to be the victim of cultural influences. There's another way. You are the most powerful influence in your child's life (even when it seems he isn't listening). The media can fake it with smoke and mirrors, but you're the real thing. Your child knows you are, whether he admits it or not. That's why he needs *you* to talk with him frankly, honestly, and often about how sex fits into the bigger picture of life.

Avoiding Mixed Messages

Woven into the fabric of our culture are a couple of distinctly different and mutually contradictory messages about sex and sexuality. The first is that sex is the most important thing in life. It's the goal of almost everything we do: how we dress and groom ourselves, how we present ourselves to other people, how we go about our daily business. And because sex is such a fundamental part of our physical and emotional makeup, there's no reason in the world why we shouldn't indulge our feelings and satisfy our sexual desires through any number of purely physical relationships.

The problem with this viewpoint, of course, is that it elevates personal pleasure above respect for God and other people. This mindset has spawned an epidemic in teen pregnancy, sexual addiction, and gender confusion, as well as STIs. And that's not to mention the "heart damage" that results from extramarital sexual activity: loneliness, hurt, depression, and low self-esteem.

An opposite but equally destructive message suggests that sex is a secret, shameful part of life that should never be discussed. In essence, this view denies that sex and sexuality are the good and holy gifts of a loving God.

The idea here is that a "good" person doesn't experience sexual temptations, sexual thoughts, or sexual feelings. Obviously, this is a lie. By divine design, sex is an integral part of life. Sexual feelings are part of our basic humanity. This negative view of sex has led to ignorance, shame, and secretiveness about sex and sexuality. Ironically, this perspective, like its opposite, translates into an increase in teen pregnancy, STIs, sexual addictions, loneliness, heartache, depression, and guilt.

Taken together, these lies leave teens between a rock and a hard place. On the one hand, sex is simply a biological and emotional drive that one has the right to gratify in any way one sees fit. On the other hand, sex is a filthy, shameful thing to be avoided at all costs. Either way, sex is anything but the beautiful, fulfilling, and holy mystery God created it to be.

If you're a Christian parent, your challenge is to equip your child with an attitude toward sexuality that's both balanced and biblical. This approach suggests that sex is part of God's plan, and if it's kept in the context of marriage and integrated into life in a healthy, productive way it will promote fulfillment on every level: physical, emotional, mental, and spiritual. Viewed from this perspective, sex is neither compulsive nor damaging. Instead, it's a gift intended to enhance the intimate "one flesh" bond between a husband and a wife.

Not Just Another Sex Manual

This book is written from this uniquely biblical perspective. The authors genuinely believe that sex is a beautiful gift, given to us for our good by a loving heavenly Father. It's not just a feeling, a physical activity, or a biological drive. It's deeply relational, emotional, and spiritual (as well as physical). We're convinced that young people who understand this can embrace their sexuality with power and knowledge.

The authors of this book address sex and sexuality with clinical experience and the support of scientific evidence. Many of them are physicians who've spent decades dealing with patients who've experienced the unfortunate results of sexual activity outside of God's design. Such outcomes include unplanned pregnancies, STIs, and infertility.

In other words, acknowledging and embracing God's plan for human sexuality can help your child avoid a great deal of emotional, relational, and spiritual anguish as well as significant physical consequences. To help you in that cause, the questions and answers you'll read later in this book will be addressed with the caring but straightforward approach of the seasoned health professional.

Here are some of the issues you'll see addressed:

- Healthy sexuality requires that every person present his or her body to the Lord as a living sacrifice (Rom. 12:1). It also implies respect for other people as creatures made in the image of God (Gen. 1:27). True pleasure comes from recognizing the worth of others and the value of deep interpersonal relationships, especially the relationship of marriage.
- Sexual health is one result of a sincere desire to please God. It's centered in a positive self-image based on a deep understanding of His love. It's marked by strong character traits such as self-control, personal responsibility, honesty, and kindness.

- Sex within the relationship for which it was designed—marriage—is healthy and good. Sex outside of this context can have devastating results.
- Sexual desires are normal and healthy. At the same time, sexual passions and desires are not irresistible. They can be controlled by an act of the will.
- Self-control is healthy and necessary for achieving sexual satisfaction. People who operate solely on the basis of their physical and emotional urges find little joy and happiness in life.
- Avoiding promiscuous sexual activity is an emotionally, spiritually, and physically healthy choice.
- Parents are the most powerful influence in a child's life. They have the ultimate responsibility for teaching biblical truths, spiritual values, and personal character to their children. They also have the primary right and responsibility to be involved in their children's education—especially about value-laden topics such as character and sexuality.

Do you feel overwhelmed as you contemplate the task of equipping your children with a healthy, biblical understanding of human sexuality? Do you fear that your puny efforts can't possibly compete with the influence of media and culture?

If so, we want to help you turn that attitude around. With God's help, you can counteract the mixed and malignant messages and train your kids in the basics of Christian character and healthy sexuality.

You don't have to be daunted or discouraged—or dreading the prospect of answering your kids' questions. Talking with them about sex and sexuality is just another adventure on your parenting journey. Believe it or not, it can be fun! And the benefits will last a lifetime.

2

THE BIG DEAL IS YOU!

Parents Do Make a Difference

When teens are asked, "Who has done the most to shape your attitudes and opinions?" rock stars and athletes don't top the list. An overwhelming majority of kids respond, "My parents." That's you.

Children are created to be relational beings. The first relationships they develop are usually with their parents. Kids want intimacy and the opportunity to communicate with someone about the most important things in life. That includes sex.

Unfortunately, many moms and dads don't feel prepared or qualified to discuss this "hot" topic with their kids. This is a common affliction, and it's not hard to see why.

Think about it: If and when your parents talked to you about "the birds and the bees," was it painful, perhaps even terribly embarrassing? If so, you've probably inherited some of their discomfort with the subject.

Some parents find it hard to discuss sex comfortably and confidently because of the sexual choices they made in their younger years—or even as adults. *How can I presume to tell my child the right way to think and act about sex when I made so many mistakes?*

Fear and lack of confidence in this area seem especially common among Christian moms and dads. Why? In many instances, these parents labor under a burden of confused theology and faulty teaching. They don't really understand the biblical view of human sexuality.

Some believers have been taught to associate sex with sin. Others have been told it's a gift from God, but find that modesty forbids them to talk about it and guilt prevents them from enjoying it. Many confuse the use of sexual terms with vulgarity and are too embarrassed to be specific. Some have been sexually abused by church leaders or volunteers, and as a result their view of the relationship between faith and sexuality has been warped. Still others are so used to fighting battles over sex-related issues—sex education, same-sex marriage, abortion, pornography, sexual content in entertainment—that they've become conditioned to see sexuality itself as negative if not downright dangerous. In some cases, fears that their children might lose their innocence or abandon the faith have compelled parents to adopt a controlling and sheltering style of parenting that squelches free inquiry and discourages honest conversation.

Let's face it. If we want to equip our kids with a healthy, balanced, biblical view of sex, we're going to have to acknowledge these hang-ups and misconceptions and resolve them—or at least work around them. We're going to have to learn how to be frank and forthright about sex. There really is no other option.

After all, times have changed. Our sexually saturated culture doesn't allow us the luxury of *not* talking with our kids about this basic aspect of human life. If we don't do it, the media, the peer group, and society at large will. We can choose to initiate and direct the conversation, or we can let the culture dictate our children's beliefs and values. Ignoring the issue can have disastrous results, including ignorance, pain, and loneliness for our kids in the future.

Rather than seeing this as a threat, though, you can see it as a tremendous opportunity. You have the power to provide your child with accurate, biblical, God-honoring information about sexuality. Your child desperately needs you to do this. Whether she knows it or not, she's looking to you to shape her attitudes, not just physically and emotionally, but also in the areas of character and faith. And you're in an unparalleled position to make a real difference in her life.

The Journey Begins with Four Steps

Exactly how should you go about meeting this challenge? Here are four steps you can take, and they all have to do with *knowing*.

1. *Know God.* It all starts with building a healthy, Christ-centered relationship with your child. To be as stable and effective as possible, the connection between you and your son or daughter should be rooted in your relationship with the Savior. It must be three-cornered, with the parent-child bond forming the base of the triangle and God Himself at the apex. If you put everything else, sex included, under the umbrella of His eternal truth—if you consciously make Him the focus of all you are and do—then your perspective on sexuality and sexual behavior will fall naturally into its proper place.

That perspective includes the fact that sex is the God-given mechanism whereby a man and woman become "one flesh" within the bonds of marriage (Gen. 2:24). The delights of sex, when experienced within that context, are just one of the many pleasures God grants to those who submit to His authority and live according to His plan (Ps. 16:11). Let these biblical ideas form the basis of all your interactions with kids on the topic of sex.

2. *Know yourself.* No parent is perfect. No parent has every issue figured out. We're all sinners in God's eyes, and we all have baggage from the past. That's standard for everyone who's ever lived, moms and dads included. The truth is that life is hard, and it's the rare person who gets to the stage of raising kids without accumulating bruises and scars. Parenting isn't a call to be perfect—just to be real. You don't have to ignore your pain and confusion. Make up your mind not to let your fears and failures taint your child's future.

If you're married, keep your marriage strong and maintain open lines of communication with your spouse. Kids need to see that while Mom and Dad don't always agree, they can express their differences respectfully and talk sensibly and civilly about all kinds of issues—including sexuality.

If you're no longer married (or never were), it would be helpful to keep talking to your former spouse or another trusted adult about your child's growth, character development, and sexuality. Parenting shouldn't be a solo flight. This is especially true when it comes to teaching children about sex.

3. *Know your child.* You can't effectively teach your child about healthy sexuality unless you really know him. Take time to get into his world, to understand and appreciate his temperament, to respect him as an individual. Take careful stock of his strengths, weaknesses, joys, passions, and fears. Avoid generic lecturing, and resist the temptation to think the job is done when you've delivered your ideas and opinions.

Developing a closer relationship with your child doesn't mean spoiling her by giving in to her every whim. It means providing her with time, attention, affection, affirmation, and comfort as well as appropriate structure, limits, and guidance. All these things contribute to a healthy sense of identity, which helps your child resist sexual pressures from culture and peers.

4. *Let your kids know you.* Relationship is a two-way street. If it's going to work, you'll need to let your children know you as well. This doesn't necessarily mean sharing all your mistakes and weaknesses, but kids need to hear how your experiences have influenced your journey. If you've felt the same emotions they're experiencing, if you've walked in their shoes, tell them in an age-appropriate way. When they see that you experienced some of the same struggles growing up and had many of the same questions, they'll be less likely to feel alone in their quest for maturity.

How much should you share? Let your words and actions be guided by a desire to give your children the information they really need for the situation at hand. Truthfulness is essential and transparency is critical, but the detail of your confessions should be determined by the child's age, maturity, and motivation for asking a question. Is she requesting that you reveal personal data, as in, "Did you and Dad have sex before marriage?" If not, ask yourself whether there's any good reason to volunteer this kind of information.

How's Your Sex Life?

Much of the instruction your children get from you on the subject of sex will be nonverbal. Attitudes toward sex are caught more than taught.

That's why it's so important to ask how *your* sex life is doing. Would you describe it as good? Great? Troubled? Indifferent? It's important to figure out how you feel about the matter. Research indicates that those who have the best and most frequent sex are people who are married, monogamous, and religious—quite the opposite of any Hollywood stereotype.[1] But that doesn't mean your experience necessarily fits that pattern.

Do you want your kids to grow up to have a balanced, healthy sex life—one that's consistent with God's design for marriage? If you're like most parents, you want your kids to have a better life than you've had—personally, professionally, even physically. One of the most powerful ways you can help your child achieve a fulfilling sex life in the future is by nurturing a healthy, wholesome, balanced sexual relationship with your spouse today.

The Right to Remain Silent?

You're the most influential person in your child's life when it comes to sexual issues.[2] Your behaviors and attitudes about sex—spoken and un-spoken—will forever be imprinted upon his life.

But some parents are scared to talk to their kids about such a personal subject. Others are unprepared academically and/or emotionally. After all, you probably aren't a physician and don't hold degrees in anatomy or physiology.

But neither do most parents. And in today's world there are plenty of resources available and places to go for advice on this topic—as long as you make sure the advice is consistent with biblical teaching and supports your understanding of the divine plan for human sexuality.

Perhaps embarrassment is keeping you from delving into sexual issues with your child. If so, consider this: Songwriters and Facebook friends aren't embarrassed to talk candidly with him about sex. Why should you be?

If fear is holding you back, it's time to ask yourself why. Are you ashamed to talk with your kids because you had many partners early in life? Does it hurt to admit the mistakes you've made?

Maybe you're not emotionally ready to talk with your son or daughter about sex because you were abused as a child, or raped, or because your child was conceived while you were under the influence of alcohol or drugs, or you weren't married when you got pregnant. Perhaps your sexual addictions or an affair have cost you your marriage and family, and you're not prepared to be vulnerable with your child about the pain.

Whatever your situation, your experiences can be building blocks or stumbling blocks for your child. Why not use them as springboards to growth and healing? Why not turn your failures into teaching opportunities?

It's understandable if one of these issues makes it difficult to speak up about sex. But that doesn't justify remaining silent. You need to deal with your issues so that you can protect your kids from the pain you've experienced in the sexual realm. Take the time to seek the healing you need. You'll be in a stronger position to help your child develop a healthy, balanced, biblical understanding of sex.

There are several steps you can take to begin this healing process:

1. *Start with an honest review of your life.* You can't hope to fix your problems until you know what they are. Face your mistakes and acknowledge the hurtful experiences of your past—especially those connected with sex and sexuality. This includes looking at how others have let you down and how poor choices you made have affected your life.

2. *Share these reflections with a trusted friend or professional counselor.* Find a reliable person with whom you can talk openly about these negative experiences and your feelings about them. Healing is unlikely to occur outside of relationships, and talking with a trustworthy friend or counselor can provide a tremendous sense of relief from the pain and sadness of your past.

3. *Forgive.* This is perhaps the most difficult part of the process. Forgive those who have wronged you, and forgive yourself. This is essential if you're to achieve freedom and help your children develop a healthy sense of self-worth and God-centered sexuality. Bear in mind that forgiving isn't the same as forgetting. It doesn't matter if the person has asked for or earned forgiveness. It's a process of letting go and moving forward. It's a gift you give yourself.

4. *Keep learning.* It's never too late to become a student again. As you talk with your kids about sex and sexuality, take the opportunity to glean new information from reliable sources so you can positively shape your children's future relationships.

It's Never Too Late to Start

If you can embrace a positive outlook on sex and sexuality, you'll be better able to communicate effectively with your child about this basic aspect of human life. Releasing your pain is the first step toward equipping your child with the skills she needs to match her sex life with God's design, and to enhance her experience of marital sex in the future. If your child is in high school and you're just starting this process, ask her forgiveness and try to correct any misinformation you may have communicated in the past.

There's never been a more exciting time to give your child the gift of a positive, strong message about her growing sexuality. She'll learn about sex from someone. The question is—will that person be you?

Parents are powerful. You're more influential than you might have imagined! So take seriously the charge God has given you. Train up your child in the precepts of His Word. Do everything you can to prepare her for a life of healthy sexuality. At the same time, bear in mind that you're not ultimately responsible for the outcome.

If you're thinking, *I've tried everything, and my child is still a disaster,* don't be discouraged. You can't force another person to embrace the truth. Only God can draw your child to Himself and inspire her with a desire to live a holy life and apply the lessons you've taught.

Don't get bogged down under a burden of false guilt. Just do your best to model a healthy life and to develop a positive relationship with your child. Then commit your efforts to the Lord—and leave the result in His hands.

3

WHAT A GIRL WANTS

Attention, Affection, and Affirmation

Talking to a daughter about sex isn't meant to begin at puberty. Long before that, moms and dads can build a strong foundation of accurate information and biblical wisdom that will serve a girl well when the earthquakes of adolescence arrive. Girls need that information and wisdom, since sexual maturation can be a confusing and frightening experience. All too often they face the onset of menstruation, breast development, mood swings, and other changes with little or no support from their parents.

Your daughter needs to understand that the transformation going on in her body is a positive transition into womanhood rather than a reason for fear, shame, and embarrassment. A girl who learns to embrace her femininity early on will be better able to resist misinformation and eventually enjoy a sexually fulfilling marriage.

What Does It Mean to Be Female?

Scripture tells us that God created two distinct sexes—male and female—and that in some mysterious way these two complementary "pieces" of

31

humanity, when combined, reflect His divine nature and character as nothing else in creation can. One of the most important implications of this teaching is the idea that men and women are different.

So what makes a girl a girl? If you've been to the movies lately, you know what a girl wants: power, prestige, beauty, wealth, and a strong man to care for her at the end of the day. Box-office hits show young women doing anything and everything men can do, but with a sensual style that can knock others off their feet. For young women to be successful, Hollywood suggests they must be smart, beautiful, athletic, adventuresome, powerful, and, of course, sexy and seductive.

Unfortunately, Hollywood's extreme view of size-two women does incredible damage to vulnerable teens in search of their identity. Many young girls are so desperate for attention from young men that they starve themselves in order to achieve the "right" weight and body shape. That's because the primary need of young women is to be *nurtured*. You don't have to be a rocket scientist to figure this out. Sure, girls want to be successful, smart, and sexy. But even more than that, they want to be loved, valued, and cherished.

This concept is worth stressing because it's under fierce attack in our culture. Some feminists and advocates of same-sex marriage—each group for reasons of its own—tell us that the distinction between male and female is nothing but an outdated social construct. If we want our kids to grow up with a genuinely biblical understanding of sex, we need to recognize and affirm the fundamental truth that girls and boys are different. They approach life from different angles, and they have different sexual needs and desires.

Girls' Greatest Traits

Like boys, girls are on a journey. They need to know where they're headed and why. Some characteristics of this journey are specific to each girl, meant to be matched with the person God has created her to be. You and your daughter can discover this together over time, writing her story of womanhood line by line.

Having said that, is it possible to describe some of the basic features of femininity in greater detail? The answer is yes.

Here's a list of several things a girl needs to make the journey toward mature womanhood and healthy sexuality with a sense of security, poise, and peace of mind. This isn't an exhaustive list, of course. And not every girl will feel or express each of these traits in the same way or to the same degree, nor are they exclusively the domain of women. Many men, for example, have nurturing personalities, while many women demonstrate this trait to a lesser extent. But each of these needs and desires express in some way what it means to be female according to God's design.

1. *Intimacy.* Girls have a greater need than boys to offer and receive intimacy—not only sexual intimacy, but a deep, emotional, personal connection. It's a sense that she is received, heard, and understood by others.

2. *Mothering.* The female brain is hardwired to mother, protect, and nurture. Providing care and comfort comes naturally to most girls whether they become moms or not. They need to be told that it's one of the greatest strengths God has given them.

3. *Caregiving.* Girls tend to have a strong impulse toward caregiving in its various forms.

4. *Emotional perception.* Closely connected with the urge to mother and give care is the emotional sensitivity of the female brain. Compared with the male brain, it's more aware of and better able to read the emotions, facial expressions, and body language of others.

5. *Talk.* Girls and women often need and crave verbal communication. Typically, they are greater word users than men. In fact, certain language-related regions in a woman's brain are larger than a man's.[1]

6. *Affirmation.* Because talk is so important to them, girls need to know they have a right to speak and to be heard.

7. *Security.* Finally, the female generally has a great need and desire to feel safe and cared for. A healthy woman is protective and seeks protection.

In light of this list, it should be no surprise that playtime for a young girl usually centers around the relational pieces of life. Many girls love to play with dolls, cook in the kitchen, and have tea parties. These activities are usually done with friends, whether real or imaginary.

If the word *stereotype* is screaming through your head at this point, consider that the uniquely female part of this equation isn't the *what*, it's the *how*. Whether a girl plays with a baseball instead of a Barbie, or creates algorithms instead of apple butter, her natural tendency is to focus on the relational aspect of the activity rather than the physical one.

The Rest of the Story

So boys and girls are different. Girls especially need intimacy, relationships, affirmation, security, and the chance to care for and communicate with others.

But what else do you need to know about girls before you start talking to your daughter about sex? Here are seven ideas.

1. *Girls need to know that sex is not a bargaining chip or a weapon.* Product developers and advertising experts spend millions trying to capitalize on young women's desire to be nurtured. The pitch: How to catch the right man. In commercials and music videos, women more often do that by talking with their hips than with their lips.

Unfortunately, most of the messages young women receive about their role in society emphasize the physical and leave relational issues to chance. Worse yet, they often suggest that if you have the physical package, the rest will automatically follow. Plastic surgeons and injectors of Botox profit from women's desperation to look more attractive. These cultural influences reinforce the falsehood that young ladies can get their needs met by looking and acting seductive.

If you want your daughter to have a healthy, balanced, biblical view of sex when she's married, it's important to help her understand that sensuality and sexuality aren't the same thing. Teach her how to accomplish her goals without using sex as currency or a cudgel.

2. *Girls need different things from Mom and Dad.* In more ways than one, the respective roles of mothers and fathers are differentiated along gender-distinct lines.

A mother's love is primarily one of nurturing and caring for her young daughter. If a mother truly invests in nurturing her daughter as she grows, that girl will realize she's valued and worth being cared for regardless of her outward appearance. If you're a mom, you're inundated with messages about your own appearance and may subconsciously respond by commenting on your daughter's weight. Don't fall into this trap. If you do, it will lead your daughter to believe that it's her physical appearance that makes her valuable. Instead, compliment her on character qualities such as courage, sensitivity, and integrity.

A father's love involves protectiveness. For the most part, a girl experiences this as affirmation and security during her growing years. The more time a father gives to his daughter, the more he teaches her that she's valuable. It's not hard to understand that when a father's love is missing, a young woman will look to other men to meet these basic relational needs. In doing so, she may become seductive, flirty, or even sexually active at an early age because she desires and needs the protective, affirming love a father should give. The greatest gifts a father can give his daughter are attention, affection, and affirmation.

3. *When Mom or Dad is missing, girls need other role models.* For example, if you're a single mother and your daughter's father isn't involved in her life, it would be a good idea to seek out a positive male role model to meet her needs in that area. You might consider asking an immediate family member, a teacher or coach, or a leader in your church to block out some time to spend with her each week.

One-to-one time spent with a trusted and trustworthy male figure can make a wonderful and lasting difference in a young lady's life, but your daughter's interactions with an older man would probably best occur as part of her interaction with the man and his wife rather than with the man alone. A man who's willing to commit to showing a girl positive attention while modeling healthy relationships may help make up for the loss of her father.

4. *Girls need to see how men and women are supposed to relate to each other.* Another critical component in preparing your daughter for a positive and God-centered sex life is to be sure she has a chance to observe healthy marital relationships up close—in other words, relationships where a husband and wife show respect for each other. If you're not married, it's important to identify and expose your daughter to thriving marriages so that she understands how they work and the benefits they provide for each partner. In the process your daughter will see firsthand how a woman is supposed to be treated by a man. This in turn helps her set realistic expectations for her future marital relationship.

5. *Girls need to know that the cost of sexual misbehavior usually hits them harder than it does boys.* You should tell your daughter that while promiscuous sex hurts both boys and girls, it almost always hurts the girl far worse than it hurts the boy. If a girl becomes sexually active outside of marriage and has multiple partners, she's the one most likely to suffer, both physically and emotionally—in terms of unwanted pregnancies, sexually transmitted infections, and other consequences.

6. *Girls need to know that pornography is off-limits to them, too.* Pornography isn't just a guy's problem anymore. Sadly, a growing number of girls are intentionally viewing porn—especially on the Internet. They're reaping the consequences in a distorted view of sexuality and in damaged relationships.

7. *Girls need to find their worth in their relationship with God.* As a young woman sees positive relationships modeled through her parents and other important mentors, it's also important that she learn to value herself. She needs to know that her worth as a person is tied directly to the fact that she's been created in the image of God. It has nothing to do with her specific talents or beauty.

As your daughter matures, a Christ-centered sense of self-worth and self-esteem will protect her against the lure of inappropriate relationships and dangerous situations that may hurt her and destroy her self-confidence. You can help by reminding her that she doesn't need to be seductive and aggressive in seeking male affection. Her value is dependent upon God's love alone. This will be a challenge, especially in light of the cultural and peer pressures she'll face in a sexually saturated society.

Up to the Challenge

As a parent, you play a vital role in your daughter's life. She needs you more than you'll ever know. You can meet her needs by reminding her of her inherent God-given value every day.

If you don't, someone else will step in and take advantage of the situation—and the results may rob her of the personal, spiritual, and sexual satisfaction that could be hers in the future.

Fortunately, as a parent who cares enough to equip yourself with the answers in this book, you're in a great position to keep that from happening.

4
....

LET THE ADVENTURE BEGIN

The Makings of a Man

Want your children to experience the blessings of God's plan for marriage and sex? It's hard to help them do that without recognizing and affirming the distinctions between male and female. The latter also comes in handy when you want to encourage your kids to grow and develop along healthy, gender-distinct lines.

That's why the previous chapter looked at the needs and traits of girls. This chapter considers the other side of the coin: boys.

Moms and dads need a firm handle on this subject, since—as with girls—sexual maturation can be a confusing and frightening experience for many boys. All too often young males go through puberty, sexual awakening, wet dreams, and erections without any support, education, or advice from their parents—especially their fathers. Your son needs to be informed about the physical changes occurring in his body so that he understands that they're a positive transition into manhood rather than a reason for fear, shame, and embarrassment. A boy who learns to embrace his masculinity early on will be better able to resist misinformation and eventually enjoy a sexually fulfilling marriage.

What Boys Are Made Of

Sticks, stones, guns, swords, bats, and balls—from culture to culture, these are the kinds of toys we associate with the play of young boys. Stereotypes can be misleading, of course, and we don't want to fall into the trap of shoving anybody, male or female, into a restrictive box. At the same time, it can be useful to think about the symbolic significance of these typically male playthings.

That significance might be summed up in a single sentence: Boys of all ages desire adventure, conquest, and competition. Compared with their female counterparts, they're far more likely to be aggressive risk takers. Their play focuses less on nurturing and caring for people and more on venturing out, conquering, and exploring their world. As a boy grows and matures, his physical, emotional, and even sexual drives will be more intense than those of a girl. Relationally, he may not require the hours of intense interpersonal connection that his sister does, but he desperately needs guidance from his parents. He needs someone to help him choose his battles wisely and show him what quests to undertake.

Many boys seem driven to defy any limits placed on them. This is what makes parenting them such a delicate art. Cultural influences aren't much help, of course; most advertisements geared toward men focus on adventure and sexual fantasy, whether the product is the trendiest beer or the latest stuffed-crust pizza. Since young men are targeted day and night by sexual messages from the mass media, it takes vigilant parents to help a son realize that sex is not a question of conquest or mere physical encounter.

What Makes a Man?

Healthy men don't just happen. They're usually created in healthy families, and it's an intentional process. It might be fair to say that the institutions of marriage and the family are declining today because society has forgotten how to develop good men.

Solid Christian manhood can be defined in terms of a few key qualities: service, protection, and respect. A true man demonstrates his strength through self-control. He chooses *not* to do certain things, such as intimidating others for no reason, bragging, putting people down, or resorting to violence as his first course of action.

If he's to achieve this kind of character, a boy must be taught early in life that he's on a journey to a particular destination. He needs to know where he's headed and why. Some aspects of this journey are unique to every individual; the goal of manhood in your son's case has to be defined in terms of the person God has created him to be. This is something you'll have to work out with him over time, building his model of ideal manhood brick by brick.

In general, though, there are several things a boy needs if he's to complete his journey to masculine maturity:

1. *Significance.* A boy wants to feel he's doing something important, that he's making a difference in the world.

2. *Mission.* Most boys have a need to "save the world." They yearn to devote themselves to a cause that aims to make things better. In the process, they need to learn perseverance.

3. *Reformation.* These world-saving boys want to *destroy* the world—at least what's *wrong* with the world. They're eager to smash evil, break down barriers, take things apart, and put them back together again. Moms need to let them do this, and dads need to show them how to do it safely.

4. *Mental competence.* Boys want to know they're smart. When they struggle with academics, they need to be encouraged to do their best, but also understand that there are different kinds of "smarts."

5. *Physical confidence.* Boys need to see their bodies developing well and their strength increasing. They want to understand the physical, hormonal, and sexual changes that come with puberty and manhood.

6. *Independence.* A boy needs to be innovative, to solve problems, and have plenty of chances to build things from the ground up.

7. *Discipline.* To do what they want to do, boys need to learn discipline and self-control. A boy with an aim in life usually doesn't want to be a slacker. Mom and Dad can help put him on the right track.

8. *Challenge.* Boys need to have the good called out of them by other men. They need positive role models and mentors.

9. *Honor.* To be honorable is to place oneself in the service of others. Boys need opportunities to serve others from a position of strength and ability rather than weakness.

10. *Acceptance and respect.* A boy needs to feel accepted and respected by his peers and elders. But he should understand that this respect has to be earned, and that it implies being respectful toward others.

These aren't the only things you'll need to teach your son if he's to grow into a healthy, balanced, productive, well-adjusted, sexually fulfilled man. You probably can come up with other male qualities that match the character and personality of your boy. The important thing is to design the journey so that it meets the needs of the individual.

Family Matters

This is why the family structure surrounding young men is so important. If you want your son to adopt a healthy, biblical view of sexuality and to experience the God-ordained blessings of sex in a loving and lasting marriage, you'll need to show him—by example—what this means.

A mother plays a crucial role in her son's life. No one else possesses the same ability to nurture him and to meet his physical and emotional needs during the early years. This nurturing love encourages a boy to grow and become strong mentally and emotionally. Mothers also can have a unique and extremely significant impact on a son's relationships with the opposite sex. Dad can and should instill standards of appropriate behavior toward girls and women, but Mom is usually in a better position to serve as an adviser in matters of the heart. A lovesick son who struggles with a relationship that's tying his emotions in knots often finds that a woman's perspective offers insight and comfort.

A father's love is just as important, of course. Some would say it's even more significant to a boy. There's an affirming, protective side to a father's love, but dads also love their children "more dangerously," because they usually play rougher and are more likely to encourage risk taking. They often provide kids with more diverse social experiences and introduce them to a wider variety of ways to deal with life.

By tending to stress rules, justice, fairness, and duty in discipline, fathers teach their sons the objectivity and consequences of right and wrong. They give insight into the world of men and prepare boys for the challenges of life. They demonstrate by example the meaning of respect between the sexes; research indicates that a married father is substantially less likely to abuse his wife or children than are men in any other category.

Dads are uniquely qualified to help their boys understand the world around them. This love is essential to the emotional and sexual health of a young boy. When a father makes the effort to spend time and play with his son and protect him from the dangers of the outside world, it contributes significantly to the young man's growing sense of self-worth. Fatherly love helps a boy become comfortable in his own skin. Where this love is missing, it should come as no surprise that a young man will probably spend the rest of his life looking for that affirmation and protection from others.

Generally speaking, fathers encourage competition, thus engendering independence; mothers promote equity, thus creating a sense of security. Dads emphasize conceptual communication, thus helping kids expand their vocabulary and intellectual capacities; moms major in sympathy, care, and help, thus demonstrating the importance of relationships. Dads tend to see their child in relation to the rest of the world; moms tend to see the rest of the world in relation to their child.

Neither style of parenting is adequate in and of itself. But taken together, they balance each other and equip the up-and-coming generation with a healthy, well-rounded approach to life. That includes a balanced, God-centered approach to sex and sexuality.

Boyz II Men

One of the most difficult challenges you'll encounter along the road of your son's sexual development will be helping him distinguish between *talk* and *truth*. Locker rooms are full of boys bragging about their accomplishments—on or off the playing field. You can help your son understand—if he doesn't already—that boys exaggerate, especially in the realm of sexual activity. Remind him that not everybody is having premarital sex, and that his friends may be talking trash to build their own self-esteem.

Most importantly, you can help your son see that a genuine Christian man lives to please God and serve others in the name of Jesus. As part of this process, he demonstrates self-control to accomplish long-term goals. For boys, sexual satisfaction is typically a short-term goal. Often they don't think about the potential long-term problems that might result from having sex outside of marriage just one time. Parents need to teach them that we really do reap what we sow.

That can happen long before puberty, too. Pornography, for example, is likely to invade your son's world far earlier than you might anticipate. Many experts believe that most young men have been exposed to their first pornographic images by the time they're eight years old, whether it's through the web, movies, or magazines. Talk with your son about the power of pornography. Tell him, in an age-appropriate way, that research shows strong neurochemical reinforcement in the pleasure center of the brains of pornography viewers makes it powerfully addictive. Help him understand that pornography can seriously warp his view of sex and keep him from experiencing a healthy sexual relationship with his future wife.

Finally, you need to prepare your son to withstand peer pressure from his female friends. We're used to the idea that girls need to be warned about predatory males, but in today's culture it isn't uncommon to hear about girls being sexually aggressive toward boys. Young men need to be prepared to say no to physical advances, cell phone sexting, and other forms of temptation.

Real Men Need Real Parents

Too often adolescents—especially boys—are left to discover their sexuality with Hollywood and their peers as their only teachers. You can make sure this doesn't happen to your son.

To empower the next generation to experience sex as God intended it, moms and dads can set to work equipping boys with a biblical understanding of human sexuality and marriage. They can provide sons with models of healthy relationships and realistic expectations. Above all, they can help boys understand that the greatest experience of sex awaits the man who reverences God, respects His plan for marriage, and loves his wife as he loves himself.

Talking about those concepts is a lot easier when you know how to really communicate with your child. That's the subject of the next chapter—one you'll want to read whether you have boys, girls, or both.

5

RULES OF ENGAGEMENT

Ways to Listen so They Will Talk

Talk is cheap—or so the saying goes. That may be true in some situations, but when it comes to kids and sex, talk can be one of the most valuable and effective tools at a parent's disposal. Besides, in this particular instance, *not* talking may end up costing you far more than you bargained for.

It's especially important that you, as your child's mom or dad, should be the one doing the talking. Why? Because too many kids learn about sex from everyone but their parents. Playground slang and obscenity, a distorted description of intercourse from the tough kid up the street, a chance encounter with a pornographic website—any of these can provide a child with his or her first jarring glimpse of sex. Even efforts by public schools to correct misinformation generally leave out the most critical ingredient: the biblically based moral framework within which the facts about reproduction should be presented.

For all these reasons, we believe the best place for a child to learn about sexuality is at home with those who care most about him. In the school of sex education, the faculty should be *you*. Anyone can teach the basic facts about reproduction in an hour or two (or they can be read in any of several reference books), but *you* are in the best position to put this information in the proper context and give it the right perspective over a period of time.

Can You Relate?

Sex is a deeply personal and relational topic. Talking about it can't be a one-time event. And how it happens depends on how you and your child relate to each other.

As he learns about his sexuality, let your child know that you want to be his guide on this very important and exciting journey. If he's older, it may take him some time to warm up to the idea—but you shouldn't be offended by his unenthusiastic responses to your initial efforts. Instead, remember that your relationship with him is the factor that determines how much he wants to know from you.

All relationships, especially the parent-child kind, should be grounded in a healthy respect for one another; your primary concern is what's in the best interest of your child. If you're a Christian parent, it's also vital to find ways to place your relationship with Jesus Christ at the center of the parent-child connection. Whether spoken or unspoken, there needs to be an acknowledgment that He is the unseen participant in all your conversations—whether you're discussing sex or football or piano lessons or chores.

How do you develop a healthy relationship with your child? There's more than one way to answer this question, but one of the most important factors in building any relationship is a willingness to enter the other person's world. If you want to connect with your child at a meaningful level, begin by finding out what her current needs, interests, and passions are. Play with her. Ask her to work alongside you. Talk to her and listen to what she has to say. Work hard to understand what she thinks and how she feels.

If you make the effort to lay this foundation, you'll find that it eventually becomes a springboard to all kinds of interesting and spontaneous conversations. As your child matures, she'll have more questions about sex and sexuality. They might be prompted by a scene in a movie, exposure to pornography, a friend's romance, or reports of sexual abuse in the community. In every case, a healthy relationship with your child will provide a great opportunity. Because of the bond between you, you'll be able to answer questions boldly and affirm the thoughts, ideas, and growing identity of your child.

As you prepare to talk with your child, it's important to understand the difference between the kind of conversation you're contemplating and mere "sex education." As a Christian parent you can't be content to explain the "mechanics" of sex. Your goal is much higher: teaching your child about the very essence of life and the meaning of human relationships. Among other things, this will involve discussing your faith in God and the reliability of the principles He's set down for us in His Word.

As your son or daughter approaches puberty, you'll shift gears from talking about sex in general to more specific briefings on the subject of his or her own sexuality. Whether you make this a specific conversation or include it as part of a more extensive explanation of what lies ahead, you'll want your child to be ready for the changes that are about to take place—mental, emotional, and spiritual as well as physical.

Tips for Success

Communicating with your child about sex, sexuality, and biblical sexual ethics is an art, not a science. It's a delicate skill, and you have to grow into it as your child grows.

Initially, the answers you provide may be very simple. But as your child matures, you'll want to explain how relationships and feelings are connected to the biology. You'll also want to tie your discussions to bigger issues such as character, holiness, morality, spiritual truth, and what it means to offer one's body as a "living sacrifice" to God (Rom. 12:1).

Whenever possible, provide affirmation and permission to ask more questions in the future. You might say something like, "I'm glad you asked that. I know it's a difficult subject to understand. Let's take a closer look at it together."

Many parents wonder how they can more effectively influence their child's attitudes on sexuality. Here are some principles and strategies to keep in mind:

- Begin by affirming your love for God, your understanding of the Christian worldview, and your confidence in biblical moral principles. Never underestimate the power of the Holy Spirit and a lively faith when it comes to your child making a decision about becoming sexually active.

- Remind yourself that giving a child facts about reproduction, including details about intercourse, does not rob him of innocence. Innocence is about attitude, not information. A school-age child who understands the specifics of sex—and that it's an act which, in the proper context, expresses love and begins new life—retains his innocence. A child who knows very little about sex can have a corrupt mindset if he's been exposed to the subject in a degrading, mocking, or abusive way.

- If you feel squeamish or inhibited about broaching this subject with your child, reflect for a moment on your own attitudes. Do you harbor any feelings that sexual activity, even within the context of marriage, is somehow disapproved by God? If so, it's never too late to address such issues with a qualified pastor or Christian counselor.

- Don't try to tell your child everything you know about sex during a single, intense marathon session. If possible, details should be released gradually during many conversations over a period of several years. Start early and work your way into it gradually. Practice your communication skills by discussing health and safety issues as your child grows. These might include hygiene, dealing with strangers, resisting peer pressure, avoiding substance abuse, and anticipating puberty changes. It will be easier for both of you to talk about sex if you've already developed a rapport and a pattern for discussing sensitive subjects. In most cases, you'll be dispensing information on a need-to-know basis.

- If your child asks questions you can't answer, don't be afraid to say, "I don't know." Admitting that you don't have the answer could be the one thing that helps your relationship thrive. You'll gain more stature in your child's eyes by being candid than by bluffing, and he needs to hear you admit your limitations. Rather than letting this slow you down, use your lack of knowledge as an opportunity to research the issue in more depth together.

- Believe in your child and help him build his confidence and self-control. Make it clear to him that everybody *isn't* "doing it"; both kids and adults tend to overestimate the number of teens who are sexually active. Never assume that your child is incapable of resisting temptation. Instead, equip him with knowledge, confidence, and unconditional love and support. Help him establish high goals and expectations for himself. Inspire him with a desire to please God in everything he does. Praise him regularly for his success.

- Look for teaching opportunities and use them. Many parents have a hard time finding a good starting place for a discussion about sex. But if you're observant, you'll find natural launching pads all around. They might include a provocative commercial on TV, a popular singer's attention-getting wardrobe, or graphic sexual content in a movie.

- Relax and create an open environment for talking (and listening). Your child can tell when you're tense. To foster an environment that encourages meaningful discussion, be as calm and confident as you can. Urge your child to ask anything he wants, and thank him when he does. If you don't, he'll probably seek an answer somewhere else. Don't overreact to what he says, even if it's not what you expected to hear. The goal is to make your home the preferred place for discussions. Don't just talk; ask questions and listen to his responses.

- Give accurate, age-appropriate information. Listen closely to the questions you're being asked, and be ready to say, "What exactly do you mean?" Don't get lost in details if your child asks a very general question. Consider his age and what's appropriate for him to know, but also remember that kids today experience puberty earlier than ever. They're also exposed to sexual imagery and vocabulary more freely and at a much younger age.

- Anticipate the next stage before it happens. It's always better to be proactive than reactive. You can be an even stronger advocate for your child by preparing him for what's ahead. This approach tends to create more opportunities for discussing responses to situations that might arise.

- Consider how your approach to these conversations might affect your child. For instance, as you become more comfortable talking with him about sexual issues, be careful not to bring the subject up when it might embarrass him—such as when friends are around.

- As you talk to your child about the importance of saving sex for marriage, don't forget to tell him *how*. Provide him with practical strategies

47

for managing his emotions and physical desires as well as avoiding tempting situations. You'll find some suggestions later in this book.

- Many young people skip the friendship phase when they begin seeking a relationship with the opposite sex. You can avoid this by teaching your child how to develop good, strong, non-romantic relationships. Show him what genuine friendships look like.

- Encourage your son or daughter to listen to trustworthy, spiritually mature adults in addition to yourself. These people can serve as great role models, sources of information, and supporters of your child's psychological and emotional growth.

- Love your child unconditionally and remind him constantly that you do. Tell him that you love him for who he is, not what he does. If he blows it, don't take his mistakes personally. Step up to the plate and help him through the crisis.

- Finally, keep in mind that the overarching theme of your discussions about sex should be the importance of respect—for God, one another, our own bodies, the wonders of reproduction, privacy in sexual matters, the present and future well-being of others—and for marriage as the appropriate context for sexual expression.

Any Questions?

As you digest this information and delve into the rest of this book, remember that the answers provided are merely a foundation to get the conversation started. Be creative and open to exploring conversations you never dreamed of having with your child.

Your kids are listening. Will you be the one talking?

6

QUESTIONS, ANYONE?

What Parents Need to Know

You probably heard this repeatedly when you were in school: "There's no such thing as a stupid question." Nothing could be truer when dealing with sex and sexuality.

Among other things, this statement implies that questions of all kinds should be encouraged. As a parent, you need to do everything you can to draw your child out and help him acquire the information he needs. If he shows signs of interest, respond before that interest fades. If he's reticent to broach the subject—as many kids are—watch for opportunities to bring it up yourself.

Above all, be careful not to squelch his curiosity. Don't let your own lack of confidence forestall the conversation. Parenting, after all, is a journey of humility; instead of getting flustered if you don't know all the answers, you can find them together with your child.

If you're like most people, you probably don't have fond memories of discussions with your parents about sex. If you did have such conversations, it's safe to assume that they stopped just short of getting interesting. In the absence of sound parental counsel, you may have found answers to your sexual questions on the playground or from an early boyfriend or girlfriend. Or perhaps you avoided premarital pitfalls and waited to experience sexual intercourse as it was meant to be, with your spouse on your honeymoon. One way or another, you pieced together enough information to make it to adulthood with a working knowledge of the fundamentals of sex.

Want to equip your child with something better than this haphazard, ad hoc, patchwork sort of sex education? If so, you're aiming at the right target.

Unfortunately, good intentions don't always guarantee satisfactory results. They don't ensure that you have the words you need to answer the questions that may come up in conversations with your kids about sex. That's where this book comes in. It might even provide answers to questions lingering in the back of *your* mind—questions you've never found the courage to ask.

So let the conversation begin! Don't be afraid to kick-start it if you have to. If it starts of its own accord, stand back and let it take to the road in a relaxed and natural way. Surprisingly, talking with your kids about sex may become one of your fondest parenting memories. If you don't know how to initiate the discussion, don't beat yourself up over it. Just take your time, lighten up, and wait for the opportunity to present itself.

Why is it important for my child to learn about sex from me?

Your child is going to learn about sex from *someone*. Why not you?

After all, you know him better than anyone else does. You probably have a good sense of his needs, maturity level, and degree of interest. You can gauge how much information is too much too soon. This makes you an ideal teacher on the subject.

Sexuality is one area where the correct information, delivered in the correct context in the correct emotional atmosphere year after year, is crucial to healthy growth. Ignorance about the true meaning and purpose of sex is dangerous. Talking thoroughly about this subject is a long-term project for someone who's signed on for the duration—not one that can be condensed to a classroom lecture, weekend retreat, or semester syllabus.

Discussing sex and sexuality is a dialogue that should continue throughout your child's growing years. Because you know him so well, you can boost the impact of the discussion by tailoring it to address his immediate situation. If he's been exposed to overtly sexual messages during a movie, for instance, you can respond on the spot to address and counter the inappropriate information he's received.

For Christian parents, any discussion of sex has to take place in the context of your family's commitment to Christ. The biblical principles outlined in chapter one need to shape every aspect of the conversation. Since God invented sex, we can't understand what it's all about unless we pay serious attention to what He has to say on the subject.

For the health of your child, it's essential that the emotional and moral tone of his sex education be compatible with your Christian worldview. Research strongly indicates that young people who make the worst decisions are those who have no spiritual foundation on which to build their own moral structure later in life.[1] Facts are important for the conversation, but they're not nearly as important as the larger context in which they're delivered.

When should I start teaching my child about sex?

Now. Talking about sex and sexuality needs to begin as early as possible. If you have eyes to recognize opportunities as they arise, the conversation can start in a relaxed and natural way—for example, as you respond to your child's normal curiosity about his or her body. If you have a daughter, for example, she may seek information about what it means to be a girl. She may be curious about her body parts, and that curiosity is almost certain to grow as she does.

If you start talking early about these issues, it will make the process much easier. After all, your goal as a parent is to teach your child about the world, and sexuality is just one of the many important topics you need to address.

Can I tell my child too much too soon?

In our culture, sexual images and sexual talk are everywhere. Sexual awareness is foisted upon most kids far sooner than most parents would prefer.

In this atmosphere, you face the challenge of preparing your child to understand sexual issues without burdening him with facts and feelings he isn't ready to handle emotionally. Any discussion of the details associated with sexuality should be customized to fit your child's level of mental and emotional development.

Give this aspect of your task some careful thought, but don't sweat it too much. If for some reason you present information that's over his head, it probably will roll off him like water off a duck's back. The spontaneous questions he asks will provide you with the best idea of where he is and what he wants to know.

What are the dangers of teaching too little too late?

There are a number of reasons why it's important for parents to accept the responsibility of teaching their kids about sex, and to step up to the plate as early as possible. If you aren't timely in sharing the facts of sexuality with your child, her first impressions could come from an uninformed peer, a predatory older child, or a sex education program that contradicts Christian values. If you don't give her the information she needs, the day may come when she finds herself confronted with sexual situations she isn't intellectually or emotionally prepared to handle.

What can I do to feel more confident when talking to my child about sex?

The more you talk, the better you'll feel.

Yes, talking to your kids about sex can be embarrassing. But it can also be fun. Don't act like you have all the answers. Treat this as an educational journey, and both you and your child will benefit greatly.

Don't be afraid to say, "I don't know." And don't be afraid to admit you've had your share of personal failures if you think such confessions are in your child's best interest. Understand, though, that such admissions shouldn't involve details. The idea is to build connection and support, not evoke mental images in the mind of your child.

Once you start talking about sex and sexuality, you'll be surprised at how easy it can be. Don't expect your first conversations to go perfectly. Start early, talk often, and be open. Your confidence will develop gradually.

If you're still dealing with your own attitudes about sex, it's time to work through the issues. If necessary, get help from a trained Christian counselor. There's no time like the present to become comfortable with your own sexuality; you may have been sexually abused or wounded in other ways, but now is the time for a fresh start. Your child deserves the best, and he deserves to hear about sex and sexuality from you.

How important is our family life to developing a healthy attitude toward sexuality?

The quality of a child's family relationships plays a vital role in your child's developing sense of her own sexuality. In fact, the overall atmosphere of the home may be more important than your ability to present the facts. A home where a child feels accepted and where family members are comfortable with their sexuality sets the stage for healthy sexual attitudes in the future.

On the other hand, if the atmosphere in the home is cold, inconsistent, or lacking in role modeling or unconditional love, a child will have difficulty developing healthy sexual attitudes even when presented with the very best sexual education.

A healthy, loving home, then, is the first step to a healthy understanding of sex. And a Christian home, where Jesus is Lord and where family members strive to live according to God's Word, offers your child the greatest advantages of all.

How can I help my child have a wholesome attitude about his body?

As we've noted earlier, attitudes are largely caught rather than taught. Your child will generally mirror *your* attitudes when it comes to his body and his sexual self-concept. If you're ashamed of your body and uncomfortable with your sexuality, he may follow suit.

On the other hand, if you're at ease with these aspects of the way God has designed you, he probably will be as well. You can reinforce healthy attitudes by talking matter-of-factly with him about the beauty of the human body.

I'm a single parent; does that affect how I talk to my children about sex?

Many parents are rearing children without the help of a spouse. Singleness makes many aspects of parenting harder, but the task is not impossible. As a single parent, like any other parent, you'll need to prepare yourself with the facts if you're to answer your children's questions effectively. There may be times when you have to say, "I haven't had that experience, but here's what I think."

If this is your situation, you might consider enlisting the help of a trusted relative or other adult to supply necessary information on gender-specific issues when a parent of the opposite sex isn't available. Being single doesn't mean that you can't or shouldn't talk about sexual issues. Your children want to hear from you. Your opinions and experiences are valuable.

I didn't start talking to my child at an early age. Is there any way I can catch up?

It's helpful to start talking about sexuality early with your child. But if you missed those first stages of sex education, you can always begin where you are and make a clean slate of it. It's better to start now than to remain silent.

With a teenager, you can initiate the conversation by apologizing for dropping the ball. Then ask him if he has any questions. If you're honest about your failures, you'll find that your kids are more forgiving and flexible than you thought possible.

Which age is most important when it comes to teaching about sex?

This question is difficult to answer because each stage of development is important and unique.

The preschool period is critical in establishing comfort in talking about the body and sexual issues. Subconscious attitudes and feelings are rooted here.

The school-age years are the best time to provide factual information about the body, reinforce a positive self-concept, and establish boundaries in relationships with both sexes.

The preteen and teen years are crucial from both an educational and a behavioral standpoint. During this stage of development, the physical facts of anatomy and bodily function will be spelled out in greater detail for the rapidly growing adolescent. This is a period of emotional upheaval when sexual curiosity and desire become powerful driving forces. In view of the surging hormones inside a teenager's body and the temptations in society, parents need to be vigilant during this phase and work hard to supply their kids with generous amounts of information and support.

What is a healthy attitude toward sex, anyway?

As far as we're concerned, this question can only be answered fully from a specifically Christian and biblically based point of view. God is the Creator of all things, and sex is His idea. A healthy attitude toward sex acknowledges this. It says that sex is good because God invented it and gave it to men and women as a wonderful, precious gift to be enjoyed within the context of a lifelong, male-female, one-flesh union.

Because of this, sex is something more than intercourse, animal attraction, a process of gratifying needs or longings, stimulation of the senses, recreation, a way to have fun, or a means of manipulation.

Healthy, God-centered sexuality frees us to be whole persons rather than imprisoning us and limiting our options. It's intimately intertwined with love. Sexual urges may ebb and flow, but they reach genuine consummation only in the context of a loving, committed, and permanent relationship between one man and one woman—marriage. Anything less shortchanges the people involved.

What should I teach my child to protect him from sexual abuse?

This is an important question. Several factors have contributed to this epidemic: the sexual overstimulation of our society, the breakdown of morals and behavioral boundaries, and the fact that children today are in contact with more people outside the home than ever before.

If you talk to your child about sex at all, at some point you're going to have to acknowledge that there's a dark side to this subject, at least as it's understood and approached by many people in modern society. This is another way of saying that you need to arm him against sexual abusers. The following protective steps are based in part on recommendations from the American Academy of Pediatrics:

- Talk to your child about sexual abuse. At every age, teach him boundaries for intimate contact and talk. Using age-appropriate language, help him understand that it's not right for adults or older children to behave toward him in certain ways.

- Starting when your child is very young, teach him which body parts are private and are to be touched or talked about only by the child, a doctor or nurse during an exam, or a parent who is helping the child, such as during an illness or after an injury or operation involving the body part. If anyone tries to violate this privacy, urge him to let you know.

- Listen when your child tries to tell you something. Often children won't describe directly the actions of a person who has violated their privacy. But they often hint at their concerns. Be sensitive and listen carefully when you feel that your child is trying to tell you something but is having difficulty putting it into words.

- Let your child know that you won't be angry with him when he tells you something that someone else did. Make it clear by your words and facial expressions that you won't blame him.

- Never let your child go anywhere with someone you don't know. Close supervision is a must. Take time to get to know baby-sitters, child-care providers, and the parents of your children's friends.

- Most importantly, let your child know, whatever his age, that you are always available to give attention to his concerns. Frequently spend unstructured time with him so that you'll have the opportunity to pick up on cues indicating any concerns on his part.[2]

Is it necessary to use special materials such as books, magazines, charts, or videos when teaching my child about sex?

Various teaching tools may be helpful in teaching the facts of sexuality. A picture book you can read to your preschooler may help open the door to discussions about body parts or the birth process. A color atlas of the body will clarify the presentation of information about puberty to the preteen. A video or audio series that parents and teens watch or listen to together may be a catalyst to stimulating talk with teenagers.

It's important to realize, however, that such items are only tools—not the main course of study. By far the most important tool in teaching children about sex is open dialogue between parent and child. This is true at any age.

How can I best transmit my values about sex to my child?

You have great power to influence your child's feelings, attitudes, and behaviors. You can do several things to maximize this potential. Begin by building your home on a strong foundation of commitment to Jesus Christ. Study the Scriptures, have regular devotions, and pray together as a family. Make it clear to your kids that you believe in God with all your heart and that you take following Jesus seriously.

Once you've established this spiritual context, talk with your child about sex. The more accessible you are, the more likely she'll be to look to you for answers to her most pressing questions—including those involving values. As opportunities arise, speak openly about Christian morals. Help your child understand how they relate to the sexual sphere of life. Engage your kids, particularly teens, in conversation about your family's spiritual commitments and ethical values. Use teachable moments to talk about the pros and cons of sexual practices that are all too familiar to many teens, since they see such behavior in public, on TV, or in the movies. Most importantly, live a life worth imitating.

What's the school's role in teaching my child about sex?

Parents are ideally the best teachers for their children when it comes to sexual issues. Over the last thirty years, though, schools have assumed a more prominent role in talking with kids about sex and other risky behaviors. From a certain perspective this makes sense; after all, some parents lack good communication skills, others are on poor terms with their children, and still others simply don't feel comfortable talking about the details of sex or human anatomy. It could be argued that schools

The Methods of Sexual Predators

While many people teach their children about "stranger danger," the importance of not getting in a car with someone they don't know, and not taking gifts from strangers, parents may be unaware of a disturbing fact: In an estimated 90 percent of cases of child sexual abuse, the perpetrator is known by the victim or his family.[3]

Many instances of child sexual abuse do not begin with a direct assault. Child advocates describe the following system that many abusers employ to acquire victims:

1. *Building the relationship.* In normal relationships, people get to know one another by talking, spending time with each other, and doing fun things together. An abuser may go through the same motions with the aim of "grooming" a selected child. The abuser will spend time with the family as well, hoping to engender trust. At this point of the relationship things seem normal; there is typically nothing happening that would raise red flags.

2. *Slow escalation.* After an abuser has the trust of his victim (and the family), he may engage in subtle behaviors designed to maintain that trust but which slowly move the child closer to victimization. These actions will typically not raise concerns in the child or the family. For example, the abuser may give the child back rubs, foot rubs, or close hugs in a way that's calculated to not make the child uncomfortable. He may spend more and more time alone with the child doing nonthreatening, fun activities.

3. *Testing the waters.* As the child becomes more comfortable and more trusting of the abuser, the latter will start to do small things that continue to groom the victim. The abuser's close hugs may become closer and more prolonged, or he may place his hand on the child's leg—though not directly on the child's private parts. The child may find this confusing and uncomfortable, but as this behavior doesn't cross obvious lines regarding what parts of the child's body another person is not allowed to touch, the child may not know what to think. He may be unable to process his concerns properly due to the trust that the perpetrator has already built. If a child

started discussing these vital issues precisely because many parents had abdicated their responsibilities and weren't educating their children about sexuality.

Be that as it may, some people take the view that schools are now aggressively assuming a parenting role in order to promote social conformity.

expresses discomfort, especially to family members, the abuser may back down, work to build more trust with the child, and try again later.

4. *Blatant abuse.* Once the abuser feels confident that he has established sufficient trust with the child, direct sexual abuse may begin. At this point the child may feel strong emotional conflict due to his affection for and loyalty to the abuser despite the knowledge that something very wrong is happening to him. He may feel deep shame. The abuser may threaten to hurt the child or his family if the victim tells anyone. Through fear and manipulation the perpetrator may continue abusing a child for years.

Since this type of abuse is secretive, parents should be aware of their children's relationships—especially with adults—and be on the lookout for any signs of abuse. Maintaining open, constant communication is crucial when it comes to detecting clues that a child might be the victim of a sexual predator. Children who have been sexually abused may show one or more of the following[4]:

- unusual interest in or avoidance of all things of a sexual nature

- sleep problems or nightmares

- depression or withdrawal from friends or family

- seductiveness

- statements that their bodies are dirty or damaged, or fear that there is something wrong with them in the genital area

- refusal to go to school

- delinquency or other conduct problems

- secretiveness

- depicting aspects of sexual molestation in drawings, games, or fantasies

- unusual aggressiveness

- suicidal behavior

Many schools have been pushed to become more proactive in teaching about sex in response to acquired immunodeficiency syndrome (AIDS) and other sexually transmitted infections. Whatever the reasons, there's no doubt that schools in every area of the country and for every age are teaching more and more about sex.

There are two areas where you have the right, as well as the responsibility, to observe closely what schools are doing about sex education. First, it's important in our overly sexualized society to make sure schools don't present too much sexual material too early, before children are ready to deal with it. The second area of concern has to do with presenting information about sexual behavior in a way that seems to imply morality doesn't matter and that sex in all its forms is okay as long as it is "safe sex" or "safer sex" (which generally means promoting the use of condoms). The most important thing you as a parent can do is stay involved in your child's education. Don't check out. Your involvement will go a long way toward making sure he receives the best education in all subject areas.

Are there any health implications associated with homosexuality?

Yes, particularly with male homosexual activity. The human body was not designed for anal intercourse; anal tissue does not stretch as readily as vaginal tissue and tears more easily. In addition, scientific research shows the following:

- Men who have sex with men have a greater chance of contracting many dangerous and even life-threatening sexually transmitted infections, including human immunodeficiency virus (HIV), hepatitis B, and anal cancer, compared with heterosexual men. Other STIs of concern among men who have sex with men include anal syphilis, urethritis, and a range of oral and gastrointestinal infections.[5]
- Men who have sex with men account for over half of all AIDS cases in North America.[6]
- Hepatitis A is more prevalent among men who have sex with men than among heterosexuals.[7]
- According to the National Health and Nutrition Examination survey, the prevalence rate of hepatitis B is about five times higher among men who have sex with men than among those who are exclusively heterosexual.[8]
- Herpes is one of the most common anal and rectal infections among homosexually active men. The existence of open sores from genital herpes infection enormously increases the risk of acquiring HIV.[9]

It's also worth noting that youths who identify as homosexual are two to three times more likely to attempt suicide than are their heterosexual peers, and 30 percent of all youth suicides are committed by those who identify as homosexual.[10] While many gay activist groups have been quick to link these suicides and suicide attempts to stress caused by anti-gay prejudice, it's important to understand that suicide is a highly complex issue that can't be adequately explained by social pressures alone—such as belonging to a group that may encounter discrimination.[11]

Among other things, these statistics tend to reinforce the biblical view that sexual behavior is best kept in the context of lifelong heterosexual marriage. Teens should be taught to refrain from any sexual activity outside this God-ordained context regardless of their personal feelings about sexual identification.

What's my role in helping my child develop healthy friendships, and how do those relationships help him avoid future high-risk behaviors?

Friendships are powerful influences on your child's emotional and sexual development. They're the glue of life. Helping him develop strong, positive friendships will go a long way toward building his self-esteem and preparing him for his future. It will also provide him with a solid basis on which to build healthy relationships with the opposite sex.

As your child grows and matures, so will his ability to develop friendships. Your own friendships with colleagues, your spouse, and your kids will help construct the foundation for your child's future relationships, including marriage.

Many parents believe they don't have the power to affect their child's friendships. But they do, and so do you! If you're involved in your child's life, you'll influence not only her but her friends as well.

My child doesn't seem to have the patience to wait for anything, much less marriage. How can I encourage her to remain abstinent until then?

One of the most important things you can do is to teach her the concept of *delayed gratification* from an early age. Among other things, this means you need to resist our culture's omnipresent marketing messages and train yourself not to buy her everything she wants when she wants it.

If you grant her every wish, you'll only be setting her up for future failure. She may grow up believing that instant gratification is the norm. On the other hand, if you teach her that good things come to those who wait, you'll be equipping her with the skills she needs in order to exercise self-control even when her hormones are raging.

Material Girls . . . and Boys

Many parents don't understand how teaching children about money management relates to sex education. The bottom line: If you can teach your child how to wait for the things she wants now, she'll be able to wait for things she wants when her hormones have kicked in.

Here are a few ways to help kids learn about delayed gratification through money management:

- Give your child an allowance and be clear on what you'll pay for (food, clothing, school supplies) and what she can use her allowance for (games, candy, special gifts). This will teach her how to plan ahead.

- Have your child set 10 percent aside to give to your local church. By teaching your child to tithe, you can begin to help her understand that doing the right thing can be gratifying, too.

- Your child is watching what you're spending, so model what it's like to keep a budget. Eliminate whimsical or impulse spending, avoid the trap of "keeping up with the Joneses," and let your child see that a little self-denial isn't fatal.

- Teach the value of patience. If your child wants something special, encourage her to save up for it. Let her earn a little money by doing extra chores. The investment of her own funds may make a difference in how she treats the new game or DVD, and will help her learn that good things really do come to those who wait.

For a book of creative ideas that teach money management, see *Your Kids Can Master Their Money* by Ron and Judy Blue and Jeremy White (Focus on the Family/Tyndale House Publishers, 2006).

How important is it that I teach my child about character traits?

Very. A book on healthy sexuality would be incomplete without a discussion on character development; the two are intertwined. Think about it:

- How do you wait until marriage to have sex if you have no self-discipline?
- If honesty isn't part of your character, you'll be more likely to lie to a potential sexual partner about any contact you may have had with sexually transmitted infections.
- Where there's no loyalty, the stability of a relationship is jeopardized.
- If respect is absent, sex becomes a commodity.
- If love and unselfishness are missing in a relationship, sex for one's own pleasure becomes the focus.

Character development must start early and continue throughout life. You, the parent, are the best teacher, and the best curriculum is the way you live your life every day. You can help your children understand what being a person of character is all about by using "character words" in daily conversation. Many elementary schools have recognized how important character training is to produce responsible students, but it's really our job as parents to instill these traits in our kids.

How should you go about fulfilling this responsibility?

- Be intentional about modeling character traits.
- Show humility by admitting when you've blown it and explaining what you should have done differently.
- Applaud your child when he demonstrates one of these traits by his own words or actions.
- When your child fails to live up to your character standards, use the incident as a teachable moment. Instead of punishing him, give him another chance to prove himself.
- Look for examples of positive character traits on the Internet, in newspapers and magazines, on TV, and in books that are likely to be of interest to your children.

63

What follows is a list of character traits we will discuss at greater length later in this book. At one level or another, they apply to every child at every stage of life. The list isn't complete, so don't hesitate to add to it as you see fit.

- *Honesty:* being truthful and trustworthy; not lying, cheating, or stealing. Honesty is the inner strength and confidence bred by truthfulness, trustworthiness, and integrity.
- *Kindness:* being friendly, generous, thoughtful of others; showing compassion.
- *Respect:* treating people and things in ways that recognize their value and honor. This includes manners and courtesy. It means having respect for God, His standards of righteousness, human life, differences among people, elders and parents, property, nature, and the beliefs and rights of others.
- *Determination:* setting one's mind to accomplish something; resolving to take a certain path, even in the face of difficulty.
- *Orderliness/cleanliness:* picking up after yourself and keeping things organized; taking care of one's body—hygiene and grooming.
- *Responsibility:* taking on an obligation and carrying it out. Responsibility implies being dependable, reliable, and accountable.
- *Loyalty:* remaining committed to one's family, friends, school, employment, faith, or country.
- *Courage:* facing and dealing with anything dangerous, difficult, or painful instead of withdrawing from it. Courage means doing something hard—for example, acting on one's convictions instead of following the crowd—even when it's unpopular.
- *Self-discipline:* being able to motivate and manage one's self and one's time, appetites, emotions, and health.
- *Sexual purity:* From a Christian perspective, this means following the Bible's guidelines and commands regarding sexual thoughts and actions, including the principle that God created sex to be enjoyed exclusively within a one-flesh union—marriage—between one man and one woman. Purity acknowledges that remaining sexually abstinent until marriage is the best choice for emotional, physical, and spiritual reasons.

- *Unselfishness/love:* personal caring that includes putting the other person first, placing his or her needs above one's own, and sacrificing one's self on his or her behalf.

To learn more about cultivating Christian character, we suggest consulting the following resources: *A Parents' Guide to the Spiritual Growth of Children* (Focus on the Family/Tyndale, 2000); *Raising a Modern-Day Knight* (Focus on the Family/Tyndale, 2007); and *Raising a Modern-Day Princess* (Focus on the Family/Tyndale, 2009).

As parents, we're challenged every day to educate and equip our children for the journey ahead. We've been given the task of teaching them things we may not have had an opportunity to learn when we were young—of passing along benefits received directly from the Lord rather than from our own parents. It's a hard job, but it's also a high calling—one to be embraced with enthusiasm and joy.

As you talk with your child about sexuality, remember that you're giving him tools to build a successful future and a life without regret. Fight the good fight (1 Tim. 1:18), and don't grow weary in doing good (Gal. 6:9). Press on and leave the results to God's grace!

Part 2

THE ANSWERS YOU NEED
AND THEY WANT

7

BABY STEPS

Infants to Four-Year-Olds

"Mommy, I have a penis!"

Did you laugh in amazement the first time your son made that statement? Or did you shriek in horror as you realized where his statement might lead—or where he might repeat his new knowledge? his statement might lead—or where he might repeat his new knowledge?

Whether you're ready or not, teaching your kids about sex and sexuality actually begins even before they can speak. As we mentioned earlier, your attitudes, actions, and words will profoundly affect your child's view of these issues.

For example, there's no doubt that young children derive pleasure and comfort from rubbing and touching their genitals, whether they're twelve months old or four years old. This behavior isn't sexual for the child in any adult way, but is instead part of exploring and experiencing the body. It's your job, however, to help your child understand that even though she may enjoy the touch, certain parts of the body are private and should not be exposed or touched in public. What's more, you need to teach this in a way that does not encumber your child with shame.

As a parent, you have an incredible opportunity to help your young child embrace the beauty of sexuality while at the same time teaching her the importance of bodily boundaries and the proper context and relationships for sex. As she explores her world and brings up questions about sexuality, challenge yourself to answer her questions with confidence and creativity. The investment you make now in shaping her actions and attitudes will reap amazing dividends for her in the future.

Parents' Questions

When does sexuality develop?

Giving and receiving love, which is intimately related to one's sexuality, has its roots in the earliest days of life. A child's primary need to experience love and trust is met when stable caretakers hold, cuddle, feed, and talk to the baby. Physical touch, eye contact, and soothing words give your infant a sense of warmth and security. The act of feeding, whether breast- or bottle-feeding, provides not only nutrition but physical closeness and feelings of pleasure, trust, and security.

Exposure to this love and affection early in life begins the process of affirming a boy's masculinity or a girl's femininity and leads to deep, loving relationships later. Unfortunately, this type of affirmation is often not met in infants who are neglected or abused, and this may be manifest in the way a child relates to the rest of the world.

When should sex education begin?

At birth! Affirming your newborn as an individual through cuddling, touching, and a soothing voice communicates a sense of personhood and reinforces his developing identity. The messages your infant absorbs moment by moment early in life set the stage for a healthy identity throughout his life span.

When your child becomes more verbal and aware, you need to use a more deliberate means of sex education to build on this early nonverbal modeling. Then you'll be able to teach proper words for body parts as well as model healthy attitudes about the body and sexuality.

How do I teach my young child about the body and its proper functions?

In both sexes, the reproductive organs are completely formed at birth. The external genitalia of both boys and girls, however, increase little in size during the first ten years or so of life. Then, at puberty, the genitalia of both sexes experience a phase of rapid growth. Your job will be much easier if you teach your child the correct names for the genitalia and body functions at an early age.

Use proper anatomical terms rather than slang words. Boys have a penis, not a "dingdong." Girls have a vagina, not a "hole." Using precise names of body parts now will pave the way for appropriate discussion when children are older. And while words such as "pee" and "poop" may not be banished from your vocabulary, it would be worthwhile to teach your child the proper uses of words like *urinate* and *bowel movement*. This will help your child develop better communication skills regarding his or her body.

My four-year-old has taken to touching her genitals frequently at home and sometimes in public. How should I respond?

Preschoolers' curiosity naturally extends to the body and how it works. They ask questions about it: "What is my belly button for?" "Why am I different from Julie?" With their queries and actions, they're discovering how their body looks, feels, and functions.

Some degree of touching the genitals at this age is quite common and natural. You shouldn't be frightened or concerned if your toddler or preschool boy or girl touches or plays with the genitalia while taking a bath or getting ready for bed.

Such situations present you with great teachable moments. For example, you may say, "Yes, this is your penis." Pointing to the navel, you may ask, "What is this?" Later, pointing to the scrotum, you can ask, "What is this?"

On the other hand, the child who is rubbing or pulling at her genitalia in public should be corrected gently but not scolded. You might say, "It's not a good idea for you to touch your vagina (or penis) in public. That part of your body is very private. Remember, we don't touch our private parts in public." With this approach, you're giving your child guidelines for behavior but not making her feel guilty.

How do I teach my child the proper names for body parts and body functions?

Among the very first words your son or daughter learns are names of family members and personal pronouns such as *he* and *she*. Names of body parts quickly follow. Attitudes previously taught through looks, gestures, and tone of voice are reinforced by words.

Some parents are not particularly comfortable talking about the names of private body parts, either using technically correct terms or otherwise. For those parents we have this advice: Take this as an opportunity to break out of your comfort zone.

By teaching your children the proper use of the words *penis* or *vagina* you are *not* introducing vulgarities into their vocabulary. On the contrary, if your kids know the proper terms, they're more likely to use them when necessary rather than spouting embarrassing or inappropriate slang.

Bath time presents a great opportunity to teach about the body. As more water splashes on the floor than on the skin, questions and answers fly back and forth between you and your child. Nose, ears, and toes are identified. If your son touches his penis and asks, "What's this?" simply respond, "Your penis. You know, all boys have a penis and girls don't. They have a vagina."

How do I encourage my preschooler to develop a healthy identity as a boy or a girl?

A baby is never just a baby. From the very moment of birth, and often before, we think of the baby as *he* or *she*, not *it*. The most obvious difference between the sexes at any age is the uniqueness of the male and female genitalia. As children mature, secondary sex characteristics such as breasts, hair distribution, body shape, and pitch of voice also help distinguish one sex from the other.

Gender identity is defined as all those things a person says or does to define himself or herself as being either male or female. As language is learned, children see others as either *he* or *she* and see themselves as uniquely a *he* or a *she*. Healthy personal development requires a child to be comfortable with her gender, and it is consistent with God's design of humans as male and female. This healthy sexual identity is affirmed not only by identifying with adults and peers of the same sex, but also by comparing oneself with the opposite sex.

In our society, sex-specific behaviors overlap a great deal. There's no broad line dividing gender roles. You shouldn't feel that you must impose strict sex stereotypes on your children. Instead, it's helpful to reinforce a healthy gender identity by expressing through verbal and nonverbal means your pleasure in your child as a person.

Who's more important to the infant—the father or the mother?

Both parents play crucial and unique roles in the lives of infants and preschoolers.

The breast-feeding mother has an essential task in the physical nurturing of her infant. Through nursing, she also provides a sense of warmth and security through the cuddling and touch that's part of feeding. Even for women who choose not to breastfeed or are unable to do so, the nurturing interaction between mother and child promotes bonding and a sense of security. The father's contribution in bottle-feeding the baby as well as holding and loving him is also vital.

Beyond these differences in the way that feeding is carried out, fathers and mothers interact with infants in contrasting ways. While mothers tend to be comforting and cuddling, fathers tend to be active in their involvement—stimulating the infant to more motor and cognitive activity. Fathers represent the outside world, introducing the infant to life beyond mom's arms. Both roles are crucially important to the healthy development of the infant's identity.

A young child benefits when both parents are involved in teaching about sex. Since the healthiest sex education occurs spontaneously, both parents should be prepared to answer their child's questions as they arise. Children of both sexes will see their sexuality in a more natural light when both parents have served as role models and have been actively involved in conveying facts and attitudes.

Is it normal for my son to dress up as a girl?

It's normal, and even expected, that some boys of this age will enjoy the excitement of "dress up." While boys often dress up in men's clothes or action-hero costumes, some will experiment with dressing up in girls' clothing. Dressing up as a part of imaginative play is normal in the early years, and this shouldn't become a source of conflict or anxiety. At the same time, directing your son toward more appropriate dress-up play would be encouraged.

If your son wants to exclusively dress as a girl and begins to do this even in secret while frequently saying he'd prefer to be a girl, you should be concerned and seek professional help.

Why does my son prefer to role-play as a girl when he plays with his friends?

Many boys experiment with the roles of boys and girls during this age. When a boy consistently prefers to play as a girl, there's greater reason for concern. This may be because of the lack of a male role model, an overenmeshed relationship with his mother, or struggles with gender identity.

While it's important for all young boys to have a strong male role model, if your son is struggling with his gender identity it's even more important. Focus on building a healthy relationship with his father or other positive male role models. Also, encourage your son to play with boys his age, and make sure his playgroup is one where he feels safe and included. If his role-playing behavior continues, consider professional guidance.

Is having my child sleep in my bed a problem for his psychological development?

Opinions vary about children sleeping in bed with their parents. An occasional night in bed with you is not something to be concerned about. Usually your bed represents a place of safety and security, and sleeping there is considered a treat by most kids.

Generally issues raised about this practice aren't sexual in nature. But having a child in bed with the parents can have sexual implications for the adults. Bed-sharing should be discouraged when it starts to interfere with marital sexual intimacy. And while it might seem needless to say, the husband and wife should never engage in sexual activity while the child is in their bed.

A larger issue for the child who shares a bed with his parents is the necessary milestone of learning how to soothe himself and get to sleep on his own at bedtime. Learning to fall asleep and stay in one's own bed during the night is part of a healthy growing-up experience. As your child reaches school age or even earlier, this becomes a major issue and a developmental milestone.

My preschooler is always asking questions. Often they're about sexual issues. How should I respond?

Sometimes it seems a young child's questions are incessant. Every sentence begins with *why*, *how*, or *what*. Sooner or later this curiosity touches on concerns about her origins and method of arrival.

The usual query at age four is, "Where did I come from?" With this question, your child could be asking any number of things. You can assess what she really wants to know by asking, "What do you mean?" Her response will let you know if she's inquiring about birth or whether she's asking a theological question ("Who made me?") or a geographic question ("Did I come from Alabama like Johnny?").

In fact, the response "What do you mean?" is one of the best tools you have to teach your child of any age about sex. It's a way to learn several things at once. You can find out what generated the question in the first place: "Johnny told me he grew in his mommy's tummy. Did I?" You learn what your child already knows about the subject, which helps you know where to start with your answer. Once you know these facts, you can build on what she reveals to answer her question most appropriately.

How do I explain "making love" to my preschooler?

Your preschooler isn't likely to ask about this term directly unless he's heard it used by an older person or heard it on TV.

75

Again, the most helpful thing to do is ask questions: "What do you think 'making love' means? What have you heard about it?" Your child's response will clue you in to what he has heard and help you determine how you should respond.

If he seems to have a vague or general curiosity about the meaning of the term, you might reply something like this: "'Making love' is the way your daddy and I show that we love each other. We hug each other very tight and lie close to each other."

If you get the impression that your young child has some hint of the nature of intercourse, then it's important to give an accurate but simple account. You might reply, "When a mommy and daddy 'make love,' they get very close to each other, and the daddy puts his penis inside the mommy's vagina." Or, "When mommies and daddies make love, the daddy plants his sperm inside the mommy. This is the way babies are made."

What should I teach my child to protect him from sexual abuse?

See "What should I teach my child to protect him from sexual abuse?" in the previous chapter (pages 55–56).

Before I start toilet training my child, is there anything I need to know about the relationship between toilet training and sexuality?

Learning to control bladder and bowel function is a normal, necessary part of healthy child development. This control is separate and distinct from sexual function, but it's a symbolic transition, as it's the first time children are given the chance to control their bodies. A tenuous relationship does exist, since both functions (toileting and sexuality) are associated with the same part of the body and thus use some of the same language.

Toilet training may affect how a child feels about her sexuality. If shame and coerciveness are associated with toilet training, she may relate these negative feelings to her understanding of sexuality because of the anatomical closeness of the toileting and sexual functions. If she's made to feel guilty about toileting, she may transfer this sense of guilt and shame to attitudes about sexuality.

Is it okay for my preschoolers to bathe together? Until what age?

It's not uncommon for preschool siblings (of the same or opposite sex) to bathe together. Some families attempt to use bath time as a teachable moment to discuss bodies (and the differences between male and female bodies if opposite-sex siblings are involved). While this may not seem problematic to many, when children reach a certain age there are other ways this should be done.

Part of your job as a parent is to teach privacy and modesty, ideas best taught early on. For some children it may be around age twenty-four months when they begin to take baths separately from siblings. While privacy and modesty are the goals, parents shouldn't launch separate bathing in a way that conveys to children a sense of shame about their bodies. On the contrary, instill in them a sense of the specialness of their bodies and let them know the body isn't something to be put on display.

Even if your family opts not to separate bathing siblings at such a young age, your children should stop taking baths together when one or both of the children express any discomfort with it or indicate that they want more privacy.

When should I stop washing my child's pubic area during bath time?

With younger children, it's appropriate for you to fully or partially bathe your child. In fact, the young child almost always needs help. With the older child, such as early school age, you should begin to encourage privacy in bathing. You should honor her request for privacy, but be prepared to assist when your child asks for help cleaning or if inspection is needed.

In general, the goal is to have her assume responsibility for self-help activities, such as bathing, as soon as possible. Most children three and older should be able to wash their whole bodies with minimal help, except in special circumstances.

When does it become inappropriate for my child to see me naked?

Infants and toddlers are often present with parents of either sex as the latter get dressed. This is natural. As your child gets older he may start to indicate curiosity about the shape and look of your body; this extends to parents of the same sex as well as of the opposite sex. This would be a good time for you to start letting your child know that people need to be modest and private. And it's a good time for you to start modeling these traits.

Parental modesty in front of children is a good thing for your child to see at an early age. By the time your child is twenty-four months old you should not be intentionally naked in front of him.

When is it no longer appropriate for my child to run around the house naked?

Typical toddlers and younger preschoolers have no sense of embarrassment about their bodies and often love to run around the house naked. This is natural and doesn't mean your child will vacation at nudist camps in the future.

But it's best that your child's cavorting not be done in a state of complete undress. By putting some clothes on him you can begin to train him toward modesty and privacy, and give him a natural sense that being clothed is an expectation. The goal is not to impart any sense of shame about his body, so don't be upset or react with shock if you find him running around naked. Be calm and gently tell "Tarzan" that it's time to get some clothes on.

Is my young child affected by seeing sexually explicit material?

Children, regardless of their age, are impressionable and curious. You may think kids exposed to sexually explicit material are blissfully untouched by it, but chances are very good that they'll be affected. Because sexually explicit materials are themselves a distortion of what God designed, they can cause your child to develop a distorted view of sex.

Your goal should be to talk to your child *first* about relationships, sexual intercourse, and respect for others' bodies—rather than allow a movie or other media with inappropriate content to do the teaching. The proper time for some of these discussions normally wouldn't be until your child is older, so part of your job now is to protect him from exposure to material that may give him a warped view of sexuality.

It's important for you to train him to recognize inappropriate material. To do this, it's not necessary to describe sex acts in detail; explain that you're talking about pictures of naked men, women, or children. If you feel this definition might be misunderstood—by including classic paintings or statues, for example—make that distinction. Encourage your child to ask you when he has questions on this subject, and to tell you if he's been exposed to this kind of material so that he knows you're concerned.

What should I say when my son announces, "Mom, I want to marry you"?

Often when a child says something like this he's making a statement about the sense of safety he feels with you. He's conveying a desire for life to stay the way it is. He's also becoming aware of two other things: his maleness and that his future will hold a deeper relationship called marriage.

Tell your son, "Someday when you're older, I hope you find a wonderful girl to marry. When that happens, I will always be your mom and a good friend." If you're already married, point that out, too.

Should I allow children of the opposite sex to spend the night with my child?

At this age, decide on a case-by-case basis. If a child of the opposite sex is a good friend and his parents are out of town, it's not a big deal. If your child is asking for a friend who's two to three years older than she is to spend the night, that's not appropriate.

It's important to start discussing relationship boundaries with your children at this age. In this case, you might tell your daughter that her friend can come over and have dinner and then go home at bedtime.

When is it inappropriate to change my child's clothes in public?

About the time your child turns three, he'll no longer want you to change his clothes in public—but it's probably best to curtail this activity at an even younger age. This way you can help engender a sense of modesty and privacy that feels more natural to him, and he'll be less likely to infer that his body is something to be ashamed of.

You also need to listen to his cues, as well as take into consideration the people around you. If you're at a mall, for instance, look for a bathroom or dressing room to change your child in. If you change your infant in public, be discreet. It's also polite to ask the people around you if they mind.

Should my toddler see me showing affection to my spouse?

Yes! Your toddler should see you showing affection to your spouse on a daily basis. Watching you show consistent affection to your spouse (e.g., kissing, hugging, hand-holding, verbal praise) will go a long way in helping your child feel secure. It also will help model a positive marital relationship for her future.

What sort of affection for my spouse is inappropriate for my toddler to see?

Inappropriate affection to display in front of your child would include deep kissing, aggressive touching, fondling of the breasts or genitals, and other sexual behavior that should be conducted privately.

What can I do now to help keep my child from getting involved in risky behavior—like premarital sex—when he's older?

Playing with your child is one of the most important investments you can make. It not only relieves your stress, but can go a long way toward instilling confidence in your child.

He needs to engage with you at his level; it doesn't matter whether you chase him around the house, throw a ball, or spend time coloring or drawing. The time you invest playing with him today will ultimately help protect him from engaging in high-risk behaviors in the future.

I'm a single father. How important is a female role model to my child?

If you're rearing your children without a positive female role model the consequences can be damaging. The adage "You can't be all things to all people" is especially true for your kids.

A positive female role model can provide your daughter with a person to help her understand what it means to be a woman and to answer questions that might embarrass her to ask you. A similar woman in your son's life can help him understand how men and women function differently and help him appreciate differences between the sexes. Such a person will also offer him the opportunity to practice respect for women. Most boys want to learn how to get along with the opposite sex, but they need a female role model to actually practice this.

Without stereotyping either gender, it's generally true that a female role model in a boy's life can help him learn about gentleness and tenderness as well as answering questions about the many "mysteries" of girls. Having both male and female role models in a child's life demonstrates the complex beauty of how men and women complement one another.

I'm a single mom. How important is a male role model to my child?

A positive male role model is important to both boys and girls. The appropriate attention of a trustworthy man can help your daughter understand that she doesn't need attention from boys to feel valued. A male role model can help your son develop his masculinity. Often single mothers shelter their sons from rough play, and this decision can affect healthy male development.

A trusted, trustworthy, positive male role model also can help your daughter understand how to avoid clothing and actions that can "turn on" boys. In addition, he can help your son understand how to control his impulses and respect women.

Questions Children Ask

Where did I come from?

With this question, your child may be asking a number of things. He may be raising a geographic question, wanting to know what city or town he came from. Often he's seeking assurance that he belongs to the family by asking, "Who do I belong to?" He may be asking a spiritual or philosophical question, especially if he's heard that God made people and is trying to find out if God actually made *him*. Of course, many preschoolers who ask where they came from are wondering how they were made—and have a vague idea of the truth.

So before plunging into a long explanation of pregnancy and childbirth, it's best to ask your child, "What do you mean?" If it's apparent he's curious about the birth process, you can answer this way: "You grew in your mother's body. All mothers have a special place where babies grow. It's called the womb or the uterus. When you were ready, you came out of your mom's body."

How do babies get out?

Mommies have a special opening between their legs called the vagina that allows a baby to come out when the time is right.

When a baby comes out, how can you tell if it's a boy or a girl?

Boys and girls have different kinds of bodies. When a baby is born, parents can tell by looking at the penis or the vagina if the baby is a boy or a girl.

How does the baby get inside the mommy's body?

Mommies make tiny eggs in their bodies. The eggs are released, and when the egg meets up with the sperm from the daddy, the egg begins to grow into a baby. It takes both a mommy and a daddy to make a baby.

How does the daddy's sperm get inside the mommy's body?

When mommies and daddies make love, the daddy puts his penis inside the mommy's vagina and passes sperm from his penis. When one sperm joins with one egg, a new life is formed.

Will I have a baby, too?

If a girl asks this question, you can answer, "Not everyone gets married or has a baby. When you grow up and get married, you probably will have one.

Or you might even adopt one. That means inviting a child whose parents can't take care of him or her to be part of your family." If a boy asks this question, you can answer, "No, boys don't have a special place for babies to grow like girls do. But after they get married they often become daddies and take care of the babies along with the mommies."

Why do mommies have breasts?

Women have breasts so that they can feed newborn babies. Breast milk is the perfect food for babies.

What is a penis?

The penis is the fingerlike part of the body that hangs down between the legs of boys and men. It's how boys urinate. When a boy grows up, his penis gets larger.

Will my penis fall off?

No, God made your penis to be part of your body for your whole life. It's like your nose or your ears; it will grow bigger but never fall off.

Can my friend touch my penis?

No. Your penis is a part of your body and belongs only to you. It's private. No one should touch your penis unless something is wrong with it and it needs to be checked by your doctor or your parents. You shouldn't touch another boy's penis either. And you shouldn't touch a girl's vagina.

Why do I have a belly button?

A belly button is where your umbilical cord was attached when you were inside Mommy. That cord made it possible for you to eat and drink while you were in Mommy's belly.

Does it hurt to have a baby grow inside the mommy?

Not usually. Sometimes mommies feel the baby kick, but it's not painful. Often mommies will feel pressure as the baby gets big, and they get tired a lot.

Why do mommies go to the hospital to get the baby?

Mommies don't get the baby at the hospital like people get food at the store. The baby first grows inside the mommy. She goes to the hospital so that the doctor can help the baby come out.

Luke and I [a boy] are going to get married when we grow up.

You and Luke may be best buddies now. But God designed boys to marry girls, and girls to marry boys. I'm glad Luke is your buddy, and I hope you're friends for a long time; but you want to marry a girl so that you can have children like your daddy and I had you. Right now, you may not like girls very much. As you get older, you'll find that you see them differently, and will like them in different ways than you do now.

Mom, I'm [a girl] going to marry Billy when I grow up.

Many girls don't have the benefit of having great friends like Billy, and it's nice that you already feel you want to marry Billy when you grow up. Finding someone you love and want to be with will be an important decision. The best way to make an important decision is after a lot of thought and prayer. If you and Billy change your minds before you're grown up, that's okay.

Why do girls sit down to go to the bathroom?

Girls go to the bathroom sitting down because their genitals are inside their bodies and their urethra (the tube that moves the urine) is between their legs.

Why do boys stand up to go to the bathroom?

Boys can go to the bathroom standing up because their urethra (the tube that's attached to the bladder and moves the urine) is in the penis. Since the penis is on the outside of the body, a boy can urinate while standing up. Boys do sit down to have a bowel movement.

8

FIRST COMES LOVE

Five- to Seven-Year-Olds

L ogan and Lauren sitting in a tree, K-I-S-S-I-N-G. First comes love, then comes marriage, then comes baby in the baby carriage."

You may remember this childhood taunt from your days on the playground. And you might have noticed that little boys and girls aren't as innocent as they were when you were in first grade. Times have changed; unfortunately, kissing games and much more have made their way to kindergarten.

This is a wonderful age to find out how your child sees the world around her. Take time to ask questions about her friends; dig a little deeper into the games she's playing. While children this age aren't exploring many questions about sex, they often use their imagination and playtime trying to create perfect relationships between boys and girls.

This is also the age of bold exploration and excitement about their bodies and what their bodies can do. Modesty and privacy may become an issue. Don't be offended if your child doesn't want you to join her in the bathroom anymore. Keep your eyes and ears open, and be ready to be inspired by her confidence and newfound independence.

Parents' Questions

What effect do outside influences have on my school-age child when it comes to sex?

Outside influences will definitely shape your child's view of sex. It's up to you to determine whether those influences will be positive or negative. If you're working to prepare him for the world he'll live in, these outside influences can be great teaching tools.

As he enters school, it's a good idea to get to know his teachers and his friends' parents. If you know he's been exposed to a movie you don't approve of or to foul language, take the opportunity to explain to him why what he's been exposed to doesn't reflect your family values.

Communicating openly with your child during this stage of life is very important. Your being involved in his activities and getting to know the people around him will not only protect your child but also prepare him for the world.

How can I guard my child from the unhealthy influences that seem to be all around us?

Your goal should be to prepare your child for—and protect your child from—the world she'll encounter. You need to talk about the unhealthy influences she might experience and role-play responses that will help her react appropriately.

This isn't the time to exit your child's life. More than ever, she needs you to stay involved. Volunteer in her classroom. Invite her friends over and get to know their parents as well. When she spends time with other families, talk to the parents about your standards for movies, TV, video games, and the Internet. This can help them avoid exposing her unnecessarily to negative influences.

Listen to your child to gain insight into how she sees the world. Ask questions about what she thinks and you'll learn a lot. The bottom line is to be involved in your child's life and let her know you're available and want to be with her.

Finally, hold fast to the confidence that comes from knowing God has your child's future in His hands. Even though you should diligently monitor the media and personal influences that affect your child, the fact is that you can't control every aspect of your child's life—and being overcontrolling and overprotective of your child can introduce its own problems. Teach your child to be discerning about the influences around her, and trust God to allow your teaching to bear fruit when your child needs it most.

How can I build my child's self-confidence and help him to resist peer pressure and negative influences?

Teaching your child about God's design for sex and sexuality is critical, but what your child does with that knowledge is determined to a large extent by his self-confidence. Self-confidence is a trait every child needs in order to navigate the difficulties associated with peer pressure. Investing in your child's confidence now will protect his sexuality in the future. Kids who have a *can-do* attitude are usually able to withstand peer pressure and make good choices.

Modeling self-confidence is the best thing you can do for your child. After all, actions speak louder than words. Make an effort to affirm your child as well. Tell him you love him for who he is; show him affection with hugs and kisses. Celebrate his achievements. Focusing more on the process and character building than on the visible result tells him he is capable and worthy.

What should I do if I don't know the answer to my child's questions?

Say, "I don't know." Then use the experience as a teaching opportunity.

If your child has the attention span to do so, invite her to research the answer with you. If not, let her know you'll start looking for the answer and get back to her as soon as you find it.

Make sure to set a time to talk about the issue again. Your failure to follow through could eliminate future conversations on the issue.

When should I start talking to my child about sexual intercourse?

A few children at this age might come right out and ask the "big question" about sex or how a baby gets made. It's important to understand what your

---

Getting a Head Start on Date Nights

Since most children think about being married someday, it's never too early to start talking about and modeling how to treat the opposite sex. When your kids are in grade school, it's good for each parent to institute a "date night" with each child of the opposite sex. It could be once every few months or on special occasions.

One family had each child take his or her parent somewhere special on the parent's birthday—at the parent's expense. (This could be expensive, so set your parameters carefully!) The point is to show your children how to treat their date and teach them the ropes of courtesy and conversation.

If this starts in grade school and has been fun, when your child hits preadolescence he or she may still want to have a date night—even if it means being seen with a dreaded parent.

Research shows that if a girl's father is involved in her life, she's less likely to initiate sexual activity during high school.[1] Since girls have more issues with self-esteem, body image, and friendships than boys do, an attentive dad can build his daughter's confidence by encouraging her to be a beautiful young woman on the inside. A dad can also provide cautionary insight on how certain clothes and behaviors "turn on" boys.

It's equally important for sons and moms to discuss what girls are looking for in a guy as the boys get more interested in the opposite sex.[2]

---

child is looking for by asking additional questions. He might be looking for something very simple, not "What is sexual intercourse?" If he clearly wants the straight facts, a simple answer is in order.

In addition to discussing body parts, it's very important to discuss context (that is, "when you are a grown-up and married") and that sex is something very special between two people who love each other and are married. Whatever you communicate to your child you should *ask him to repeat back to you*, since kids at this age often have vivid imaginations.

How do I explain the process of "making love" if my child should ask?

At this age, most children don't want a long, drawn-out, moment-by-moment explanation of sexual intercourse. Usually they just want to know how babies are made and what "making love" (or any other term they're questioning) actually means.

This is a great opportunity to tell your child how special love can be between a husband and wife. The fact is that you love each other so much that you want to hug and kiss and be as close as possible. When you're alone together, you sometimes like to be naked when you hug, and there are special feelings that happen when Dad's penis is inside Mom's vagina. It feels good all over. It's a great way for a husband and wife to say, "I love you."

Remind your child that sex is intimate and special and meant for marriage. She might give you a range of reactions, from "gross" to just plain "okay" and then run off to play. When discussing sexual issues, stress to your child that she shouldn't talk about these things with her friends or siblings. Again, *ask her what she heard* to make sure she didn't think you said something you didn't.

What if my child isn't asking any questions about sexual matters?

He's normal! Most children this age don't bring up questions about sex. If your child does, reply with simple and short answers; then ask if he understood what you said. Most kids aren't looking for long dialogues, but just want to get something confusing sorted out.

If you want to bring up a sexual issue and your child isn't asking, initiate a conversation based on something you've both heard or seen recently. Life offers plenty of opportunities to talk about love, respect, and sex; just look around your neighborhood or at the TV.

What should I do if my child walks in while I'm naked?

If your child saw you naked while she was younger, this incident won't be a big deal—especially if you're of the same sex. Ask her to step out of the room for a moment while you reach for a towel or something to cover up, and then talk with her about knocking before entering your room. There's no need to convey any sense of shame about the human body, but take this opportunity to talk about closed doors and privacy.

What should I do if our child walks in while we're having sex?

If your door isn't locked and your child is suddenly in your room during sex, ask him to leave because you want some special time alone together. If he's in shock from what he's seen, tell him this is a way parents show affection for one another.

Don't overreact! It will make an uncomfortable situation worse. Often your child's response to the situation will mimic yours. As traumatic as it is for you, it probably will be more confusing for your child. You can discuss what he did or didn't see once your clothes are back on.

Prevention is the best approach to this embarrassing situation. Install a lock on your door. Tell your child that if your door is closed, he should knock and be given permission before entering.

When should I introduce the subject of HIV/AIDS to my school-age child?

HIV and AIDS are complex subjects that an early elementary-age child might not run into or ask about. You don't need to bring up the topic at this age unless your child's school addresses it in the classroom. If there are any children in the school with HIV, it should be brought up to all classes so that misinformation isn't spread around the playground. (See "What should I tell my child about HIV/AIDS?" in the next chapter, page 112.)

What should I say and do if my child has been sexually abused?

If this is the case in your family, no doubt you're facing a whirlwind of emotions—anger, sorrow, and grief, among others—all of which are completely normal under the circumstances. As painful and shocking as this discovery must be, the fact that it's come to light now rather than later may provide you with some measure of encouragement. Child sexual abuse is often covered up for years; when that happens, the victim usually ends up carrying a heavy burden of shame, guilt, and damaged self-esteem into adulthood; what might have been an isolated incident can carry consequences from one generation to the next. You have an opportunity to break that chain by taking firm, appropriate action.

If your child has already confided in you, you're ahead of the game. If, on the other hand, this information has come to you from some other source, you'll need to sit down and broach the issue with your child in a sensitive and caring way. Don't blame or condemn or get angry. Instead, let her know you're on her side. A child in this situation needs to be assured that someone believes her and is willing to fight for her.

Ask safe questions designed to draw out the details as gently and gradually as possible. Say things like, "I can't tell you how deeply it hurts me to know this has happened to you. Who has been doing this to you? For how long? Is it an ongoing situation?"

Once you've reached this stage in the process, help your child understand the importance of reporting the abuse to the police and the department of social services. Tell her that keeping a secret like this will only make things worse, and that not telling the authorities about it might allow the offender to hurt someone else. It's in the best interests of all concerned that the truth be known and appropriate action be taken as soon as possible. Let her know that you will help her make the report and that you will be with her every step of the way.

Understand that if you, as the parent, are aware that an incident of sexual abuse has taken place, you're legally obligated to make sure it's brought to the attention of the proper authorities. If you don't follow through, you could become liable to criminal prosecution yourself. For additional guidance, we suggest you contact the National Organization for Victim Assistance (NOVA) 24-hour crisis hotline at 1–800–879–6682 (800-TRY-NOVA).

What your child needs most right now is the comfort and reassurance that come from a strong support network. It's important to enlist a select group of trusted adult friends who can come alongside the two of you as you seek to deal with this disturbing situation: your spouse (unless, of course, he's the perpetrator), a teacher, a school counselor, a pastor, a youth leader, or the parent of a friend. It would also be a good idea to make an appointment with a professional counselor—preferably a trained, licensed Christian therapist. Meanwhile, make sure that your child is in a safe place where the abuser won't have access to her while you're addressing the details of the case.

How do I warn my child about sexual predators without scaring her?

As parents, we must teach our children that some adults aren't trustworthy. This is a concept that they've seen over and over in movies and cartoons. Basically, tell your child not to interact with strangers. You also need to tell her that if a stranger approaches her in a threatening way, she should run and yell that this person is not her parent. Explain that many of the "lines" predators use might not sound dangerous or threatening at all ("I lost my kitten; will you help me find her?").

It's imperative as your child grows to remind her that no one except a medical professional should touch her private parts. If someone touches or views her genitals by force or coercion, she needs to tell you immediately—even if the person specifically said not to tell her parents. This way she has your permission to come to you.

Get to know the parents of the friends your child spends time with, too. It may be hard to believe, but most predators are family friends or acquaintances. Finally, never leave your child with someone you don't know or haven't run a background check on.

How do I reinforce a sense of privacy at this age?

Often children at this age become embarrassed about nudity—yours and theirs. To show respect for your child's privacy, don't interact with him when he isn't clothed. Encourage your child to make bathing or showering a private undertaking. Rather than standing in a public restroom stall with him, hold the door shut on the outside. Respect his need for boundaries.

Privacy is something that comes naturally to most children. If your child isn't showing a need for privacy, modeling can help him get there.

Is it normal for my child to want to touch her genitalia at this age?

By and large, kids enjoy touching their genitals. It's quite normal for children to explore their anatomy and learn the correct names for the parts. This becomes a problem when your child wants to touch herself often and in public.

You need to explain that this is not something people do in public. You shouldn't punish your child, but explain that other people feel uncomfortable watching her rub her genitals and that it's not appropriate to do in front of others. If the behavior continues, ask your child to leave the room and to come back when she's able to stop.

What should I do if I find my child playing with a friend, and they're both naked?

If you discover your child and a friend playing "doctor," it's important to ask what they were doing and why. Make sure one of them wasn't forcing the other to do something uncomfortable and that they weren't simulating intercourse. (Unfortunately, many children this age have seen enough on TV, in the movies, or on the Internet to have a basic idea of what the motions look like.)

If they were simulating sex, you need to have a discussion about privacy and respect for each other's bodies. Remind your child that it's okay to be naked with his doctor and perhaps his parents under certain circumstances, but it's not okay to be naked with other people. Ask him to repeat what you said so it's clearly understood.

While curiosity shouldn't be punished, it's appropriate to have consequences laid out if the behaviors are repeated. By all means, tell the parent of the other child so that you both can approach the problem as a team. This isn't an issue you should get angry about or shame your child over. The key is to let him know that there are boundaries to all of our behaviors. You may wish to consult a licensed Christian counselor to discuss this behavior and its ramifications.

My little girl was pinched in her privates by a friend. What should I do?

Aggressive play at this age isn't uncommon, and when this play is unsupervised, sexually aggressive incidents may occur. You should take steps to address the inappropriateness of this behavior as well as affirm your daughter for telling you about the incident.

If you're cool, calm, and collected, you can give good information about avoiding aggressive behaviors and people—including peers who violate personal boundaries (such as touching, tugging, or punching one's genitals or touching one's body without permission).

If you feel the behavior is persistent and aggressive, talk to the parents of the child and even the child himself. If the activity persists, you may have to take action to separate your child from this "friend."

Should my son and daughter have separate rooms?

If space in your home permits, this is a great time to allow your children to have separate rooms. If your children must share a room, however, it's a good idea to hang a curtain or some other barrier that will allow them to have their own space.

This is the time in life when your children's sense of privacy is developing. Helping them have space to themselves allows them to develop modesty and their own sense of identity.

What types of TV shows are appropriate for my child to watch?

Here's a rule of thumb for TV viewing during this stage of development: Your child should watch only those shows whose content you're confident is appropriate.

It's very tempting to just let your kids sit in front of the TV while you make dinner and do chores. The problem is that even cartoon networks and "kid-specific" channels have programming that's inappropriate for the early-elementary audience. Children this age should watch only programs that promote positive behavior and good character traits. They do process sex, foul language, and violence, but not in a mature way. Images will be distorted in ways you don't have control over.

It's best to watch programs with your child so you can comment on the programming. This will have a great impact on how he'll interpret what he sees. Make watching TV an active event by asking questions during viewing to find out how your child is processing what's been shown on the screen. If the show your child's watching is not appropriate, you can turn it off. Then talk about why it's not a good show to watch, and what makes a show worthwhile.

Should I allow my child to go to PG-13 or R-rated movies?

No. PG-13 and R-rated movies contain material that even the entertainment industry admits will be too graphic for your child; this may include foul language or explicit sexual scenes. Unfortunately, many children's movies have PG ratings and aren't appropriate for young kids; just because it's animated, for example, doesn't mean your child should see it. Exposing her to explicit images, relentless sarcasm, violence, and foul language will only lead to behavioral problems in the future.

Remember, you're the parent. Don't just tell your child no, however; provide alternative activities and explanations that support why you don't want her to see a particular movie.

Information about movie content can be found at pluggedin.com. This website, from Focus on the Family, provides detailed reviews of movies (along with TV shows, music, and video games) so that parents can make informed decisions about the entertainment they want their children to be exposed to.

Is it appropriate to permit my child to go around the house naked?

No. Starting around age five, most children begin developing a sense of privacy and become uncomfortable when they're nude in the presence of others, or when others are nude around them. But even if your child is not uncomfortable with nudity, now is a great time to talk about personal modesty and respecting others' privacy. Without conveying the notion that the body is a source of shame, teach your child that he doesn't need to show his to other people. Encourage him to value modesty, and let him see you modeling it as well.

Should I allow my children to take baths together?

While young children often find taking baths together to be fun, by this age your child should be learning the importance of modesty and privacy. Your child is more apt to learn these if you classify bath time as a solo undertaking.

Should I allow my child to take a bath with a friend?

See answer on previous page.

What should I do if I hear my child using vulgar sexual terms?

Many children like to impress their friends and siblings with "bad words," sexual or otherwise. When kids are young, most likely they don't have a clue what the words mean.

Before you get angry, ask your child what the word means. If she doesn't know, explain that there are certain words that show a lack of respect for the bodies God has given us, for His instructions not to use "obscenity" or "filthy language" (Eph. 5:4; Col. 3:8), and for other people who are offended. If your child knows what she's saying, establish an appropriate consequence for the behavior and explain the word's meaning. Encourage your child to use correct sexual terms rather than implying that all references to sex are forbidden.

It's important to find out where she's hearing the words and make sure she isn't hearing them from you or your spouse. Since modeling is the best teacher, it's hard to scold your child if she's repeating words learned from your mouth.

How important is school when it comes to shaping my child's attitudes about sex?

Your home should be the primary source of your child's information about sex. The school should support what you're doing at home. Unfortunately, many schools have taken over the job of sex education, partly because too few parents are doing the job.

Many schools have a sex education curriculum for kindergarten through twelfth grade. As a parent, find out what your child's school teaches. You have a right to review all your school's materials, including those used in sex education. Take advantage of your right and ask to review it.

The influence the curriculum will have on your child depends on the stands it takes. If the material supports what you're saying at home, that's great. If it doesn't, you'll need to either pull your child from the class or be prepared to talk with him about how your family's values differ from what was taught in school.

The best approach, and the one that will minimize the school's potentially negative influence, is to talk about sexual issues before they're brought up at school. This will not only give you opportunity to address information about the mechanical aspects of sex, but you'll also be able to talk with your child about God's plan for human sexuality.

How do I find out what the elementary school is teaching about sex?

Ask. As previously noted, you as a parent have the right to review all your child's curriculum. You don't want to come across to her teacher as difficult and demanding, but it's important to know what she'll be taught in this area.

You may wish to ask the teacher if you can review the curriculum so you'll know how to supplement it at home in discussions with your child. Or you can volunteer to work in the classroom on those days, or ask to review books on topics that the teacher might use. By talking and working with your child's teacher in other areas, you won't seem confrontational. If you're concerned with some of the curriculum, ask the teacher why it was chosen.

Should I allow my child to spend the night with a group of kids at a sleepover?

Sleepovers have become very popular through the school years, especially for birthday parties and special occasions. In the early elementary years, children especially need a good night's sleep and don't have the desire to stay up late watching movies and gossiping about the opposite sex—so it isn't necessary to start group sleepovers at this age. There's always a concern that your child will be exposed to TV and movies you might not approve of, so if he does spend the night make sure you know what will be going on.

Organized overnights with church groups, Scouts, or others who ensure a high ratio of responsible adult-to-child supervision can be great opportunities for children to learn to be away from home for a night or two. Since some children are fearful of leaving home, this might be a good way to introduce a little independence. Spending the night at a friend's house, where you trust the family and are comfortable with its standards, is also a fun way to practice being away from home.

If your child doesn't want to "sleep away" at this age, don't encourage it. Be prepared to trek out during the night to pick him up—a moment that could be priceless in reminding you that your child isn't as mature as you thought.

Tragically, sexual abuse is all too common today. If you have even the slightest concern about a particular situation, don't hesitate to say no. Conflict with your child, or with other parents, is far better than a lifetime of regret.

Don't let your child stay overnight at a friend's house unless you know the other family, including siblings, very well—and understand what the sleeping arrangements will be. You and your child should discuss in advance how she'll respond if asked to do something she's uncomfortable with or that violates your family standards. She should also know that she has complete freedom to call you at any time, and that you'll come and get her without hesitation.

Should I be concerned if my child tells me about her friend who has a boyfriend or girlfriend?

Kids today are exposed to so much talk about "boyfriends" and "girlfriends." Ask what your daughter means when she says her friend has a boyfriend or girlfriend. Most of the time at this age it means something simple; perhaps her friend just thinks her "boyfriend" is cute. Usually there's no real relationship beyond being friends. Most of the time they don't even speak to each other! Occasionally kids might brag about having kissed each other on the lips, but they may see it as more of an accomplishment (one to be discouraged by parents) than a true reflection of any feelings.

Take this opportunity to discuss relationships in general with your child. What does it mean to be a boyfriend or girlfriend or a friend in general? What's the difference? Emphasize that looks aren't what makes a good friend, and that character and Christian virtues are important to look for in others as well as to develop in oneself.

Also, take this time to introduce your family's position regarding when it's appropriate to begin dating. Keep your ears open for future conversations on this topic, because it will come up often over the years as your child redefines these terms.

What should I tell my child about his father's new girlfriend living with him?

This is a difficult concept for kids to grasp after a divorce. In addition to trying to have a normal relationship with each parent, kids secretly desire that their parents will reunite. As parents start to rebuild their lives, the process often will include a new relationship.

Unfortunately, cohabitation is a living arrangement that many singles adopt for a number of misguided reasons. Some people consider it an opportunity to "try out" a new relationship to see if it works, with the option of walking away if things don't go well. Others believe—mistakenly, according to social research—that cohabitation will somehow increase their likelihood of having a successful future marriage. Still others simply use cohabitation as a way to avoid real commitment.

Whatever reason your child's father has for living with his girlfriend, it sets a poor example for your child—and makes it awkward when it's time for your child to visit. Have a discussion with your child (with respect for the other parent) about God's design for relationships and His plans for human sexuality. Let him know that you wish things were different with his father.

It's very important that you not try to influence your child's opinion of his dad (or mom), but your input will help him process the differences at his father's house. Be sure to listen to his feelings before and after the visit. Encourage him to share his feelings with his father as well, if appropriate. If your child is uncomfortable, you might talk with your ex about how to remedy the situation.

Is it normal for my son to play exclusively with girls?

No. At this age, it's the rare boy who prefers to play with girls only. Starting around age six, boys typically give up the companionship of opposite-sex friends and move into an "I hate girls" mindset. This is the time when boys want to build clubhouses and don't want girls around. It's not sexism; in fact, it's part of healthy and normal gender identification.

If your son wants to play only with girls, it would be wise to seek input about his behavior from a professional who shares your Christian values. Many parents may be uncomfortable with their son's behavior but choose to ignore it because others will insist it's not a problem. This preference could be a sign that your son needs more one-on-one time with his father.

This also would be a good time to help your son interact with boys who have similar interests. And if you have the time and resources, you may want to identify an individual sport, such as bowling, biking, tennis, or swimming, that your son can excel in to boost his confidence.

Is it too early for my child to show signs of gender confusion?

No. Gender confusion can certainly manifest itself between the ages of five and seven. It isn't common for a boy this age to consistently prefer to play only with girls, be overly attached to his mother, dress up like a girl, or consider himself a girl. The most important thing you can do as a parent is to not panic or react in a way that communicates rejection. Instead, express love to your son, affirm his masculinity, and seek ways to build confidence and connection with other males. You should also seek help from a licensed Christian counselor.

A "tomboy," on the other hand, usually doesn't require such intervention. A girl who likes to play athletic and aggressive games while avoiding more "girl-like" activities isn't of great concern unless she's convinced she is actually a boy.

Children this age need strong, supportive relationships with parents and adults of both sexes. They also need clear direction and boundaries for behavior and activities. These adults need to be committed to affirming the children for the gifts and temperament that have been given them.

How can I prevent gender confusion in my child?

Questions about one's gender may be unavoidable when a child, boy or girl, isn't stereotypically "all boy" or "all girl." Some identity issues arise from feelings and confusion within the child. These questions should be addressed by parents who are affirming and loving to their child, helping that child to understand his or her maleness or femaleness while avoiding behaviors that reinforce the image of gender confusion (such as encouraging your son to play with baby dolls or allowing your daughter to only dress in boys' clothing).

Other children may experience gender confusion simply because of questioning or ridicule by peers, adults, or even parents. Children in this situation need affirmation, strong role models, and possibly professional help.

How do I prevent my son from experiencing gender confusion while helping him appreciate his "less manly" gifts?

The first things you can do if you see your son acting differently from other boys are to appreciate his special gifts and stay involved. If your son is sensitive, kind, social, artistic, and gentle, this doesn't mean he won't grow up to be a strong man. The primary factor that affects a young boy's identity is how his father responds to his personality. If his father doesn't appreciate his gifts, a boy may identify with his mother, and then he may experience some gender confusion.

Mothers need to allow their sensitive boys to be boys. If your son is being teased or pushed around, don't rush in to save him; without being overprotective, let him learn how to express himself. Fathers need to avoid ridiculing their sons for being artistic; rather, dads should spend time exploring the hobbies their sons enjoy. Embrace your boy's personality, affirm his masculinity, and help him experience your world with his giftedness in mind.

At this age your son is very aware of his differences, and counseling may be necessary to help him understand his strengths.

As a mom, what should I do if my son doesn't like—or rejects—his father?

Sometimes young boys don't identify with their fathers because the dads are away most of the time or ignore their sons when at home. Before you react harshly or encourage your son's dislike for his father, dig more deeply into the reason behind the boy's statement. Often young men choose to shun their fathers because they've felt rejection from them.

Boys desperately need three things from their fathers in order to bond with them: affection, attention, and approval. If your son isn't getting his needs met, he may interpret his father's behavior as personal disinterest in and rejection of him. If he's feeling rejected, the natural thing to do is to reject his father.

By all means, don't encourage this behavior. Does your son's dad love him? If so, remind your son of this. Then talk with your husband (or son's father) about your boy's actions, and encourage him to invest more time with his son and to look for opportunities to bond. Encourage your son to not reject his father, but rather to give his dad the opportunity to be involved in his life.

How can I, as a father, develop a strong relationship with my son?

Cultivating a strong relationship with your son will take a lot of commitment and involvement on your part. This starts when he's young and continues through his adolescence. Start early by engaging your son in roughhouse play. Let your son tackle you and believe that he's taken you down. Affectionate physical play of this sort will go a long way in reinforcing your son's sense of masculine identity.

Take your son with you on errands. Let him help you wash the car. Take him to the hardware store or out to buy flowers for Mom. This will communicate to your son that he's special.

Finally, be the last person to tell your son good night. Read him a story and say a quick bedtime prayer. Your being the last person in his room will provide him comfort and emotional assurance that he'll be safe through the night.

Questions Children Ask

Where do babies come from?

One way a husband and wife show how much they love each other is by hugging each other very close. To be as close as they can be, they hug without any clothes on, and a tiny cell, called a sperm, comes from the husband's penis and swims up into his wife's uterus and joins one of her eggs. Together these two cells start a baby!

The baby grows inside the mom's uterus until it's ready to come out through the mom's vagina. The uterus gets bigger as the baby grows, just like blowing up a balloon. Once the baby is born, the uterus gets small again. All of this takes nine months to happen, and it's quite an amazing process!

Why do boys have a penis?

The penis helps a boy go to the bathroom and later in life helps make babies. Just behind the penis is a sack of skin, the scrotum; inside it are two small, round objects called testicles, where sperm cells are produced.

What is sexual intercourse?

Sexual intercourse is one way that a husband and wife show each other how much they love each other. You might see a married couple kissing, holding hands, and giving hugs. But sex is getting even closer together than that. In fact, a husband and wife usually lie together naked in bed (it seems to be most comfortable and private there) and get so close that the man puts his penis into his wife's vagina. (For more information, see "What is sexual intercourse? Is it the same as sex?" in the next chapter on pages 124–125.)

How does a baby get inside a mom's tummy?

A baby's life starts when a dad's sperm and a mom's egg join together. This happens when the mom and dad hug close together so that the sperm from his penis goes into her vagina to find her eggs.

This tiny beginning of a baby moves into the mom's uterus, a place inside a mom especially made to grow babies. The baby will spend about nine months growing in the uterus before it's ready to be born.

How do babies get out of the mom?

After spending nine months growing inside the mom's uterus, the baby is ready to be born. The uterus opens up into the vagina, and the vagina is the passageway that the baby comes out of. It's between the mom's legs, close to the opening in her body that she uses to go to the bathroom.

When the baby is ready to be born, the mom goes into labor for a number of hours. During labor, the mom pushes her baby through the passageway so her baby can come into the world.

What is a vagina?

Girls and women have three openings in their private areas. The first is near the front and allows urine to come out. It's called the urethra, and the opening is very small.

The second one, in the middle, is larger and is called the vagina. The vagina allows babies to be born from a woman's body.

The third opening is in the back; it's called the anus. It's medium-sized and is where bowel movements come out.

What is AIDS?

AIDS is a disease caused by a dangerous virus that makes the body so weak that it can't fight off other germs. It's hard for most children to catch the AIDS virus, since they normally don't do the things that would cause them to get AIDS.

What is a period?

A period is the flow of blood that a woman has about once a month that comes from her uterus and through her vagina. A period shows that a woman's body is able to take care of a baby inside her uterus if a man's sperm comes together with one of her eggs.

Why don't boys have breasts?

Boys do have breasts, but they don't grow like a woman's breasts. The main purpose of a woman's breasts is to make food for newborn babies. Since boys don't give birth to babies, they don't need to make breast milk. That's why boys have breasts that don't grow.

What is sex?

Sex can mean a few different things. There are two sexes—male and female. Sex can also mean sexual intercourse, also known as "making love" and several other slang terms you might hear.

Sexual intercourse is an activity that should be enjoyed by a man and woman who are married. One of the reasons a man and woman have sex is to make a baby and start a family. God's plan is for people to have sex and to have babies only when they're married. Many people who aren't married have sex, but they often experience a lot of problems because of their choices.

9

BREAKING FREE

Eight- to Ten-Year-Olds

Soccer games. Boy Scouts. Karate. Homework. Video games. Sleepovers. Do you remember a simpler time? A time when your Saturdays were spent watching cartoons and making breakfast for your kids? Those days have been replaced with games, practices, multiplication tables, and more and more activities.

Whether you like it or not, your baby isn't one anymore. He or she has become a confident student or athlete or artist (or thinks so). Now's the time to start talking about his or her future, if you haven't already done so. As your child longs for independence, it's your job to teach him or her the responsibility that goes hand in hand with it.

This is also a time when you can build confidence by showing interest in what your child likes to do, rather than forcing him or her to be involved in your interests. Many kids this age are dying for their parents to show an interest in their dreams and desires. Even though your child longs to be grown-up, he or she secretly wants you to quit work early and come home to play catch or bake brownies together.

Your mission during this stage of your child's life, if you choose to accept it, is to start letting go—while at the same time providing him or her with the skills to make good decisions. The fatal mistake many parents make at this juncture in their child's development is to gradually drop out altogether. Your child needs your affirmation and help to make sense of the world. As he or she begins to change physically and emotionally, your son or daughter needs you to be there with encouragement and support. This is indeed a pivotal time in your child's development.

Parents' Questions

When does puberty begin for boys and girls? Is it the same for both?

Puberty is defined as the time of life in which boys and girls physically begin to change and develop into men and women and become able to have children. Puberty begins, on average, between ages nine and eleven for girls and ten and thirteen for boys. Some start developing even later than that, and a very few begin earlier (which could be a sign of a hormonal problem).

When should I start talking to my child about puberty?

You certainly want to talk to your child before puberty begins. Since you don't know when that will be, this conversation should happen earlier rather than later.

If you have a daughter, start discussing puberty between ages eight and nine. If you have a son, start between ages ten and eleven. If you have a family history of early development, you might want to consider even a year earlier.

Your child may resist a conversation about puberty, but your attitude can play a role in her comfort level. Be positive and let your child know that you want to tell her about something very important that will be happening to her body. If she shuts down or seems disinterested, set another time and make it special for her. How she reacts is out of your control, but your responsibility is to let her know she can come to you with her questions.

Should I use books or charts to illustrate the physical facts of puberty?

Pictures are very helpful in explaining puberty. Showing your child illustrations of his anatomy will help make an abstract issue more concrete. These books can be found at the local bookstore, library, or physician's office.

How will puberty affect the personality of my son? My daughter?

Puberty is often a time of turmoil. Generally kids feel frustrated with what's happening to their bodies and don't have much control over their emotions. This anxiety can lead to moody behavior for both boys and girls. Your child might not be able to pinpoint what's wrong, or he may lash out, sulk, or withdraw for no apparent reason.

Fortunately, his basic personality is still intact. Rest assured that it will reemerge when puberty ends, and may even be present throughout. Patience and understanding are needed to survive this stage of your child's development. That doesn't mean you should put up with disrespectful behavior, but spending more time listening and asking open-ended questions without seeming to pry lets him know you still care about him and are just trying to understand his world.

Is it inappropriate for my child to see the opposite sex naked?

At this age, your child should desire privacy when in the bathroom and dressing. Even if she doesn't, modesty and respect for others' privacy should be encouraged (and modeled) in the home.

It's not unhealthy or inappropriate if she sees her baby brother's body while she helps Mom change his diaper. Her natural curiosity will be satisfied without embarrassing anyone. It's not appropriate, however, for her to see siblings (or other children) of the opposite sex naked if they're beyond toddlerhood.

How much roughhousing play is appropriate for a father and daughter?

Once your daughter starts to go through puberty, it's time to curb this kind of activity. In this day and age, it's easily misunderstood, and it might embarrass your daughter.

Hugs and kisses are still called for. In fact, daughters *need* appropriate touch from their fathers. And it's always okay to ask your daughter what she's comfortable with and what she enjoys doing with you. If she doesn't mind the roughhousing, let her determine how long it should continue.

What should I tell my child about HIV/AIDS?

AIDS, or *acquired* (not something you're born with, but due to infection) *immunodeficiency* (inability to fight off infection) *syndrome* (an illness with various symptoms), is a disease caused by a powerful virus called HIV (human immunodeficiency virus). It makes the body so weak that it can't fight off other germs.

It's hard to contract HIV, and children usually don't do the things that could normally cause them to get the virus, like having sex or taking illegal drugs with needles. Some teenagers and adults do things that could cause them to get HIV. A child can get the virus if his mother has it when she's pregnant and passes it on to her child during birth, but this is uncommon if the mother is being treated with the proper drugs.

You can't catch HIV from someone just by touching or hugging him. But it's possible to catch the virus from someone else as a child if you come into contact with blood from someone with HIV and you have a cut, scratch, or tear in your skin. So never touch anyone else's blood. If your friend is bleeding, get an adult to help stop the bleeding.

How do I encourage my child to use appropriate language rather than slang when referring to body parts or functions?

Modeling is usually the best way to teach. The place to start is making sure your language is appropriate when referring to your child's penis or vagina. If you haven't used those words in the past, now's the time to correct that.

If you're embarrassed to use correct terminology, now is also the time to get over it for the sake of your child. If you're not flustered, your child probably won't be, either.

If your child uses slang to name a body part, gently say, "You mean your . . ." and stress that it's best to call it what it is. This shows respect for one's body, which is an important principle to teach at this age.

What should I do when my child uses vulgarity or profane language?

Many late-elementary kids try to show off to their friends by using profanity they've heard. Often they're uncertain about what's really being said.

Most kids try not to let the words slip out when an adult is around, knowing they'd get into trouble. If you happen to overhear an unacceptable word from your child, talk first about what he thinks that word means, and examine what he's really trying to communicate. It's best to initially keep the tone nonjudgmental.

Let your child know that your family follows certain rules of respect, and that includes no foul language. If you're a Christian, explain that such language is not consistent with your faith. Ask your child not to repeat it, and help him find some other, more suitable term that expresses his feelings. Discuss with him your expectations and the consequences of not following your rules. If your child continues to use this type of language, make sure you follow through as promised!

Do I really need to monitor the websites, movies, TV shows, music, and video games my child sees and hears at this age?

Absolutely! As your child starts to become more independent in the later grade-school years, you may be tempted to stop keeping track of what she watches on TV, explores on her computer or tablet or smartphone, plays in video games, or listens to on her MP3 player. The influence of her friends' older siblings starts to filter down and may expose her mind to things she hasn't seen or heard before.

Beware! It's important to think about and hold to your standards for media consumption. Now is not the time to let your child start seeing

Managing Your Media

The Internet, TV, movies, and MP3 players bring several sets of new "friends" into a child's home. These "friends" have a profound influence in kids' lives. Within hours or days, young people across the country can pick up the latest trends, styles, and products that have been promoted through viral videos and social networking.

Think of how many millions of dollars are spent on advertising during the Super Bowl. That's because advertising influences buying decisions. If the media can convince a three-year-old to beg his parent to purchase Scooby Snacks instead of the generic brand, why wouldn't sexually immoral and indecent content desensitize our kids beginning at an early age, too?

When it comes to the effect of such content on young children, most parents seem to assume it "goes right over their heads." As long as it doesn't involve nakedness, these parents think their kids don't get it. Unfortunately, that sentiment doesn't hold water. Research shows that violent behavior and exposure to media are deeply connected, and the connection is even stronger between entertainment and sexual decision-making.[1] Furthermore, graphic images aren't the only ones that influence children; some movies with a PG rating show unmarried couples living together and having sex—just without nudity.

As a parent, you can't afford to give in just because "everyone else is watching it." If you want to curb the influence the entertainment industry has on your family, try some of these tips:

- Limit your children's TV and video exposure (including noneducational computer time). Research links childhood obesity, among other things, with TV viewing and time spent online. Institute a "no TV" week or

PG-13 or R-rated movies (even some PG ones are inappropriate), thinking she won't comprehend all the sex, language, and violence. Seeing sexually explicit material will arouse her curiosity and imagination.

It's still best to sit down with your child and watch TV together. If you don't agree with the values you see or hear, comment on them or turn the show off and say why. And don't forget that many video games are loaded with toxic content, from sex to language to drug references (not to mention pervasive, realistic violence). Be sure to check the ratings on the video games you buy.

"Internet day off" every so often; it might just bring your family closer together.

- If you want your child to have a cell phone, consider getting him a "feature phone" rather than a smartphone. Smartphones provide access to the Internet that's usually harder to monitor and control than it is on a typical computer.

- Be proactive in choosing TV shows and movies the entire family can watch. Ask your kids questions about what they thought of the characters and overall message of the show or movie. Give your opinion at the end, especially if you don't agree with what you saw.

- If you happen to turn on a raunchy movie, don't hesitate to turn it off. Your kids might complain, but explain your reasons for turning it off and start a conversation; more likely than not, your children will learn to imitate your behavior.

- Use ratings only as a starting point. Research TV shows, video games, music, and movies ahead of time so that if you don't approve, you'll have an alternative. You may want to start with Plugged In Online, an outreach of Focus on the Family. It's designed to help families evaluate media messages and teach discernment in media consumption. At the Plugged In website (www.PluggedIn.com) you'll find critiques of music, films, television shows, and video games that offer in-depth information on both the positive and objectionable themes presented.

For more information on how to guard your family against damaging media influences, visit www.FocusontheFamily.com/safety. You may also want to read the book *Plugged-In Parenting* by Bob Waliszewski (Focus on the Family/Tyndale House Publishers, 2011).

Are children affected by seeing sexually explicit material at this age?

So often parents think, *My children are clueless; what they hear or see won't have much influence.* But kids, regardless of age, are impressionable and curious.

Because sexually explicit materials are themselves a distortion of what God designed, they can cause your child to have a distorted view of sex. Your goal should be to get there first (which means now, if not sooner) when talking about relationships, sexual intercourse, and respect for other people. Train your child to recognize inappropriate material and tell you about it.

Keep asking your child if he has any questions in this area, which will encourage him to look to you as an authority. If you discover him with a magazine, book, or movie that's unacceptable, discuss why you don't think he should be exposed to it. That goes for sexually explicit or otherwise inappropriate songs and websites you may have noticed him visiting.

What types of clothing are appropriate for my child to wear?

As children reach the later years of elementary school, they're much more aware of and opinionated about how they look and what they wear. Especially with girls, the latest styles are what they want. Boys also become aware of the trends, though this may occur a little later than with girls.

But don't fall for fads that are inappropriate for your child's age. Let her choose as much as she can, but hold your ground on clothing that's immodest. Eight- to ten-year-old girls don't need to be oversexualized by dressing like models and wearing clothes that don't cover enough skin. You may get some flak when you take a stand, but it can start a discussion about modesty and how the way you dress influences what people think about you.

Should I allow my child to attend a sleepover with his friends?

Sleepovers become a favorite for birthday parties and special occasions at this age. The problem is that very little sleep occurs at sleepovers, and they may wipe your child out for the rest of the weekend. Saturday nights wipe out Sundays, when your family may attend church and children need to get homework done.

If your child does spend the night at a friend's house, it's best to know the family well, know what its standards are for movies (this is an age when a lot of children start seeing R-rated movies their parents don't know about), and ask about plans for the night. Let the parents know your limits on movies and other entertainment.

If a pattern develops and your child is exhausted for the duration of the weekend, you might let him stay until ten o'clock and then pick him up. It's also okay to have a limit of only one overnight a month or quarter so that you're not battling a cranky child every weekend.

Should I be concerned about my son being exposed to pornography at this early age?

Yes! Most boys in our culture are first exposed to porn around age eight. Brain imaging studies indicate that pornography can be as addicting as cocaine or heroin. The earlier a child is exposed to pornography, the more likely he'll later experience addictive behavior and damaged relationships.

While pornography is often presented as a boys' problem, in recent years more and more girls have become involved in viewing it. Even girls who haven't developed a habit of doing so can have their perceptions of God's gift of sex drastically altered by accidental exposure.

Children who regularly use the Internet frequently run into pornographic sites. Since kids this age—especially boys—have a heightened curiosity about sex anyhow, this is the time to be diligent about what your child is being exposed to. Take the following precautions to reduce your child's likelihood of exposure to Internet pornography:

- Have an open and honest discussion with your child about online safety and responsibility, and make sure he or she clearly understands any guidelines you establish.

- Encourage your child to talk to you immediately if he or she happens upon any explicit material on the Internet.

- Put your family computer in a central location so that you know when your child is online and can easily see what's being viewed.

- Don't allow your child to have an Internet-connected computer in his or her bedroom.

- Install filtering and parental control software on your family computer (visit FocusontheFamily.com for more information).

- Draft an Internet safety contract that explains your rules and expectations for your children when they're online; talk through each point with them and have them sign it.

If, in spite of your best efforts, you discover your child has been viewing pornography, it's time to have a frank discussion. Don't shame your child for being curious about or interested in the opposite sex, but make sure he or she is aware that pornography is destructive and can seriously warp one's view of sexuality. Explain that porn exploits others; in a real way, it represents the sexual abuse of the person in the photo or video. Help your child understand, too, that sex is designed to be beautiful and freeing in the context of marriage—not the distorted thing that pornography depicts.

Determine the consequences your child will face if he or she views pornography again. Talk with him or her about those consequences, and be ready to follow through.

Finally, if your child repeatedly views pornography or you have even the least concern that he or she has a problem, be prepared to seek the assistance of a licensed Christian counselor who deals with this issue.

My daughter doesn't do many things that I think of as "feminine." What should I do?

Before you do anything, Dr. Joseph Nicolosi (a doctor who works primarily with gender-identity issues in young people) suggests answering the following questions with your spouse or with a trained counselor:

- Is your daughter markedly gender atypical?
- Does she reject her sexual anatomy?
- Does she go to her mother with questions? Does she ask her mother to do things with her? Does she show Mom her toys, games, and activities, or does she prefer to go to Dad? Does she have a comfortable relationship with her mother? Does she enjoy doing "girl things" with her mother?
- To what extent does your daughter interact and relate comfortably with other girls?
- Does your daughter adamantly reject the possibility that she'll grow up to be married and have children someday?
- Does her father encourage her feminine development?[2]

If your daughter is expressing herself in feminine ways at home—but not away from home—you should keep your eyes open, but don't panic yet. The reality of life for girls this age is harsh. It's easier for a young lady who hasn't "blossomed" to hang out with the boys, because the teasing and rejection isn't as tough. You may remember the pains of growing up; unfortunately, girls today are exposed to harsher criticism about their looks and behaviors earlier than ever. Stay involved in your daughter's life, and remind her that she's loved for who she is and who she will be. If you're concerned, seek help from a qualified Christian professional.

How can I talk to my son about sex when he rejects me? I'm his dad and live in the same home; sometimes it seems like I should just give up and let his mom take care of it.

Don't give up on your son. And by all means, don't let his mother take exclusive care of him. Pursue your son and get past his defensive detachment. Put your own feelings of rejection aside and try to find ways to identify with him.

Many fathers give up on their sons because they don't want to be intrusive. Be intrusive; you matter to your son and his future. Sooner or later, he'll soften to your efforts and let you back into his life. If you feel discouraged and want to abandon ship, seek professional help for guidance and encouragement to stay the course.

Sometimes my son seems depressed about having to compete with other boys. Once he said he wished he were a girl. How seriously should I take this?

There are several markers that can help mental health professionals determine if a child has a gender-identity disorder:

- Repeatedly stated desire to be, or insistence that he or she is, the other sex.
- In boys, a preference for cross-dressing or simulating female attire. In girls, insistence on wearing only stereotypical masculine clothing.
- Strong and persistent preference for cross-sexual roles in make-believe play, or persistent fantasies of being the other sex.

- Intense desire to participate in the stereotypical games and pastimes of the other sex.
- Strong preference for playmates of the opposite sex.[3]

If you notice any of these behaviors in your child, it would be wise to talk with his physician or a professional counselor who shares your Christian beliefs and values.

What happens to boys during puberty?

Pubertal development is a relatively simple process for boys. The first physical sign of puberty in boys is the enlargement of the testicles and the thinning of the scrotum. Hair appears on the face and chest, under the arms, and in the genital area. Also, a boy's voice begins to deepen; during this time it may crack and squeak.

While these external changes are taking place, internally the testicles begin to produce sperm that are transported through the epididymis and onward to the penis through the vas deferens. The prostate then begins to produce seminal fluid, which carries the sperm out of the body during ejaculation.

During puberty, boys also have a growth spurt and tend to experience rapid weight gain—while losing body fat.

What happens to girls during puberty?

While puberty for boys is fairly easy to describe, girls undergo a greater number of changes. Some would say it provides an excellent excuse for the moodiness and poor behavior they tend to display during this phase.

The first visible sign of puberty for girls is the development of breast buds. This usually begins about two years before a girl's first menstrual period. As her breasts continue to grow, hair appears on her legs and genitals and under her arms. Her hips become wider, while her internal reproductive organs grow and mature.

After all this is complete, a girl experiences her first period—known as *menarche*—and in most cases is capable of having babies.

Questions Children Ask

What is puberty?

Puberty is the time of life in which boys and girls physically begin to become men and women and are then able to have children. Puberty for most girls begins somewhere between ages nine and eleven. For most boys, it's a little later—on average between ages ten and thirteen.

Girls develop breasts; hair appears in their genital area. About two years after puberty begins, a girl's period starts. She grows a lot before that happens, and then keeps growing a little more after that.

Boys also start developing hair in their genital area and eventually body and facial hair as well. Their voice begins to deepen, and their penis and testicles begin to enlarge. Muscles bulk up as well. The growth spurt in boys starts a lot later than in girls but can continue longer.

What happens to boys when puberty begins?

Puberty is marked by the fact that testosterone (the main male hormone) is flooding through a boy's body. When this happens, he starts growing quickly, his shoulders and chest start to fill out, and his penis gets thicker and longer. His voice may also begin to get deeper. Eventually, curly, dark hair begins to grow in his pubic area and under his arms. The penis and testicles continue to grow larger, and facial and body hair also gets darker and coarse. A downside of puberty is that acne may show up.

Puberty is a very normal process. When it's finished, boys look more like men than they did before. All boys go through puberty, usually starting somewhere between ages ten and thirteen. Boys continue to grow throughout the teen years and some grow into their twenties.

What happens to girls when puberty begins?

Puberty in girls usually starts earlier than in boys; sometimes it can start as early as age eight, but it generally begins between ages nine and eleven. Most often, a breast bud (a bump under the nipple that can be a little tender) shows up first. It can appear in one side before the other. (Don't panic;

the other side will eventually develop.) Sometimes the first sign of puberty is dark, coarse hair in the pubic area on a girl's labia (the lips outside the vagina) as well as in her armpits.

A girl usually grows a lot before her first period starts, and she'll continue to grow for a couple of years after her period, but at a slower pace. She may develop some acne (pimples) on her face. In addition, a young woman's hips and shoulders round out, and her breasts continue to grow. Generally, by age sixteen girls start looking more like women.

Why do some kids start puberty before others?

All kids go through puberty, but the timing varies from person to person. Sometimes when your mom or dad was very late in going through puberty, you'll be late also. Your genetic makeup can play a role in this process. That also means you might not follow your mom or dad at all!

What are hormones?

Hormones are amazing substances produced in various glands throughout the body. They flow through the bloodstream to all parts of the body, stimulating growth.

During puberty, several sex hormones that start the process of changing the body from that of a child to an adult are released from the pituitary gland in the brain. Testosterone is the main hormone during puberty for boys, and it's made in the testicles. Estrogen and progesterone are the main hormones for girls, and they're released from the ovaries. Hormones are responsible for pubic and underarm hair growth, breast development, testicle and penis growth, acne, moodiness, and all the other things that make puberty a unique experience.

What is a menstrual cycle?

A menstrual cycle lasts about twenty-eight days, but it can be shorter or longer. When a teen girl begins to have a period, it means her body is capable of having a baby. The first year of her periods may not be very regular, meaning she could go several months without one.

As a young lady develops, eggs start maturing in her ovaries. Those eggs are released about once a month. If a sperm from a man finds its way to the released egg and they unite in the fallopian tube (which connects the ovary to a woman's uterus), they travel together down the fallopian tube and settle in the lining of the uterus—resulting in pregnancy.

Even if a pregnancy doesn't happen, a woman's body knows that a potential baby needs a tremendous blood supply for nutrition. So as an egg travels toward the uterus, even if it doesn't meet a sperm, the uterus gets ready. But when a sperm doesn't fertilize the egg, the uterus releases the blood that's been collected for the potential baby from the uterine lining, and it flows out the vagina. This is what causes a period.

Early on, a young woman may not experience a lot of blood flow each month. But it can vary from girl to girl. Most girls wear a maxi pad that can stick to their underwear to absorb the blood.

A girl will usually experience a period two years after the onset of puberty. When you start to experience a growth spurt, hair growth, and breast development, it's a good idea to be prepared by carrying a thin pad in your backpack in a nontransparent small plastic bag. But if you're caught off guard at school or camp, find an adult and she'll be able to help you. It's also not unusual for the blood to overflow onto your clothes if you don't change your pad often enough. Try not to be embarrassed; it happens to every girl from time to time.

What is a virgin?

A virgin is a person who's never had sexual intercourse (oral, vaginal, or anal). Many teens falsely assume they're virgins if they've "only" had oral or anal sex. This is simply not true. In the broad sense of the term, the word *virgin* means that a person is without experience. By having oral or anal sex a teen has definitely gained sexual experience.

When thinking about what makes a person a virgin it's more important to consider God's plan rather than technical definitions. His intent is that sexual experience of any kind be shared only between a man and a woman within the relationship of marriage. You should understand, too, that the Bible talks a lot more about our thoughts and attitudes than it does about which specific acts may cause us to "lose our virginity." Looking at it this way, you can see that it's better for you to remain sexually pure in your thoughts and actions than it is to see just how far you can go sexually while still technically remaining a virgin.

Even if a person has already been sexually active, he or she can decide not to engage in sexual activity again until marriage. This is sometimes called secondary virginity.

How does a girl get pregnant?

For a girl to become pregnant, several things need to happen. First, she needs to have matured enough to be having periods (rarely a pregnancy will occur before a first period). Next, an egg needs to be released from the ovary into the fallopian tube; this generally happens during the middle of her menstrual cycle. Finally, she needs to have sexual intercourse with a man who releases sperm into her vagina, and these sperm—millions of them—make their way up through her uterus and into her fallopian tube. It only takes one sperm to unite with her egg to start a baby. The joining of a sperm and an egg is called fertilization; conception is another term that is often used for this event.

What is sex?

Sex includes the very broad topic of how our bodies work as male and female. Sex can also refer to "making love" or sexual intercourse.

What is sexual intercourse? Is it the same as sex?

Sexual intercourse is the scientific term for "having sex," "making love," and a whole host of other names. But what really happens during sex, or sexual intercourse?

Most anyone who's old enough to have gone through puberty is physically able to have sexual intercourse. But sex is an activity that's meant to involve the entire person—heart, mind, body, and soul. Research shows that the best sex happens when two people love each other and commit to one another in marriage.

This evidence supports God's design for human sexuality. Having sex before marriage cheapens sex by taking it out of the setting that God intended for it—marriage. Premarital sex can also put both parties at risk for an unwanted pregnancy or a sexually transmitted infection.

When a couple loves each other so much, they want to hug and kiss as closely as they can. That means they take their clothes off. When this happens, the husband's penis enlarges and hardens because he's very excited to be so close to his wife. The wife's vagina gets moist, and she lets her husband put his penis inside her vagina. It feels very good for both of them. At the same time that the man feels great pleasure being inside his wife, his penis shoots out a sticky fluid that contains millions of sperm.

Sex is an activity that allows couples to show one another just how much they love and care for each other. This is such an intimate activity that it should only be between a husband and wife. You won't want to let anyone pressure you into sharing it with him or her.

At what age is it okay to have sex?

This is a reasonable question. But it's more important to ask, "When is it the right *time* to have sex?"

When you get married is when it's okay to have sex. (By the way, regardless of age it's never okay to have sex if the other person doesn't want to. This is called rape or child abuse.)

Many people say, "When you're ready, you'll know it," but there are so many things besides the physical act that you need to think about. First and foremost, saving sex for marriage is God's design, so that's how we really know what the right time is—when you're married. But even apart from what the Bible explains about God's plan, it's easy to see that there are lots of emotional dangers that can arise when people have sex before marriage.

Some girls want to be loved, so they'll have sex with a boy in hope that the boy will love them. But often boys just want to have sex, so sex outside of marriage sets someone up for getting hurt. Emotions can fool you when you're a teen and you think you're ready for sex.

Then there are the physical problems that go along with sex. A girl can get pregnant when she doesn't want to. A girl or a boy can get a sexually transmitted infection that may be hard to treat or even incurable (see Appendix A in the back of this book).

Finally, don't forget how these things can change your future. If you become a parent as a teen, will you finish high school, go to college, or be able to get a job and work while rearing a child? How will your behavior affect your parents or other family members? Will you feel guilty or lose your self-respect?

The best time to start having sex is when you've found the love of your life and are married. Research shows that the best sex happens in marriage, when having sex is a part of what it means to love each other for the rest of your lives. You'll never regret that you waited.

Is sex a good thing or a bad thing?

Sex is a great thing. God created it for people to enjoy, and it's healthy and normal for married people. Unmarried people, however, sometimes choose to be sexually active—which isn't part of God's plan and isn't healthy.

For teens, sexual activity can cause both emotional and physical problems. These problems include infections that may lead to painful disease, or that might not allow them to have children in the future. Another problem is teenage pregnancy—which affects girls (and guys) for the rest of their lives.

What is homosexuality?

Homosexuality is having sexual or romantic attraction toward the same sex, engaging in sexual activity with a person of the same sex, and/or identifying oneself by those attractions or behaviors. Men attracted to other men often identify themselves as "gay," while women attracted to other women may identify as "lesbian." Some younger adults may identify as "queer" or "questioning."

God's plan for sex is that it be expressed between a man and woman who are married to each other. Sex between two men or two women falls outside that plan.

Still, homosexual men and women, just like everyone else, need to be treated with respect. There are many slang words that insensitive people use to refer to homosexuality. Using these words is cruel and demeaning.

Some teens have fleeting sexual or romantic attraction to members of the same sex. This does not mean they are homosexual.

What is AIDS?

See "What should I tell my child about HIV/AIDS?" on page 112.

Why do I have a lump growing under my nipple? Should I be worried?

Usually when puberty starts, many girls (and some boys) discover a lump under one or both nipples as the first sign of their bodies changing. When it's only under one nipple, one on the other side will usually show up in the next several months. These bumps aren't harmful, and the tenderness will go away. As you develop, these bumps will turn into breasts—or, if you're a boy, will eventually go away.

What is pornography?

Pornography is websites, books, magazines, pictures, videos, phone messages, video games, movies, or other material depicting men, women, or children naked and in sexual situations. Pornography is usually used by people to experience sexual excitement with or without a sexual partner.

Being exposed to pornography can lead to a very damaging view of sex that can hurt you and others. The Bible teaches that God cares not only about whether you're physically sexually active, but He cares about your thoughts and attitudes about sex as well. Here's one of the reasons pornography is wrong: It encourages you to focus on thoughts that oppose God's design for sex.

127

If you find a pornographic magazine or video or web page, tell an adult. It's not wrong to discover pornography by accident, but it's dangerous not to get rid of it right away. You can become addicted to pornography, just as people become addicted to drugs, tobacco, and alcohol.

What does it mean to ejaculate?

Ejaculation happens when, during sex, men release a burst of fluid containing sperm cells; it's accompanied by tremendous physical pleasure.

What is oral sex?

Oral sex describes the act of partners using their mouths on each other's genitals to physically excite one another.

Is oral sex really sex?

Yes. Oral sex is sex. Sexual activity occurs when one person touches another person's genitals and causes that person to get sexually excited. Any type of sex outside of marriage, including oral sex, goes against God's design for human sexuality.

Some teenagers experiment with oral sex because it can be pleasurable and won't lead to pregnancy. But just as with penetrative sex (when the penis goes into the vagina), they can contract infections from oral sex.

Are you a virgin if you've had oral sex?

A virgin is a person who's never had sexual intercourse (oral, vaginal, or anal). The term applies to both girls and boys.

Many young people falsely assume they're virgins if they've "only" had oral or anal sex. This is simply not true. In the broad sense of the term, the word *virgin* means that a person is without experience. By having oral or anal sex a teen has definitely gained sexual experience.

When thinking about what makes a person a virgin it's more important to consider God's plan rather than technical definitions. His intent is that sexual experience of any kind be shared only between a man and a woman within the relationship of marriage. You should understand, too, that the Bible talks a lot more about our thoughts and attitudes than it does about which specific acts may cause us to "lose our virginity." Looking at it this way, you can see that it's better for you to remain sexually pure in your thoughts and actions than it is to see just how far you can go sexually while still technically remaining a virgin.

Even if you've already been sexually active, you can decide not to engage in sexual activity again until you're married. This is sometimes called secondary virginity.

10

TELL ME MORE

Eleven- to Twelve-Year-Olds

Remember that song in the movie *Grease* where the girls and guys sing in high-pitched voices, "Tell me more, tell me more"?

Those lyrics likely summarize the thoughts swirling through your preteen's mind. Puberty is just around the corner, so take advantage of this momentum and get a head start on preparing him for the turbulent times to come.

Of course, not all teens will experience turbulence. But just in case, consciously continue to develop a relationship with your child—thinking of it as an investment in the future. Is there a sport or hobby he excels at that you can do together? If so, get involved with him. The time you spend together will help prevent some of the headaches you may experience tomorrow.

As your child approaches puberty, remember to celebrate the changes. Whatever you do, don't make fun of your child or minimize the emotions he's feeling during this transition. If you do, you'll likely sever the trust you've developed over the years.

Remember, with hormones in control, this isn't the time to poke fun at him. Be sensitive, respectful, and available. Doing so will allow you to experience the reward of watching your child blossom into a young adult.

Parents' Questions

How do I explain to my child the process of making love?

There are many ways to approach talking with your child about the mechanics of sex, but if you want to satisfy her curiosity as well as plant seeds of expected behavior for the future, it's important to discuss this in a context she can understand.

First, start the conversation with the question, "What do you understand making love to be?" Since many kids this age have friends who are experimenting with sexual play, you might be surprised by the answer.

Then offer your own, something like this: "Making love is an activity that most often happens between a husband and wife as an expression of their intense love for one another. When a person is touched by a person he or she loves and is attracted to, the brain releases chemicals that cause a physical response throughout the body. A person may get the tingles or become incredibly relaxed. During this process, an individual's sensory system is in full gear, and the slightest touch or kiss is completely enjoyable. As the body becomes excited, a man and woman will embrace and continue to caress, during which time the husband's penis will fit into his wife's vagina. The sensation during this process is enjoyable and causes a chain reaction known as an orgasm throughout the body."

How will my child be different now that he's going through puberty?

As mentioned before, your child's behavior will change almost daily. Some days will be great; your child will be the same person you knew prior to puberty. Other days won't be so great.

Regardless of behavior, your child desperately needs your support as he moves through this difficult stage of life. Try to remember what you felt like when you were going through puberty. Be your child's advocate during this transition.

How concerned should I be about the movies, music, and other forms of entertainment my child is exposed to?

Regardless of your child's age, media and entertainment should definitely be something you're concerned about. One of the problems with today's entertainment industry is that it often portrays casual sex as normal and acceptable. Not only does this fail to honor God and His design for sexuality, but it could have an impact on your child's choices about having sex.

Screening the movies your preteen watches is very appropriate. Also, watching TV and listening to music with your child can provide a great springboard for communication and an opportunity to express values you feel are important.

One of your goals at this age should be to encourage your preteen to develop skills in making good media choices independently. In the long run, this will be much more important than supervising every exposure.

Is it too early to promote sexual abstinence to my child?

Promoting sexual abstinence to your preteen is something that can never be done too early or too often. In fact, research shows that kids want their parents to establish what the acceptable norm of behavior will be in the home.[1] Boundaries should be set for all risky behaviors (drinking, violence, drugs, and sexual activity) early and often.

I'm divorced. How do I talk to my child about sex?

Your being divorced doesn't mean that you don't have the right to talk with your child about sex. In fact, you may have learned valuable lessons from your failed relationship that you can pass on to your child in the hope that she can avoid the same mistakes.

Promoting sexual abstinence until marriage is still the best advice about sex that you can give her. As with all things, your actions will speak louder than your words. Even if you've made mistakes in the past, it's important for you to set a good example for your preteen in your current behavior. If you want her to remain abstinent, it's important that she see you modeling sexual purity.

How do I protect my daughter from growing up too fast—you know, being exposed too early to sexual pressure and behavior?

It's natural to want to protect your daughter from growing up too fast. Unfortunately, you have no control over how quickly your child physically develops. Still, you can help protect her from overexposure to the wrong influences before she's ready to handle them.

One way of doing this is to know your daughter's friends. Make your home the place where her friends want to hang out. If their behavior or speech is inappropriate, you'll need to intervene.

Making an effort to connect with your child and staying involved will help you keep a pulse on whether she's growing up too fast. Based on your insight, you may encourage your daughter to make new friends or find new activities for her to be involved in.

How do I tell my child about the need for physical boundaries without frightening him?

Knowledge is power. Kids in this age group deeply want to be trusted; they struggle with the desire for independence. Because of your child's need for trust, this is a great time to revisit previous conversations about talking with strangers, setting physical boundaries, and other safety issues.

Use stories from the news to emphasize things you want him to do to be safe while he's not with you, that there are people in the world who want to hurt children, and that he's not invincible. If it's within your family's means, you may wish to consider getting a cell phone that he can carry with him in case of emergencies.

How can I present the facts about puberty and the dangers of sexual experimentation without overprotecting my child?

Presenting facts about pubertal development and the dangers of premature sexual activity is in no way "overprotecting" your child. The opposite is true. If you don't give her this information, you're actually placing her at risk. There are many consequences associated with premature sexual activity, including physical (sexually transmitted infections and nonmarital pregnancies), emotional, intellectual, social, and spiritual ones.

These consequences should be discussed with your child throughout her growing-up years. Conversations will occur naturally if you're spending time cultivating a relationship with her.

My daughter says she has a boyfriend; should I be concerned?

At this age, don't just shrug the "boyfriend thing" off. Bringing it up may be her attempt to talk with you on a more grown-up level.

During this stage of preadolescence, girls are usually much more interested in boys than the reverse. You shouldn't get too worked up, but rather realize that your daughter has started noticing the opposite sex. Find out what you can from her about the boy and what the relationship means; if necessary, you may be able to gather more information from other parents or teachers.

This is a good opportunity to have a discussion with your daughter about your family's standards regarding the age at which dating can occur and the circumstances under which dating is appropriate. You may also wish to start talking about boundaries in dating relationships.

In some communities, kids this age are experimenting with sexual play. Gently probe to find out what your daughter knows about this and whether she has friends who are engaged in this—and whether she's involved in it herself. If you're concerned that she may be engaged in sex play at this young age, seek help from a licensed Christian counselor. Sexual activity at this age has the strong potential to produce warped and lasting views of sex and sexuality.

Should I be concerned about my child being exposed to pornography at this age?

See "Should I be concerned about my son being exposed to pornography at this early age?" in the previous chapter, pages 117–118.

Porn in Your Home?

Pornography is a multibillion-dollar industry, and porn is accessible in virtually every home and neighborhood in our culture. Whether it's in print, film, television, or online, porn is destructive because it promotes sexual stimulation and expression apart from the most important element of human sexuality—an intimate relationship with a real person, specifically within the context of marriage.

Porn is an attack on both genders, but especially for boys and young men whose sexuality is more sensory than relational. To resist this attack, try the following:

- *Protect.* Begin at home. Keep your home free of printed pornography; set careful boundaries about movies, other entertainment, and even dress. Draw up a contract that details your expectations about Internet use and ask your child to sign it. Use filters on your computers and with the Internet. Monitor e-mail in and out.

If a child has a personal computer, place it in the living room where it can be monitored, too. Many children and teenagers are quite savvy about getting around web filters, so persistent vigilance is in order. Visit FocusontheFamily.com for resources on pornography—and to learn more about Internet filtering software as well as tools to take some of the worry out of watching TV and DVDs with your family.

- *Prepare.* Educate your children about pornography's dangers. Open and honest discussions about sex, sexuality, and the risks of pornography

---

Should I allow my preteen to go to the mall with a group of friends but no parental supervision? I'm worried about movies I haven't okayed, meetings with boyfriends or girlfriends I don't know about, and sexual predators.

Before you decide, ask yourself a few questions: Where do you live? What's the community like? Will there be adults at the mall who can watch over your child?

The reality of today's world is that there's no safe place for kids to roam. It might be wise to go to the mall with your child, allow him to wander should be part of every parent-child relationship. This atmosphere combats the secrecy and shame inherent in pornography use.

If your child is mature enough to understand, let her know that pornography increases sexual curiosity and drive outside the bounds of a healthy, nurturing marriage relationship with a real person; it can become a substitute for healthy relationships and grow addictive. In fact, anything that takes the place of a healthy relationship will, by nature, become addictive. Explain that brain imaging studies show porn to be as addictive as cocaine or heroin. Then encourage healthy friendships, which help meet the need for relationship, and activities like sports and hobbies that satisfy the need for achievement and purposeful activity. As your child grows, support from other adults and families who share your values and beliefs will be increasingly important.

- *Nurture.* Parents are the first and foremost source of nurturing for children and teenagers. This includes affirming and respecting the child, teaching boundaries and character, and celebrating the maleness or femaleness of each child.

Nurturing builds the self-esteem, confidence, and trust needed to seek healthy relationships. Nurturing is challenging work, and requires parents to form healthy relationships for themselves, too.

Most kids genuinely seek to be loved. Meeting your child's needs for love, affection, and attention at home is the best way to keep him from looking to counterfeit sources, including pornography.

with one or more friends and a cell phone, and have him check in from time to time. Remind him that your decision about going has nothing to do with trust, but rather with your concern for safety.

Should I allow my child to attend coed parties at this age?

Coed birthday parties are one thing. But parties at a friend's house on Friday night that aren't occasion-oriented should be suspect. It's important to know the family involved and what's planned.

Most kids this age aren't completely interested in the opposite sex anyway. In general, it's more fun for them to attend same-sex parties.

How can I know if my child is participating in oral sex with peers?

Some preteens these days *are* participating in oral sex. But there's usually no physical evidence.

In addition to the moral implications of premarital sex, it's important to realize that oral sex isn't a safe practice; it can be associated with sexually transmitted infections such as gonorrhea of the throat and genital herpes. The latter is often—but not always—transmitted from cold sores.

Having an open line of communication with your child is important. Here's a relatively nonthreatening way to bring up this topic: Tell her you know some kids her age are participating in oral sex and ask if she's heard anything about such activities around school. Also, talk with other kids' parents and administrators.

Enrolling your child in after-school activities is a good way to keep her busy. Studies show that most sexual activity in this age group occurs during the afternoon when kids are unsupervised because parents aren't home from work.[2]

How can I help my child resist sexual pressure from peers?

The best way to help your child is to stay connected. Most kids find out about sex and other relational issues from friends because parents are afraid to talk openly about these things. If your child is prepared with information before joining friends on the playground, he or she will be less tempted to follow the crowd.

Also, spend time helping your child find activities he or she excels in. A confident child is more likely to be an independent thinker—and leader—who doesn't need peer approval to feel good.

Research also shows that kids who are involved in religious activities and deeply committed to their faith are less likely to fall victim to peer pressure.[3] Foster your child's involvement with a church youth group, be actively involved in his or her spiritual growth and development, and strive to be a model of Christian character. When your children see that spiritual maturity is important to you, they'll be more likely to see it as important for themselves.

How do I bring up the topic of opposite-sex relationships with my child?

Go to the movies with your daughter, listen to her music, take her with some friends on an out-of-town adventure, and listen to her conversations. More than likely, she's already talking about dating and boys she likes. All you have to do is watch a teen movie to know dating's on the brain.

It's usually easier to bring up these issues with a daughter than with a son. When girls start calling your son, use these phone calls as a conversation starter.

Other than using them as a conversation starter, what should I do if my son is being bombarded with phone calls from girls at school?

First, ask your son what he'd like you to do. Try to find out if he likes getting the calls or not.

If he's overwhelmed by the calls, let him use you as a scapegoat. Tell him to tell the callers his parents don't allow him to receive calls from girls. If he's too embarrassed to initiate this conversation, offer to tell the callers for him. Then, when he's feeling pressure at school, he can shift the blame to you.

If, on the other hand, your son finds the calls flattering and doesn't mind them, now's a good time to talk about boundaries in relationships—not only boundaries *he* should have, but ones that *girls* should observe. If you're concerned that the behavior of these girls is too aggressive, let him know.

I've discovered that my son has been accessing pornography on the Internet. What should I do?

God created males to be visually stimulated, so don't shame him for being curious or interested in viewing the female body. Ask whether he has any questions about sex or anatomy. How often does he view pornography? Does he understand just how harmful and addictive it can be?

Now's a good time for a frank discussion about the destructive nature of pornography. Porn produces strong neurochemical reinforcement in the pleasure center of the brain, making it powerfully addictive. Let your son know that it can seriously warp his view of sexuality.

Explain to him that porn exploits others, and that, in a real way, it represents the sexual abuse of the person in the photo or video. What may seem exciting in an image is actually degrading and humiliating for those involved. Try to help him understand that sex is designed to be beautiful and freeing in the proper context of marriage—not the distorted thing that pornography depicts.

Take the steps listed earlier (see "Should I be concerned about my son being exposed to pornography at this early age?" in the previous chapter, pages 117–118) to help avoid further exposure. Determine the consequences your son will face if he views pornography again. Make sure he understands what they'll be, and follow through on the penalties.

If this is not a first-time offense and you have even the least concern that your son may have developed an addiction to pornography, seek the help of a licensed Christian counselor who deals with this type of problem. To some this may seem like an overreaction; it's not. Because pornography is so damaging and addicting, it's important to address the matter squarely as soon as possible.

What should I do if I find women's clothing in my twelve-year-old son's drawer?

Be calm and find a quiet time to address this issue with your son. This isn't necessarily a sign of an intractable sexual problem, but it's definitely an opportunity for you to talk with your son about the appropriate expression of sexual feelings.

Boys this age experience a significant increase in their sexual curiosity and sexual drive, and may develop secret ways to deal with this drive. Women's undergarments often have an attraction because of their feel and can serve as aids to masturbating and other experimental sexual behaviors. Even lingerie ads can serve a similar purpose.

Share with your son that sexual curiosity is normal and that he won't be punished for the normal feelings he's been given. There are, however, boundaries for sexual behavior. Anything, whether it's underwear or porn, that increases involvement with masturbation or sexual fantasy is dangerous to the healthy development of one's sexuality. Encourage your son to ask questions, get appropriate information, and direct himself toward healthy relationships with both sexes.

Gender confusion is a greater concern if a boy is secretly dressing up in women's clothing. If you fear your son is experiencing this type of confusion, be prepared to seek the help of a licensed Christian counselor.

My son has been pinching other kids in the genitals. What should I do?

This behavior can be the result of out-of-control playfulness, or it may be a sign of struggle with sexual impulses. Ask your son about his behavior, looking for clues as to why the behavior is occurring and whether he understands other people's responses.

Talk with your son about self-control and appropriate expression of feelings, emphasizing the inappropriateness of the behavior and the need to take into account the effect one's behavior has on others. Even if your son truly considers his actions playful, you should impress on him the fact that others may see the situation more seriously. Some schools, for example, view such behavior as sexual harassment and respond by suspending the offending student; in other cases a student may even be charged with assault.

Encourage your son to be involved in appropriate friendships and activities. If this behavior persists, seek professional help.

How should I approach the issue of body odor with my child?

Body odor is a natural part of life, and there should be plenty of opportunities to bring up the discussion with your child. If she participates in sports and other outside activities, encourage her to shower after the event is complete.

As she enters puberty, a frank discussion about the importance of deodorant and toothpaste is advised. Use your own hygiene as a conversation starter. Remind your child that taking care of her body not only benefits her but will help her show respect to others.

When should I encourage my son to start shaving?

Shaving in our culture is a milestone for many adolescents. Not every young man will want to shave. But one who's eager to cut his first crop of facial hair should start shaving when the hair on his face is no longer peach fuzz but darker and coarse.

This will happen sometime during the adolescent years. It's a great issue for a father or other positive male role model to handle.

When should I allow my daughter to begin shaving her legs?

Believe it or not, how you answer this question may affect whether or not your daughter will feel comfortable talking with you about her other developmental issues.

Most girls in our culture desire to shave their legs during the middle-school years. Between the ages of ten and thirteen, depending on where you live, your daughter may be surrounded by peers who are already shaving. Before you make a decision about this issue, find out why your daughter wants to shave. If you determine it's appropriate for her to begin, buy her a nice razor and teach her how to use it—in order to avoid unnecessary bleeding.

What goes on during the menstrual cycle?

The menstrual cycle is an intricate process that includes thousands of details and has been explained in hundreds of books. If you prefer a thorough explanation, take a look at Focus on the Family's *Complete Guide to Baby and Child Care*.[4]

Basically, the menstrual cycle is cued to start by the hypothalamus. This structure at the base of the brain regulates basic bodily functions such as temperature. It also signals the body to start the reproductive cycle. The hypothalamus informs the pituitary gland (which tells the organs what to do) to get the ovaries in gear. The ovaries serve two functions: releasing the eggs each month and secreting estrogen and progesterone.

Once an egg is released, it travels through one of the fallopian tubes to the uterus. The fallopian tube serves as a meeting place for the egg and sperm. If the egg is fertilized, the resulting embryo travels to the uterus and continues to grow there until birth. If the egg isn't fertilized and no additional hormones are released, estrogen and progesterone levels fall, resulting in a spasm of the blood vessels in the uterus. This causes the lining of the uterus to die and be sloughed off. Blood, mucus, and the uterine lining are then passed out through the vagina in what is known as the menstrual flow, or *menses*.

What is PMS?

Premenstrual tension is experienced by 90 percent of women, while around 25 percent experience more severe symptoms known as premenstrual syndrome (PMS). This is not the same problem as menstrual cramps; women can have cramps with a period, and some may experience them during the middle of a cycle. PMS occurs during ovulation, not menstruation.

The cause of PMS isn't known. Symptoms may include bloating and fullness in the abdomen, breast tenderness, backache, fatigue, and dizziness. Some of the emotional symptoms associated with PMS include irritability, anxiety, depression, poor concentration, and difficulty making decisions.

When should I be concerned about my daughter's irregular periods?

Your daughter should see her physician about her irregular periods if they're occurring every three to four months after more than a year has passed since her first period; if she's having more than one period in a month; if her period lasts more than eight days; or if she's experiencing heavy soaking of more than eight pads or tampons per day.

There are many underlying causes for these issues, and they shouldn't be ignored. Failure to take action could result in serious long-term consequences to your daughter's health.

My daughter shows very few signs of "typical" feminine behavior. Should I be concerned?

There's a great deal of variety in how children's temperament and play preferences are expressed. Affirm your daughter for who she is—her character, personality, temperament, and talents, including athletic ability—while encouraging comfortable relationships with girls of the same age.

Keep the lines of communication open; this is how she'll begin to understand herself and her relationships with boys and girls around her. Be sure to offer empathy and comfort if she experiences ridicule for her gifts or interests.

Why are girls this age obsessed with their bodies? Is this a sign of sexual abuse?

Most likely this obsession isn't an issue of sexual abuse. Early-adolescent girls experience tremendous changes during puberty. During this transition, most girls have questions, concerns, and outright fears about their bodies. They also seek to connect with their peer group; in so doing, they usually begin to compare their bodies with those of others.

To minimize a young woman's obsession with her body, encourage her to communicate with trusted adults—and to maintain strong friendships.

Should I be concerned if my child is smoking? Is it a sign that he'll probably make unhealthy sexual choices, too?

Some children experiment, trying one or two cigarettes and then stopping. If the smoking continues, this should be cause for concern. Studies show that kids who smoke are more likely to engage in other risky behaviors, including sexual activity.

If your child is smoking, this isn't an issue you should ignore. Talk to his physician. Discuss the matter with your child and monitor his activities closely.

Questions Children Ask

What is puberty?

Puberty is the time of life in which boys and girls physically begin to become men and women and are physically able to have children. Puberty for most

144

girls begins somewhere between ages nine and eleven. For most boys it's a little later—starting between ages ten and thirteen.

Girls develop breasts, and hair grows in their genital area. About two years after puberty begins, their period starts. A young woman will grow a lot before her period starts and then keep growing a little more after that.

Boys will start to develop hair in their genital area and eventually will grow body and facial hair as well. Their voice begins to deepen, and their penis and testicles begin to enlarge. Muscles bulk up as well. The growth spurt in boys starts a lot later than in girls, but can continue longer.

Why do some kids start puberty before others?

All kids go through puberty, but the timing varies from person to person. Sometimes when a mom or dad was very late in going through puberty, his or her children will be late also. Your genetic makeup can play a role in this process. That also means you might not follow your mom or dad at all!

Unfortunately, much of the science surrounding puberty is still a mystery. So don't be worried if you're a late bloomer.

What are hormones?

Hormones are amazing substances produced by numerous glands through-out the body. They're distributed by the bloodstream to other parts of the body where they cause various reactions.

During puberty, several sex hormones are released from the pituitary gland in the brain. These start the process of changing the body from that of a child to that of an adult. Testosterone is the primary hormone during puberty for boys, and it's made in the testicles. Estrogen and progesterone are the primary hormones for girls, and they're released from the ovaries.

Hormones are responsible for pubic and underarm hair growth, breast development, testicle and penis growth, acne, moodiness, and all the other things that make puberty a unique experience.

What is a menstrual cycle?

A menstrual cycle lasts about twenty-eight days, but it can be shorter or longer. The first year of your periods may not be very regular—meaning you could go several months without one. When a girl begins to have periods, her body is capable of having a baby.

As a young woman develops, eggs are being made in her ovaries. An egg is then released about once a month. If a sperm cell finds its way to the released egg and they unite, they travel together down the fallopian tube, which connects the ovary to a woman's uterus. If they settle in the lining of the uterus, a pregnancy is begun.

If the egg isn't fertilized—if no sperm joins with it—the uterus releases the blood that's been collected to nourish the potential baby. This blood is released through the vagina.

Am I supposed to have my period at the same time every month?

Adult women of childbearing age generally have regular periods. But as your body progresses through puberty, your periods may be erratic. A mature menstrual cycle takes place every twenty-eight days. Your periods may come every twenty-eight days or every six weeks. It just depends, because every woman is different.

Can I swim or exercise during my period?

You can swim or exercise during your period if you use a tampon. Tampons collect blood within your vagina and can be removed while going to the bathroom.

Unfortunately, many young women feel bloated and uncomfortable during their periods, so they don't want to swim. But if you feel healthy and don't mind wearing a tampon, feel free to swim.

How does a woman produce an egg, and how many are there?

The number of eggs a girl or woman has is actually determined at birth. Eggs are contained in the ovaries and are part of the female reproductive system. There are thought to be about two million eggs in the ovaries. A woman will never use this many, and most eggs will either die or just disappear.

Usually the ovaries prepare and release one egg during each menstrual cycle in response to hormones in the body. The release of the egg by the ovary is called ovulation.

Can you see the eggs?

The eggs are too small to be seen with the naked eye; however, they can be seen with a microscope.

How old do I have to be to use tampons?

Age really isn't a factor for tampon use. Tampons are made in varying sizes to fit women of all body types.

Many young women hesitate to use tampons because they fear inserting them into the vagina. For many others, tampons are comfortable and convenient. The main problem with tampons is that they should only be used for periods of four to six hours at a time and shouldn't be used overnight. Leaving a tampon in place too long can lead to toxic shock syndrome—a rare but deadly disease.

Before you start using tampons, talk with your doctor or parent about proper use. It's also wise to alternate tampons and pads in an effort to avoid toxic shock syndrome.

How do I keep the blood from staining my clothes?

The proper use of tampons and sanitary pads will help you avoid ruining your clothes during your period. Fortunately, you'll learn the signs that your period is coming and will be prepared.

If an accident happens, you can remove the blood from stained clothes by soaking them in cold water. If you're having your period and are worried about an accident, tuck an extra pair of shorts or pants in your backpack so you can change if necessary.

How does a penis fit into the vagina?

When a woman is aroused, her vagina will become moist and lubricated and allow for any size penis to penetrate the vaginal cavity. People who haven't had sex often worry about this issue, but it's usually not a big deal. Just as nature allows for the penis to become erect, a woman's body changes to allow for the penis to fit in her body. The first few times a woman has sex can be painful, however, until the vagina stretches.

What is the clear stuff coming out of my vagina?

Around the time of ovulation, a woman's body produces a clear discharge called mucus. This usually occurs in the middle of the menstrual cycle or roughly two weeks before the start of the menstrual blood flow. For some women, the discharge may be heavy; consider wearing a minipad to keep your underwear from becoming moist.

How does a girl get pregnant?

If a girl has sexual intercourse around the time of ovulation and if a sperm penetrates the egg, pregnancy results. When the sperm penetrates the egg, it's called fertilization. This process occurs in the fallopian tubes. The fertilized egg travels down the fallopian tube to the uterus and then implants itself in the wall of the uterus and continues to grow.

It's possible for a girl to get pregnant even if the boy's penis doesn't go inside her vagina. If the boy ejaculates—releases sperm—outside the vagina and any of the fluid gets inside, an egg could still be fertilized by the sperm in the fluid, and pregnancy could occur.

What is a wet dream?

"Wet dream" is another name for nocturnal emission. During the night, while sleeping, an adolescent boy may have an erection of his penis followed by the release of semen. This is normal and happens in all boys from time to time.

What should I do if I get an erection at school?

An erection can happen when a guy just thinks about a girl—or for no reason at all. Fortunately, it's unlikely anyone will notice it, and your penis should lose its hardness in a few minutes. It may seem embarrassing, but it's normal and nothing to worry about.

Why do I get an erection when I just think about girls?

When you're going through puberty and growing into a young adult, the hormonal system in your body is very sensitive and can be set off without much stimulation. As you become more interested in girls, these hormones are responsible for your erection.

Fortunately, your body will get the message that it can go no further, and your penis will get soft in a few minutes. Usually nobody will notice what's happened, and you can play it cool. It happens to all boys and even men and is normal.

What is homosexuality?

Homosexuality is having sexual or romantic attraction toward the same sex, engaging in sexual activity with a person of the same sex, and/or identifying oneself by those attractions or behaviors. Men attracted to other men often refer to themselves as "gay," while women attracted to other women may identify as "lesbian." Some younger adults may identify as "queer" or "questioning."

God's plan for sexuality is that it be expressed between a man and a woman who are married, and sex between two men or two women falls outside that plan. Still, homosexual men and women, like everyone else, need to be treated with respect. There are many slang words that insensitive people use to refer to homosexuality. Using these words is cruel and demeaning.

Some teens have fleeting sexual or romantic attraction to members of the same sex. This does not mean they are homosexual.

What is a virgin?

A virgin is a person who has never had sexual intercourse (oral, vaginal, or anal). Many teens falsely assume that they're virgins if they've only had oral or anal sex. This is simply not true. In the broad sense of the term, the word *virgin* means that a person is without experience. By having oral or anal sex a teen has definitely gained sexual experience.

When thinking about what makes a person a virgin, it's more important to consider God's plan than technical definitions. His intent is that sexual experience of any kind be shared only between a man and a woman within the relationship of marriage. You should understand, too, that the Bible talks a lot more about our thoughts and attitudes than it does about which acts may cause us to "lose our virginity."

Looking at it this way, you can see that it's more important for you to remain sexually pure in your thoughts and actions than it is to see just how far you can go sexually while still technically remaining a virgin.

At what age is it okay to have sex?

This is a reasonable question. But it's more important to ask, "When is it the right *time* to have sex?" *When you get married* is when it's okay to have sex. Having sex before you're married is a bad idea.

Many people say, "When you're ready, you'll know it." But there are so many things besides the physical act that you need to think about. First and foremost, saving sex for marriage is God's design, so that's how we really know what the right time is—when you're married.

But even apart from what the Bible explains about God's plan, it's easy to see that there are lots of emotional dangers that can arise when people have sex before marriage. Some girls want to be loved, so they have sex in the hope that the boy will love them. But often boys just want to have sex, so sex outside of marriage sets people up for getting hurt. Emotions can fool you when you're a teen and you think you're ready for sex.

Then there are the physical problems that go along with sex. A girl can get pregnant when she doesn't want to. Both girls and boys can get a sexually transmitted infection that might be very hard to treat or even incurable (see Appendix A in the back of this book).

Finally, don't forget how these things can change your future. If you become a parent as a teen, will you finish high school, go to college, or be able to get a job and work while rearing a child? How will your behavior affect your parents or other family members? Will you feel guilty or lose your self-respect?

The best time to start having sex is when you've found the love of your life and are married. Research shows that the best sex happens in marriage, when having sex is a part of what it means to love each other for the rest of your lives. You'll never regret that you waited.

What is intercourse?

Intercourse is usually described as a man's penis being inserted into a woman's vagina. Anal intercourse is a penis being inserted into the rectum. Oral intercourse is when the penis is inserted into the mouth or the mouth covers the vagina for the purpose of stimulation.

Is oral sex the same as sex?

Yes! Oral sex is sex, vaginal sex is sex, and anal sex is sex.

What actually happens during sex?

During the process of sexual arousal when a man "gets excited," blood vessels in the penis are filled (engorged) with blood. This causes the penis to get longer and harder and is called an erection.

When the penis is erect and inserted into the woman's vagina, it can be incredibly pleasurable. At the height or climax of these pleasurable feelings—called an orgasm—the penis releases semen (fluid containing the sperm). This is called ejaculation. The woman may also experience an orgasm, but usually no fluids are released by the woman's body.

What is "making out"?

"Making out" has no single definition. Some refer to kissing and hugging as making out, while others consider it to mean having sexual intercourse.

When is it okay to kiss my boyfriend?

First, you need to consider carefully what dating means, and when it's appropriate (see the questions about dating in the next chapter). Second, making a choice to kiss someone should never be done lightly. Research shows that physical activity such as hugging and kissing releases chemicals in the brain that cause emotional bonding, and at your age you just don't need this type of connection. Kissing also can lead to other sexual play.

Before you decide to kiss a boy, decide what a kiss means to you. Understand that it might not mean the same thing to the person you're kissing. Some people think kissing is no big deal, but it's often one step on the road toward intimate physical activity.

What is dry sex?

Dry sex is sexually stimulating another person with clothes on. In the early stages of a physical relationship, kissing can lead quickly to a desire for more physical excitement. A boy and girl may decide to stimulate one another with their clothes on—the idea being to prevent intercourse.

Even though the activity may appear to be "safe," you're moving your relationship closer to sexual intercourse. You're also engaging in activity that doesn't honor God's design for sexuality. God's plan for you isn't about seeing how far you can go and still remain a virgin. It's about living a life of purity in thought and action.

11

DIVING IN

Thirteen- to Fifteen-Year-Olds

Don't be worried if the only "hello" you get from your son is a grunt. You're probably used to it by now anyway.

If you were expecting your boy to be a fountain of conversation during his early teen years, you can send those dreams packing. The cute little athlete you remember from elementary school may appear more gangly than attractive, and your brilliant scientist may have found sanctuary in his bedroom.

As the parent of a young man, you may find it hard to keep him talking, but don't give up. He still needs to eat and still needs you to tote him around to practice and extracurricular activities. Take advantage of the time you have together; listen to his questions. Be careful not to be too intrusive or over-talk.

On the other hand, if you're the parent of a budding young woman, you'll probably be up to your ears in conversation—though not always involving you. We've all seen the commercials featuring early teen girls talking, texting, or tweeting incessantly to their friends about everything from brushing their teeth to shaving their legs. Remember: By keeping lines of communication open and staying engaged in conversation with your daughter, you'll discover many great opportunities to answer her questions about relationships and sex.

Regardless of your child's gender, it's time for the big leagues. No longer will he look to you for approval—though he desperately needs it. No longer will she consult you for fashion advice—though her makeup may still scream "Help!"

This is the stage in your parenting journey to be diligent and involved. Keep your ears tuned in and your social calendar light, because parenting takes on a whole new meaning during this season of life. You're no longer wiping bottoms, but chances are you'll be cleaning up messes. So jump in with both feet and enjoy the process of ushering your child into a new stage—one where his thoughts, opinions, and ideas desperately need an audience.

Tune in and keep cheering.

Parents' Questions

What are the physical facts that a boy or girl should know by this age?

By the early teen years, both boys and girls should fully understand the events that take place during puberty. They also should understand not only the reproductive aspect of sexual intercourse, but also the relational and enjoyment aspects of sex that occur within the deep intimacy of a lifelong, committed marital relationship.

Finally, you need to discuss the consequences—emotional, physical, and spiritual—of nonmarital sexual play. That's especially important when current trends among some young adolescents include experimenting with mutual masturbation, oral sex, anal intercourse, and even reenacting porn flicks and other videos at coed parties.

Remember, the facts about sexual physiology and mechanics are just a starting point. Don't let the conversation end there.

Is it appropriate for my son or daughter to start dating at this age?

Most Christian parents tend to fall into two main camps when it comes to teen dating. Some, believing dating is never appropriate, encourage their children to follow a courtship model (see Courtship vs. Dating on page 157). Others believe dating can be a safe and positive experience for teens provided they're mature enough and the parents know and trust the dating partner.

Before deciding how you're going to proceed, it's crucial to realize that contemporary dating isn't what it was when the majority of today's parents were kids. Sexual promiscuity is more common, even among Christian teens, and many young people receive little or no moral guidance from their parents. Binge drinking and date rape are more common, too.

In light of this, it's risky for boys and girls under the age of seventeen to participate in one-on-one dating. Younger teens should be encouraged to participate in group dates with Christian friends who share their moral and spiritual values. Even then, mom and dad should be well acquainted with the other kids in the group and their parents.

Whether or not your young teen is eager to start dating, sit down with him or her and map out specific guidelines for relationships with the opposite sex. Encourage your child to mingle with both boys and girls in a setting such as a church youth group. Talk about pursuing a commitment to sexual purity. Help your child understand that, for the time being, unsupervised dates are not an option. You can promise to revisit the dating question in a few years if your child displays the necessary signs of maturity and sound judgment.

I know it can be risky to let young teens date, but I've decided to allow mine to do so. What ground rules should I set?

When you set ground rules, include your child in the process. If she's ready to date, talk about her expectations and desires; then set the rules according to her maturity.

Discussions should include appropriate boundaries, curfew, attire, group dating, financial responsibilities, expectations regarding family time, and what to do in an uncomfortable or dangerous situation. Concerning the latter, remind your child that you'll always be available to help find a way out—even if it means picking her up anywhere, anytime.

Here are several dating standards you and your child may find helpful for the healthiest early dating relationships:

- Set your physical intimacy boundary *before* you go on the date.
- Boys and girls are jointly responsible for setting and maintaining limits.
- Verbally communicate your boundary to your date.
- Exercise self-control.
- Consider your manner of dress, as it will communicate a lot to your date and may send signals you're unaware of. Modesty should guide clothing decisions.
- Use nonverbal and verbal refusal skills if needed.
- Avoid dangerous or tempting situations like being alone in a house.
- Remember that your body and your relationships belong, ultimately, to God. Consider Him in every decision you make.

Your child should know that if things do start to get physical, she has the right to stop it. Forcing physical intimacy on someone is assault or rape, and it is never acceptable. Likewise, talk with your child about the dangers of drugs and alcohol—that they impair judgment, especially in dating relationships. Again, remind her that if she's ever in a situation where drugs or alcohol become part of the mix, you'll be available to pick her up.

How can I teach my child what to expect from a date?

Sometimes it's useful for a father (or other male role model) to take his daughter on a date. This could start with sending your daughter flowers, ringing the doorbell, escorting her to the car, and going out to dinner or a movie. Treat her the way a gentleman should treat a lady, including holding the door for her. This can be not only a fun time, but one of meaningful conversation and a chance to talk about the pitfalls of not being in control on a date.

A mom could have her son pick her up for a date. (Dad could slip his son a few bills for dinner.) Or let your children accompany you on a date with your spouse. If you're a single parent, enlist the aid of family and friends. Help your kids think of great things to do on a date, too.

Courtship vs. Dating

Teens today are steeped in a dating culture that places a premium on sexual gratification and freedom from commitment. To be sure, not all teens dating today are focused on fulfilling physical desire at the expense of personal convictions and virtues. In fact, a lot of Christian teens are thoughtful about what they want to happen (and not happen) in a dating relationship and are committed to sexual abstinence. In recent years some teens even have begun revisiting a time-honored approach to male-female relationships called courtship.

Dating today revolves largely around the pursuit of a relationship for the sake of exciting romantic feelings. Even when appropriate physical boundaries remain intact, dating tends to give emotional fulfillment a higher priority than other important concerns. Because of the intensity of feelings encouraged in dating, young people can be blinded to issues in each other's lives that might indicate a problem down the road. Dating purely for short-term enjoyment is more of a pastime than a thoughtful approach to long-term relationships.

Courtship, on the other hand, isn't self-centered but God-centered. It aims first to develop friendship between a guy and a girl. Courtship prizes spiritual growth and encourages each person to respect the emotional as well as physical boundaries of the other.

Dating tends to isolate couples from friends and family, but courtship engages families and spiritual mentors. Its goal is not to get away from everyone else but to seek wisdom and guidance from others who might see the relationship from a different perspective. It encourages the boy and girl to honor each other's parents and other family members.

Of course, two people may get into a courtship relationship and determine that they shouldn't marry each other. That's fine; the purpose of courtship is not to make sure that two people get married, but to lay the groundwork for a stable, loving, God-honoring marriage at some point in the future.

Most marriages in Western society are the result of one-to-one male-female relationships formed through dating. Courtship has distinct advantages that could lead to more successful marriages. All too often, dating resembles a recreational sport.

For more information on courtship, see *I Kissed Dating Goodbye* by Joshua Harris (Multnomah Publishers, 2003).

Purpose-Driven Dating

Whether or not dating is a good idea for teens in this age group, dating as a "recreational sport" at a young age can lead to negative consequences—including early physical experiences and heartaches for which a young teen might be emotionally unprepared.

When your child is ready to date, discuss the following goals of dating:

- To choose a marriage partner and prepare for a lasting relationship.
- To develop a sense of independence.
- To learn to feel more at ease in a male-female relationship and enjoy friendship with someone of the opposite sex.
- To get to know other people—their likes, dislikes, values, ways of communicating—and yourself.

Why should my child wait until marriage to become sexually active?

The main reason is simple: God's design for humanity holds marriage as the only appropriate context for sex. He didn't prescribe marriage to keep people from having fun. As research shows, the best, most fulfilling, and most frequent sex occurs between married partners.

There are other good reasons to wait. The obvious physical consequences of sex outside of marriage are pregnancy and sexually transmitted infections; longer-term there may be additional problems such as infertility or cervical cancer. And since sexual intercourse isn't just a physical act but involves the whole person, emotional damage is likely to occur from sexual activity, especially when the person goes from one relationship to another after a painful breakup.

The social cost to individuals and society for nonmarital births and STIs is tremendous. Teen girls who have babies at this age are more likely not to finish high school and to live in poverty. While it's hard to know what comes first, teenagers who are sexually active are more likely to smoke, use alcohol or drugs, have trouble with the law (even serve time in jail), and experience depression or suicide. Teens who have faith are likely to experience guilt or withdraw from their faith if they're sexually active.

If and when your child marries, the baggage of multiple sexual partners may prevent experiencing a truly intimate and satisfying marriage. The purpose of encouraging kids to wait for sex is not just to help them avoid STIs or nonmarital pregnancy, but also to provide them with the skills to enjoy marriage and have a great sex life in the future—free of guilt, scars, and memories of past broken relationships.

How do I explain to my child what an abortion is?

From the moment an egg and sperm unite—an event called fertilization—the result is a very tiny, very young human life. The highly coordinated process of cell division and specialization within the developing human being are not signs of a disorganized mass of tissue. They are the hallmark of life.

The development of that very young child follows patterns and gives rise to structures we can easily recognize. For example, only three weeks after fertilization the baby's heart begins to beat, even though it's about the size of a poppy seed. By eight weeks, the fetus is only half an inch long; yet arms and legs have developed and fingers are evident.

Development continues within the uterus until the child is born, about nine months after the life of the baby has begun. All the development the child has undergone in the first nine months of its life has occurred to allow the baby to survive outside its mother's body. While early in the pregnancy the baby may not be able to survive outside the uterus, there is no point prior to birth at which the developing child is not human. It is simply a preborn human.

Abortion is the ending of a preborn baby's life. Sometimes a pregnancy ends unexpectedly but naturally. This is often called a miscarriage, but medical professionals may refer to it as a spontaneous abortion. When a procedure is carried out to intentionally end the baby's life, it's called an elective abortion or an induced abortion. From here on when the word abortion is used it refers to an abortion that's elected or induced.

An abortion can be carried out surgically at an abortion clinic, or at home using drugs that kill the baby and cause the girl's body to expel it.

In some states, surgical abortions can be provided by someone other than a doctor. In the most common kind of surgical abortion, called an aspiration abortion, the girl's cervix (the opening to her uterus) is widened to allow a suction tube to be inserted into the uterus. The baby, or fetus (Latin for *offspring* or *young one*) is then suctioned out. Sometimes the uterus has to be scraped to make sure that parts of the fetus are not left behind.

In a medical abortion, a girl takes a drug called mifepristone. This cuts off the blood supply to the growing fetus, causing it to die. Two days after taking mifepristone the girl is given another drug, called misoprostol, that causes the uterus to contract, forcing the fetus out of her body. The girl is supposed to visit her doctor two weeks later to make sure she is no longer pregnant. In as many as 20 percent of cases the girl will need a surgical procedure to complete the abortion.

Often teens who get pregnant unexpectedly feel they need to find a "solution" as quickly as possible. Abortion is aggressively marketed to scared young women who hope it will make all their problems and worries go away. A boyfriend may insist that a girl get an abortion so that he won't have to take responsibility for a child. Even some parents, worried that their plans and dreams for their daughter's future might not come true, may pressure a girl to have an abortion.

None of these is a good reason for an abortion. An abortion can never make problems just disappear; in fact, it creates a whole new set of problems for everyone involved.

What's wrong with getting an abortion?

When a sperm cell and an egg unite a new human life begins. A new person (not just a mass of cells) bearing the image of God has been created. The Bible makes clear that life isn't something that becomes important to God only *after* a child exits his mother's body:

> For you created my inmost being;
> you knit me together in my mother's womb.
> I praise you because I am fearfully and wonderfully made;
> your works are wonderful,
> I know that full well.

My frame was not hidden from you
    when I was made in the secret place.
When I was woven together in the depths of the earth,
    your eyes saw my unformed body. (Psalm 139:13–16a)

These aren't just words from an old book that doesn't mean anything anymore. They tell us something important about how God sees each of us. God *knows* and *loves* each person from the earliest moment. Abortion, tragically, ends the life of a precious person.

While the incredible worth of a preborn child is enough reason not to have an abortion, consider the following additional reasons.

Some people describe abortion as if it were a simple procedure with no complications to worry about, but that's not true. Girls take several physical and psychological risks when they have an abortion. A surgical abortion is a surgical procedure, and every surgical procedure carries some risk. In this case, an abortion can result in tearing of the cervix, rupture or puncturing of the uterus, or infection. Those are just the immediate dangers.

Research shows that women who've had an abortion are more likely to have a premature birth in later pregnancies; babies born prematurely face many possible health problems. Women who've had an abortion are also at greater risk later of *placenta previa*, a condition in which the placenta (the structure inside the uterus that helps provide oxygen and nutrients to the baby) can fully or partially cover the opening to the cervix. This can be very dangerous to the mother and the baby, as it can result in severe bleeding and require life-saving treatment.

Scientific studies also indicate that women who've had an abortion may face increased risk for a number of other physical problems, including miscarriage and possibly even breast cancer. With a drug-induced abortion, a woman has a small chance of getting a serious infection that could result in death. And because a woman who is sexually active may acquire an STI that could prevent her from getting pregnant in the future, an abortion could end the life of the only child she may ever have.

Many emotional problems also can come from having an abortion. Women who undergo abortion have, on average, a higher risk of depression, emotional distress, substance abuse, and suicide. A woman may experience a form of post-traumatic stress disorder after an abortion;

some professionals call this *post-abortion syndrome*. Feelings of guilt, anger, and grief can continue for years. Depression and guilt can extend to a man, too, especially if he pressured a woman into ending the life of his child.

You can find more information about the physical and emotional consequences of abortion at the website of the Elliot Institute (afterabortion. org) and the American Association of Pro-life Obstetricians and Gynecologists (aaplog.org).

What are the alternatives to abortion?

It's easy for a teen facing an unexpected pregnancy to feel alone, but she doesn't have to.

Some agencies attempt to convince a young mother that the best option for her and her "unwanted child" is to terminate the pregnancy. But there are other organizations that value the life of both mother and child and are ready to assist in a number of ways. Pregnancy medical clinics (PMCs) and pregnancy resource centers (PRCs) provide care and services free of charge and can help a woman as she's deciding what to do next. It's easy to locate a center or clinic near you at OptionLine.org.

PMCs and PRCs both provide free pregnancy tests and support services, but PMCs also offer limited ultrasound services to confirm a woman's pregnancy and determine how far along she is. For a young woman choosing to give her child a chance at life, both offer confidential counseling to help her decide which option is best for her: parenting the baby herself or providing parents for her baby through an adoption plan with a loving family. Each option requires careful consideration.

A young woman considering parenting a baby from an unexpected pregnancy needs to ask herself a number of questions. Will she marry the baby's father? If the father is willing to marry her, will he be a responsible dad and husband? Sometimes choosing marriage can complicate an already difficult situation. If she's considering raising the child herself, is she prepared to take on the role of a single parent? Does she have the means to care for a child? Does she have a plan to involve positive male influences and role models in her child's life?

What Is Post-Abortion Syndrome?

Post-abortion syndrome (PAS) is a form of post-traumatic stress disorder (PTSD). PTSD is the result of having suffered something so stressful and traumatic (usually a life-threatening event or being a witness to death) that the person's normal ability to process the event is shut down. A variety of coping mechanisms (like repression or outright denial) help the person to numbly keep moving forward in life, but eventually reactions begin to surface that are outside the person's ability to control.

The path to healing after an abortion includes the willingness to identify and name the trauma; finally processing the strong emotions (guilt, anger, grief) that have been frozen in time, mourning the loss, and reintegrating back into one's life.

Here are some symptoms of post-abortion syndrome:

- depression and thoughts of suicide
- deterioration of self-esteem
- disruption in interpersonal relationships (psychological numbing)
- sleep, appetite, and sexual disturbances
- "anniversary syndrome" (an increase of symptoms around the time of the anniversary of the abortion and/or the due date of the aborted child)
- survival guilt
- re-experiencing the abortion (while awake or through nightmares)
- preoccupation with becoming pregnant again
- anxiety over fertility and childbearing issues
- disruption of the bonding process with present or future children
- development of eating disorders
- alcohol and drug abuse
- other self-punishing or self-degrading behaviors (abusive relationships, promiscuity, avoiding medical care, deliberately hurting oneself)
- brief reactive psychosis (an episode of drastically distorted reality within two weeks of the abortion, not followed by a psychotic break)

For more information, see *A Solitary Sorrow* by Teri Reisser, MFT, and Paul Reisser, MD.[1]

The other option is adoption. Many young women selflessly give their baby an opportunity to be cared for and raised by a loving adoptive couple. With the prevalence of open adoptions, a woman can get to know the adoptive family and stay informed about how her baby is doing. There may even be the option of contact with the child, depending on the specific arrangement the mother has with the adoptive couple.

The decision for adoption is not necessarily an easy one, but good parents make difficult choices in order to provide the best for their child. The choice for adoption is a generous act of love toward the baby. For more information on adoption, visit http://www.heartlink.org/pdf/imightconsideradoptionif.pdf.

What if someone has already had an abortion?

By some estimates, at current rates about 30 percent of US women will have had an abortion by the time they are forty-five years old.[2] A lot of them, though, won't talk about it. For these women, the decision to abort a child conflicts with their sense of right and wrong, and the guilt they often feel keeps them silent.

Guilt, anger, and grief are common responses to an abortion. Many women experience these feelings years after an abortion, and are unable to identify, much less grieve, their loss. Unable to process their emotions, they can find it difficult to face the choices they made and to find peace with God and others who were involved in the pregnancy or the abortion. They may experience depression or anxiety, especially around an anniversary related to the aborted child, such as the date of the abortion or the child's due date. These women may also engage in self-destructive behaviors such as eating disorders, substance abuse, or sexual promiscuity.

How can a person who's experienced an abortion find healing?

Counselors tell us there are several steps:

1. *Acknowledge the pain.* When the emotional pain is denied or covered up, the difficulties can persist and fester. The girl or woman needs to find a safe environment where she can talk about her abortion experience.

2. *Accept forgiveness.* She needs to realize that God wants to be fully reconciled with her. There is no sin that is beyond His forgiveness. A person may accept the idea that God forgives her, but she may find it difficult to extend forgiveness to herself. She needs to recognize that before she ever existed God knew her, loved her, and paid her debt in full. God has promised to draw near to her when she makes any move toward Him.

She also needs to realize that any consequences she's experienced as a result of the abortion—infertility, for example—are not the same as God's punishment. We all face the consequences of our actions, for good or bad. God's forgiveness brings us back into fellowship with Him so that we don't face His anger for our sins. When we experience the ongoing consequences of our choices, God is beside us to help us carry on.

3. *Identify and release anger.* A girl or woman may feel anger against herself, the abortionist, someone who pressured her into an abortion, or even someone who she felt could have protected her from having the abortion but didn't. If she never acknowledges the anger she has, she will never be able to get rid of it.

4. *Grieve the loss.* This may be especially difficult when a person considers that she ultimately made the choice to end the life of her child. There are a number of ways she can work through this. She may wish to write a letter expressing her feelings to her child. She might hold a private memorial service for him. Connecting with others who've undergone abortion can provide an opportunity for healing. Many pregnancy resource centers host confidential support groups for those who've gone through abortion.

Each of these steps can be difficult. The help of a licensed Christian counselor can be valuable in the journey toward healing.

Would a stricter curfew help my teenager avoid sexual temptation? How should I handle curfews?

During the early teen years, which correspond to middle school, it's relatively easy to set curfews since the kids don't drive. But the bottom line is that you, the parent, should be in charge of curfews—not your teen, his friends, or his friends' parents.

While you're ultimately in charge of this decision, take the time to listen to your teen. He may actually prefer an earlier curfew than you would set on your own.

Many parents worry about curfews but forget to be concerned about their child's whereabouts after school—the primary time when sexual activity occurs. Be careful to set appropriate curfews for the evenings and define your expectations for the afternoons.

What can I do to encourage healthy peer relationships without exposing my child to compromising situations or overwhelming temptation?

In a nutshell, know your child's friends and whether their parents share your value system. And even if you approve of her friends and their parents share your values, you need to investigate whether they have an older child in their home who might influence your child.

Healthy peer relations with the same sex and the opposite sex are a necessary part of this developmental period, but you need to be involved. Needless to say, peers of the opposite sex shouldn't be allowed to be home alone with each other or in each other's bedrooms. If your young teen is running with the wrong crowd, you need to change her mix of friends, even if it takes a drastic measure such as switching schools or church youth groups, or moving to a new neighborhood.

What should I say about my sexual history to my child?

This is a tough question if you were sexually active prior to marriage. Each parent will have to decide how to answer if and when his or her child asks, "Mom (or Dad), how far did you go when you were my age?"

If you were a virgin when you married, you can tell your child that you're happy you made that decision and encourage him to do the same. If you were sexually active prior to marriage, you must then decide how to answer.

Sharing your story can be a powerful teaching tool. But you shouldn't go into details, and it can be very short. You might say something like,

Beginning to Let Go

Here are eight things to remember about this stage of adolescence:

- Same-sex friendships will be strong. It isn't uncommon for teens this age to change friendships as they mature and deepen in their understandings of themselves. These friendships are important forces in developing self-confidence and a sense of direction for the future; they serve as a bridge for crossing into adulthood.

- Friendships are less dependent on your input or opinions. Don't give up on appropriate boundaries, but allow your teen some flexibility in his thinking and opinions.

- Remind your teen that a few close friendships are more fulfilling than superficial relationships with lots of peers.

- Strong friendships with the same sex can help prevent overdependent and controlling relationships with the opposite sex.

- Dating relationships are most likely to begin during this age. Emphasize with your teen that friendship skills with the opposite sex are more important than romantic feelings. True intimacy in later years will require friendship skills, not just romantic emotions.

- Maintain family standards, but resist the impulse to overcontrol your teen. Give him room to make decisions for himself, even if those decisions may bring unexpected or unwanted consequences. This age is the last time to experiment with freedom before total freedom actually exists.

- Instruct your teen about passionate feelings that come with opposite-sex relationships. Teaching and encouraging self-control will never be more vital than during this time of heightened passions.

- Begin to prepare yourself for the day your teen will leave home. Strengthen and maintain your own friendships and marriage as well as your identity outside of being the parent of your teenager.

"You know, I made a mistake when I was your age. I'd like to turn back the clock, but I can't. I hope you won't make the same mistakes I made." This can open the door for a meaningful dialogue between you and your child.

Even if the question isn't asked, if you feel your child is heading for deep trouble you could volunteer to share information with him. Sharing parts of your painful past could avert a disaster for your teenager. Even if you had sex before marriage and haven't experienced negative consequences yet, remember: The world is a different place today.

When should a young woman have her first pelvic exam?

There's much debate about this subject. In general, a pelvic exam is needed at any age after a girl has become sexually active. If a girl is a virgin, a pelvic exam isn't needed until sometime between the ages of eighteen and twenty-one. Some physicians, however, suggest that a girl get a pelvic exam just before she goes off to college even if she's never been sexually active, just to make sure there are no problems before she leaves home.

If a young woman is experiencing medical problems such as vaginal discharge, menstrual problems, or pelvic pain, a pelvic exam may be needed. This issue should be discussed with her physician.

What should I do if I walk in on my child while he's in a compromising situation?

If you walk in on your child while he's masturbating, it would be appropriate to excuse yourself and talk to your child about the issue later if it hasn't been previously discussed. Even if you've discussed masturbation in the past, it might be good to broach the subject again and acknowledge what happened—though most teens will be mortified by the experience and would probably prefer to let the incident be forgotten.

If you walk in on your child while he's having sexual intercourse in your home, it would be appropriate to ask him to get dressed. A brief discussion about your disappointment may also be in order. Inform the partner that you will have to tell her parents what happened.

When the other child has left and both of you have had a chance to settle down, you need to talk to your child about the situation. Some of the questions you may want to ask include these: How long has this been going on? Is this your first sexual experience? Do you know if you're at risk of pregnancy or contracting an STI?

Your child should also be seen by a physician to be evaluated for pregnancy, if female, and, in the case of either gender, sexually transmitted infections.

Love for your child must prevail over your disappointment, hurt, and anger. The key point to remember is not to let anger rule your reaction. It's

Discussing Masturbation

It's an experience universal to all young men and many women, yet it's often associated with intense secrecy and shame. Simply put, masturbation is the rubbing or manipulation of genital areas—the penis in men and the clitoris and vagina in women. It involves sexual arousal and usually orgasm.

Masturbation isn't inherently physically damaging unless excessive force or instruments are used. It can, however, be emotionally destructive and even become a substitute for relational intimacy in marriage.

Masturbation is a common and predictable event—especially in the lives of young adolescent boys. Addressing the topic with your kids requires that you be honest, open, and unshaken by the topic yourself.

Start talking about masturbation before your child enters adolescence. Describe it as a common experience. But explain that while it's pleasurable in the short term, ultimately it isn't fulfilling because it's a substitute for real sexual intimacy that should occur in a marital relationship.

Help your child understand that masturbation can become addictive. You can lessen that risk by giving your child an honest sex education grounded in the values of sexual purity and abstinence until marriage. Healthy friendships and participation in positive peer-group activities also can help keep your child from becoming obsessed with masturbation.

It's worth noting that while not all Christians agree on the spiritual dangers of masturbation, the Bible warns against lust. If a person entertains lustful fantasies while masturbating, this becomes a matter of concern. At the same time, it's destructive for your child to think that an occasional episode of masturbation is proof that he's an utter spiritual failure and hated by God. So reinforce the importance of purity in thought and action—while driving home the point that your child's value to God is never in question.

If you've discovered (or heard) your child masturbating, remain calm. Use this situation to affirm your love for him and remind him of the dangers of pornography, obsessive masturbation, and group masturbation.

possible your child let a situation get out of control and is as disappointed as you are. However, if he shows no remorse for disrespecting you and your home, a fair punishment would be in line.

Another thought to keep in mind: Have you been clear about what you expect from your child when it comes to nonmarital sexual activity? Have you taught him that God has a better plan for him and his body? Does he know that premarital sex is something you disapprove of? If not, it's time to communicate clearly with your adolescent about your hopes and dreams regarding his future, and about God's design for sexuality.

Should I be concerned about the clothes my daughter is wearing?

Absolutely! First of all, it's important to explain to your daughter how men and women are different. Explain that women are generally "turned on" by relationships, courtship, and romance. Men, on the other hand, are visual and are aroused by what they see. This explains why models sell products on TV to men. In short, men are visually stimulated and women are relationally stimulated.

The discussion of how men are visually attracted allows you to explain to your daughter that wearing revealing, sexy clothing turns boys on. It could lead to date rape or sexual involvement for your daughter—though it would never excuse such a response. At the very least, wearing immodest clothing can cause sexual temptation or frustration for the guys she encounters.

Talk about the importance of modesty as a virtue. Discuss the fact that some people make snap judgments about a girl's character and values from her manner of dress. If your daughter is unaware of this, she may be shocked by the message her clothing could send.

What should I tell my son about the way girls dress?

Educate him on the differences between males and females (see the previous question), and help him control his hormones that are kicking in during the early adolescent years. Explain why it's so easy for guys to get hooked on pornography, even so-called soft pornography.

Help your son understand that he often can't help the first look at a pretty girl wearing provocative clothing—but he can control his actions by avoiding the second look that could lead to trouble. This is a great topic for a father or other trusted male role model to cover.

Why should I be concerned about the movies, music, and other entertainment my child is exposed to?

Much of the entertainment available today doesn't reflect biblical values and Christlike character traits—especially where sexuality is concerned. If you want your teen to make good media choices, you need to be involved in his or her life. You need to know not only what websites, video games, books, and other media she's looking at or listening to, but also what's being consumed at the homes of her friends.

Remember, your ultimate goal is not to control her media consumption. It's to train her to think for herself and make wise choices about media use.

When should I be concerned about my child's delayed sexual development?

While most girls will start puberty between ages nine and eleven, it can be delayed until they're fifteen or sixteen. It's important to know when her mother, older sisters, aunts, and grandmothers started their periods. Some families tend to have late bloomers.

Boys also can come from families who tend to develop late. In fact, many men don't reach their adult height until college.

If you're worried, do your family history homework and ask your child's doctor. This is another good reason for yearly checkups with your physician. One of the tasks of a physician during a yearly well check is to see how puberty is progressing. At some point, if puberty hasn't begun, some medical tests will need to be done.

Should I allow my child to attend coed sleepovers?

No. At this age (and perhaps any), they're an invitation to disaster. Coed sleepovers are a dangerous trend.

With the possible exception of an appropriately planned and chaperoned church youth group lock-in, there's no reason for boys and girls at this age to be out and up all night together. If your child is invited to a party, allow him to attend the supervised activities—and tell him you'll pick him up later in the evening.

What should I tell my child about her father's live-in girlfriend?

Cohabitation is a living arrangement that many people adopt for a number of reasons—all of which are misguided or just plain wrong. Some people consider this as an opportunity to "try out" a relationship to see if it will work (with the option of walking away if it doesn't). Others believe—mistakenly, according to social research—that cohabitation will somehow increase their likelihood of having a successful future marriage. Still others simply use cohabitation as a way to avoid real commitment.

Whatever reason your child's father has for living with his girlfriend, it sets a poor example for your child—and can make it awkward when it's time for your child to visit. It's important not to negatively influence your teenager's relationship with her father, but you need to explain why this living arrangement falls short of the Bible's standards for relationships.

By early adolescence, most kids are aware of what their divorced parents are doing. While your ex may have a live-in girlfriend, take a look at your own relationships and make sure they model and reinforce a biblical message of purity. It's up to you and your ex to make your daughter's life less complicated by avoiding situations that cause unnecessary questioning.

I've discovered that my son has been accessing pornography on the Internet. What should I do?

See this question in the previous chapter, pages 139–140.

What am I to make of my child's physician who asks me to leave the room during an exam?

There's no need to worry or be overly concerned. The reality is that most teens don't want their parents present during the exam.

Most physicians at some point during the visit, even if the parent is in the room during the exam, will want to talk to your teen alone. This is normal and healthy, and it's to be encouraged. The time alone with your child may allow the physician to uncover risk factors you might not know about.

While it's best if your physician shares your faith and values when it comes to issues like sex, some physicians may support your family's value system even if it's different from their personal viewpoint. That can be a big support to you as a parent. It's appropriate to ask your physician about these issues, and about how he or she will handle certain situations if they arise.

Can a doctor prescribe contraceptives to my teen without advising me?

Yes. Both federal and state laws protect physicians who screen and treat minors for sexually transmitted infections as well as prescribe or dispense contraceptives. This is one reason why it's important to choose a physician who shares your values and believes that abstinence before marriage is the healthiest choice—or who at least will support those values.

Is a doctor legally bound to keep his conversation with my teen confidential?

No, but there are moral and ethical considerations if the physician has previously established teen confidentiality. Many physicians advise both adolescent and parent as the youth approaches puberty that during at least the annual physical the physician will talk to the young person without the parent around, and what they talk about will be confidential. Most physicians will explain that they can break that confidentiality if a matter is discussed that has major health implications for the teen or for society.

Should I allow my teen to attend the school's sex education program?

See "What's the school's role in teaching my child about sex?" in Chapter 6 (pages 57–60), and "Should I allow my teen to attend the school's sex education program?" in Chapter 12 (pages 207–208).

I'm a single parent with a child of the opposite sex; should I seek a positive same-sex role model for my child?

Yes, if at all possible. This might be an aunt or uncle, coach, teacher, a leader in your church, or even a friend's parent. Make sure the individual shares your values and is safe and trustworthy.

Even if you're not single, an older friend or relative who shares your faith and values can be a valuable tool in your child's development. Reflect on your life; who were the people you trusted and looked to for advice? You can't be all things to your child. Look for others in your life who also can encourage him to reach his full potential.

What else can I do to help prevent my child from becoming sexually active?

One great idea to consider is encouraging your child to volunteer for a worthy cause. Studies show that adolescents involved in volunteer activities have less time to be involved in high-risk behaviors such as drinking, drug use, and sexual activity. Besides, part of your job as a parent is to make sure your child learns the importance of thinking of others rather than just herself.

Volunteer service can be done through school, faith-based organizations, community organizations, or even just your family. Volunteering along with your child will help you model compassion for others as well as provide extra time to be with her.

How do I talk to my child about all the same-sex experimentation kids seem to be involved in these days?

Most adolescents in our society get plenty of media and peer exposure to a culture that says your sexuality can be fluid and that it's safe to experiment with sexual behavior. Gay characters in entertainment are popularized and celebrities who say they're "out of the closet" are highlighted. At some schools, experimenting with lesbian relationships is considered a rite of passage for many girls. Same-sex relationships are portrayed in the media as exciting and hip. Because of this, teens are curious and may

A Ring to Remember

A purity ring is a special piece of jewelry picked out by you or your child that he or she wears as a reminder of being committed to abstain sexually until the wedding night. Passed on to his or her new spouse on that night, it's a gift that says, "I waited for you!"

Why give a purity ring to a teen who might not make it until the wedding night? Research has shown that when teens make a commitment by signing a pledge to be abstinent until marriage, they're more likely to keep that commitment than peers who don't.[14] A ring is a daily reminder of that commitment.

When should you give this ring? A good time is during eighth grade—unless you think your child is maturing much earlier. This could be accomplished during a fun, mother-daughter or father-son weekend doing something you both enjoy. Or both parents could be present for the occasion. The ring (or other symbolic object like a "faith, hope, and love" charm) could even be given by the parent of the opposite sex.

Plan to have some good discussions about the opposite sex, dating, and marriage around this time. Talk about the reasons—spiritual, emotional, and physical—why it's important for your child to wait until marriage for sex. Allow him or her to make the decision for abstinence and to own that commitment; then give your child the ring or go pick it out together.

Tell your child that your dream is for him or her to have the fulfillment that comes from a life that reflects God's plan and design. You may want to mention that the best sex possible occurs in a marital relationship. This could also be an opportunity to challenge your child to begin praying for that future spouse.

feel no shame in experimenting with sexual feelings and behaviors with the same sex.

As a parent, you can help your child think critically about the culture's pronouncements. If you're a Christian, you can help her challenge society's assumptions using scriptural truth. You need to be able to engage in frank but comfortable discussions about sexual curiosity while strongly stating that sexual experimentation (among opposite-sex as well as same-sex peers) runs counter to God's designs for sexuality.

You should also help your child understand that while same-sex experimentation occurs among some teens who grow up to be heterosexual adults, engaging in sexual activity can establish patterns of behavior and sexual response that become deeply ingrained. Rather than being just "harmless experimentation," sexual activity often serves as a kind of programming that can be very difficult to escape.

Don't be embarrassed to discuss these issues with your child, and don't be shocked when he tells you about the presence of these events in his world. You can offer the best information and protection for your teen if you do so in a positive, affirming, and educated way.

What should I do if I walk in on my teen who's involved in same-sex experimentation?

Remain calm. Stop the behavior in a firm, nonemotional way. Talk to your son or daughter when things have cooled down.

Ask your teen to explain what was happening and how he or she got into the situation. Try to understand the power of sexual curiosity, as well as the temptation to experiment that goes with this age. Lovingly address the inappropriateness of the behavior and the potential dangers—physical, emotional, and spiritual—that go along with sexual experimentation and persistent same-sex behavior.

You should also speak with the parents of the other teen involved. While it's best not to panic or make assumptions about your teen's sexuality, you should seek help and guidance from a licensed Christian counselor.

If sexual curiosity is normal, why is sexual experimentation a problem?

Curiosity and questions about all kinds of sexual activity are predictable and healthy at this age. The key is to be an approachable parent. You shouldn't be afraid to use the support of biblical, God-honoring materials and other mature Christian adults whose value systems are Bible-based. Questions and curiosity should always be encouraged and serve as opportunities to affirm a teenager as well as to describe boundaries for behaviors.

Any sexual experimentation that involves excessive physical contact (petting, oral sex, mutual masturbation, intercourse) and the need for secrecy and shame (excessive masturbation, pornography of all types, sexual abuse) is dangerous. Sexuality is kept healthy by complete, sensible, and correct information; strong relationships with appropriate adults; satisfying friendships; and healthy activities. Healthy, integrated sexuality education that focuses on the entire person (physical, emotional, social, spiritual), friendships with both sexes, and healthy group activities will help your child mature and grow.

Questions Teens Ask

What does it mean to be sexually active?

Being sexually active with another person means to be involved in any activity that stimulates the genitals, anus, rectum, or breasts. This can involve touching, mutual masturbation, and vaginal, oral, or anal intercourse.

Is it normal for teens to have sex?

Studies have shown that over 50 percent of all high schoolers in the US have not had sexual intercourse. While most teens have gone through puberty and are capable of sexual intercourse, the widely accepted idea that "everyone's doing it" just isn't true.

One US survey of more than 5,000 teens found that 61 percent wanted to be sexually abstinent until they are married; nearly two-thirds of the teens who have had sex wish they could regain their virginity.[3]

What does promiscuous mean? Is there something wrong with it?

Webster's Dictionary defines *promiscuous* as "indiscriminate." Another definition is having more than one sexual partner.

Today, being promiscuous suggests that one has had or has multiple sexual partners. The more partners someone has, the more likely that person is to get a sexually transmitted infection. Being promiscuous also increases the risk of pregnancy. Remember, you can get an STI or get pregnant from your first sexual encounter.

Apart from these physical consequences, there are emotional consequences to promiscuity—as well as the spiritual dangers that result from ignoring God's design for sex.

I don't want to have sex now, but I feel pressured to. How can I handle this?

Perhaps you feel pressured because your friends are already sexually active. You may also feel pressure from someone you're dating.

As hard as it is to resist peer pressure, there are certain activities—such as smoking, drugs, alcohol, and premarital sex—that are worth your time and effort to avoid because it's the right thing to do and for the sake of your future health, hope, and happiness. To help you do that, it's important to choose friends who share your values. You can resist peer pressure more easily when you have friends who'll stand with you. The right friends can help keep you out of trouble, but the wrong friends will likely entice you over time to join them in these unhealthy behaviors. If you discover that most of your close friends are sexually active, you should find new ones who have values similar to yours.

If you're being pressured to have sex, there are some things you should know:

- A girlfriend who pressures you to have sex doesn't have your best interest at heart. She's being selfish and seeking to gratify her own desire for intimacy.

- If you're a girl and your boyfriend is more than two years older than you are, you're more likely to be pressured into having sex. Most teenage pregnancies occur in girls whose boyfriends are older than they are. One study by the Population Reference Bureau revealed that about two-thirds of births to teen girls in the US were fathered by men at least twenty years old.[4] If you have an older boyfriend who pressures you to have sex, and sex occurs, this is actually a crime in many states. The best way to handle being pressured by an older man is to quickly get out of the relationship.

- If you're a boy and an older woman has sex with you, that's also a crime.

- If you're dating someone your age and feel pressured to have sex, clearly let your desire not to have sex be known. If this wish isn't respected and you still feel pressured, the relationship should end.

There are many ways to avoid putting yourself in a tempting situation. Group dating, for instance, relieves a lot of this pressure. You can also avoid temptation by spending time with family and friends, not being home alone with your boyfriend or girlfriend, and not watching sexually suggestive movies together. It's very important that you're able to talk with a friend, parent, or trusted adult about your decision not to be sexually active. It's also helpful if you can put into words your reasons for abstaining—physical and emotional reasons as well as those that reflect an understanding of and healthy respect for God's plan for sexuality.

Is it true that hardly any girls go to college without having had sex?

This is simply not true. Over 50 percent of high school girls (grades nine through twelve) have never had sex.[5] "Everybody's doing it" is a myth.

Multiple surveys show that teens think more of their peers are sexually active than actually are.[6] Sexual activity, especially in guys, tends to be exaggerated.[7] And research shows that the majority of sexually experienced teens wish they'd waited longer to have sex.[8]

Why should I stay a virgin?

Here are fifteen good reasons:

1. You could get pregnant or father a child.
2. Sexually transmitted infections are at epidemic levels. Most STIs occur in teenagers and young adults.[9]
3. Abstinence is the only 100 percent effective method of preventing pregnancy or an STI. Condoms and other forms of birth control are not nearly 100 percent protective. Birth control pills and similar types of contraception offer no protection at all against STIs.
4. Some sexually transmitted diseases (particularly pelvic inflammatory disease from chlamydia or gonorrhea) can cause infertility by scarring the fallopian tubes. This means that later in life when a

woman wants to get pregnant, it may be impossible because of the damage caused by an STI.

5. One STI, human papillomavirus (HPV), can lead to cancer of the cervix.

6. "Emotional baggage"—broken trust, broken relationships—generally comes along with having sex outside of marriage. Who needs that at this or any age?

7. Sex doesn't enhance a teenage relationship; it frequently speeds up a relationship's end.

8. Most teenagers who've already had sex say they wish they'd waited.[10]

9. Having sex "casually" now could negatively affect your marriage later.

10. Many teens, especially girls, don't feel good about themselves after engaging in sexual activity.

11. Teens who are sexually active are more likely to experience depression.[11]

12. Teens who are sexually active are more likely to drink, smoke, and use drugs.[12]

13. Having sex can affect your reputation.

14. Having sex can damage your relationship with your parents.

15. Most importantly, having sex outside of marriage runs counter to God's design for sex and is a roadblock to a vibrant spiritual life.

If these reasons don't convince you, talk to a friend who's been sexually active. Ask her whether she'd wait if she could do it over. Most teens say that given the chance to make the decision again, they'd have waited.[13]

What is date rape?

Date rape is forcing someone to have sex against her or his will while on a date or in a dating relationship.

How can a girl avoid date rape?

Here are sixteen ways:

1. Go on group dates.
2. Don't date anyone you or your friends don't know anything about.

3. A blind date should be accepted only on the strong recommendation of someone you trust, and it should never be a non-group date.

4. Non-group dates—especially the first time—should take place in public places.

5. Don't drink. Using alcohol is always a bad idea for teens, for numerous reasons (not the least of which is that it's illegal). Many teen girls report that their first sexual experience was associated with alcohol. Alcohol dulls the senses and lowers your inhibitions.[15] You're likely to do things under the influence of alcohol that you wouldn't normally do.

6. Don't use drugs. As with drinking, drug use is a horrible idea. Being high lowers your inhibitions and makes you more likely to be taken advantage of.

7. Be careful with beverages at parties and other places; drink only from unopened cans, and never set your drink down unless you've finished it. This leaves no opportunity for substances such as the "date rape" drug (Rohypnol) to be slipped into your drink without your knowing it.

8. Never leave a party with someone you don't know or just met.

9. Always have money with you on a date in case you need to go home by yourself.

10. Avoid situations in which you don't feel on an equal footing with your companion.

11. Beware of expensive gifts and lavish dates. Too many guys still have the Neanderthal notion that picking up the tab for a nice evening entitles them to a sexual thank-you.

12. Watch out for the control freak—someone who insists on his way and ignores your likes and dislikes. This type of behavior indicates a potential abuser.

13. Beware of the person who tries to isolate you from your other friends and your family or who constantly bad-mouths them. This is another red flag for potential abuse.

14. Steer clear of guys who tell raunchy jokes, listen to sexually explicit music, enjoy pornography, or make degrading comments about women.

15. Don't waste your time with anyone who won't accept your limits. Any guy who pressures you for sexual favors is an abuser and most certainly doesn't love you.
16. Carry a cell phone.

What's wrong with using pornography?

Pornography devalues sex as God designed it—and can be habit forming, with increasing appetite for more sensational material. In fact, brain imaging studies indicate that pornography can be as addicting as cocaine or heroin. Exposure to pornography can also lead to unrealistic sexual expectations later in life.

For both boys and girls, watching or using pornography detaches you from the "real world" and real relationships with people. Boys who routinely use pornography eventually require increasingly hard-core material to get sexually stimulated. While pornography is harmful to single men, for married men it's a marriage killer.

Simply put, pornography destroys an individual's ability to be satisfied with sex with a real person and puts a spouse in an unfair competition. It also exploits the people who appear in it.

Is there anything wrong with watching X-rated videos?

X-rated videos are pornography, and present the same concerns as pornography.

What is oral sex?

Oral sex is stimulating the sex organs with the mouth or tongue. Even though you can't get pregnant from oral sex, it isn't "safe sex" because you can still get sexually transmitted infections. And contrary to some popular opinion, oral sex is sex.

Can you get pregnant from oral sex?

No, but oral sex is a very intimate sexual act. Most individuals who engage in oral sex soon proceed to vaginal intercourse, where pregnancy may occur. And most common sexually transmitted infections can be acquired through oral sex.

One problem with oral sex is that some teens today have taken the intimacy out of sex by making oral sex a group activity. Oral sex should be seen as an extremely intimate activity reserved for marriage—and only if both spouses are willing.

What is anal sex?

Anal sex is penetration of the anus with a penis. The rectum wasn't designed for sexual intercourse; physical problems can result, including increased risk for acquiring certain STIs such as HIV/AIDS. Anal sex is never a healthy behavior, not even in marriage.

Can you get pregnant from anal sex?

With any kind of sexual activity, if sperm is near the anus, it could be near the vaginal cavity. However, it would be highly unlikely for sperm to swim over or somehow get from the rectal area to the vagina and then up into the uterus and fallopian tubes. You can, however, acquire most STIs from anal intercourse, especially HIV/AIDS.

Can you get pregnant if you have sex during your period?

You can't get pregnant during your period if it's that time of your menstrual cycle when your body is shedding the unfertilized egg. Some girls have bleeding or spotting at the time of ovulation (when the egg is released during the menstrual cycle), and it's possible to get pregnant during this time of menstrual bleeding.

Can you get pregnant if you haven't started having periods yet?

Yes! It's possible that a girl may ovulate (have an egg released from one of her ovaries) before menstrual bleeding occurs for the first time.

Can a girl get pregnant if she's never had a penis in her vagina?

It's highly unlikely but not impossible. If any semen gets in the vagina, even though you haven't had penetrative sex, you can still get pregnant. This could occur during mutual masturbation when the sperm is near the vagina. Also, if semen is on the hand and it's introduced to the vaginal area, pregnancy becomes a possibility.

Can you get pregnant the first time you have sex?

Contrary to popular belief, it's possible to get pregnant the very first time you have sex. There are lots of other myths out there regarding circumstances under which you can't get pregnant. Having sex while standing on your head or in the shower will not keep you from getting pregnant, nor will douching with Coke. These are myths. In reality, a girl can get pregnant if a man ejaculates during intercourse (or even "outercourse") and a sperm cell makes its way into her vagina and up into one of her fallopian tubes.

How does a woman know if she's pregnant?

The most common way is by missing a period. Other symptoms include breast tenderness, morning nausea, abdominal fullness, and weight gain.

How many days a month can you get pregnant?

An egg that's been released from a woman's ovary lives for about twenty-four hours before it breaks up and can't be fertilized. This means that a woman can become pregnant for three to four days in each menstrual cycle, since sperm live between one and three days.

How many sperm does it take to cause a pregnancy?

It only takes one sperm cell out of the millions released with each ejaculation to reach the egg, clear the lining around it, penetrate a ripe egg, and start a pregnancy.

Can a person tell if another person has had sex?

You can't tell from looking at a guy's penis whether he's ever had sex (unless you happen to see lesions, sores, or penile discharge that are generally associated with sexually transmitted infections). As for women, the vagina has a covering called a hymen. When a woman has sex for the first time, the hymen is torn or broken away. Sometimes it's difficult for even a physician to determine whether a female is a virgin or has had a very limited number of sexual contacts. In many virginal women, the hymen is torn because of repeated tampon use.

How do you know if you're sexually compatible with another person?

Some may claim this as a concern, but it's not an authentic physical issue. Sometimes it's used when a person is pressuring another to have sex ("We have to know if we're sexually compatible").

It's more important to develop a relationship with a person that you're interested in, as opposed to "sexual compatibility." Talking and getting to know the other person (his goals, dreams, and desires) and having him get to know you is a far greater marker of compatibility in a relationship. What's important is that the relationship is healthy.

Sexual problems are often the result of past sexual abuse or promiscuity and can be solved by counseling and time—not by "trying it on for size." Besides, the first few times a woman has sex, it may be painful.

Do both men and women have orgasms?

Yes. They tend to be different in males and females, but both sexes experience orgasms. Some women, however—including some sexually active adolescents—admit to not experiencing orgasms during sexual intercourse.

What does an orgasm feel like?

Some describe orgasm as an explosive release after a buildup of immense pleasure. Others have compared it to a sneeze: there's the sensation of the

185

sneeze coming on, followed by a "letting go." While orgasm is hard to describe, it's very pleasurable to both partners, even though the orgasm for each sex is different not only in feelings but duration.

What is foreplay?

Foreplay is often described as sexual activity prior to intercourse. Because it's such an intimate form of contact, its proper context is marriage.

Foreplay could include a range of activities, such as deep and prolonged kissing, hands to the breasts or genitalia, and mouth to the breasts or genitalia. A modern term that essentially means the same thing is "outercourse," when a couple not intending to have penetrative sex lies next to each other fully or partially undressed.

Some believe this is a "safe" and "healthy" alternative to penetrative intercourse. This isn't true for a few reasons. Although uncommon, it's possible to get pregnant from foreplay or outercourse. You can also catch sexually transmitted infections.

Sex also tends to be progressive. Foreplay is intended to prepare the body for sexual intercourse. Most adolescents who start with foreplay or outercourse usually proceed to having vaginal intercourse at some point.

What is masturbation?

Masturbation is the manual stimulation of the genitalia. This can be done to oneself or performed simultaneously with another person (mutual masturbation).

Is it harmful to masturbate?

In general, it isn't physically harmful to masturbate, though in girls it can be associated with an increase in urinary tract infections. Masturbation can become an emotional problem if it replaces normal, nonsexual peer relationships with a fantasy world—which is common when pornography is involved.

Some Christians believe the sexual fantasy often associated with masturbation violates Jesus' command in Matthew 5:28: "But I tell you that anyone who looks at a woman lustfully has already committed adultery with her in his heart."

People may disagree about the problems associated with solo masturbation. However, masturbation with another person outside of marriage; the use of pornography with masturbation; and compulsive, all-consuming masturbation are harmful.

Is it normal to have wet dreams?

Yes. A wet dream is another name for a nocturnal emission. During the night while sleeping an adolescent boy may have an erection followed by the emission of semen. This is normal and happens in all boys from time to time.

What is an aphrodisiac?

An aphrodisiac is something that's thought to enhance sexual arousal.

What's the normal size for a penis? Can it be too big? Too small?

The normal size varies. It can depend on the age and sexual development level of the teenager. The penis in the erect position becomes much longer.

The concept of a penis being too big is a myth. And with very rare exceptions, a penis is never too small.

In reality, the size of the penis doesn't matter. What matters is having sexual intercourse in the context of marriage. When this occurs, sex can be wonderful and fulfilling to both the male and female regardless of the size of the penis.

How much body hair is normal?

This varies with age and genetics. To have no body hair is abnormal. Some people have a small amount of body hair; others have lots. Both are normal.

Today, in some cultures, it's trendy for both boys and girls to shave their body hair, especially in the pubic region.

Are you supposed to shave your pubic hair?

The majority of women don't shave their pubic hair, though more and more do. Some shave around the edges during the summer so that their hair 'doesn't show when they're wearing a bathing suit.

Shaving pubic hair causes the skin to be itchy. Sometimes women can get minor skin infections or irritation after shaving. That's why most shave only around the edges when necessary.

Why are my breasts different sizes?

It isn't unusual to have different-sized breasts. Occasionally this may be extreme, but usually it's subtle with only minor differences.

I'm a guy. Is a lump in my breast normal?

It's not unusual for teen boys to have some initial breast development. This may start as a lump under the nipple and may occur just on one side. It's a normal part of adolescence and almost always goes away.

Why do some boys have some breast development?

Adolescent boys, particularly younger ones, may have some development that usually resolves on its own over a period of several years. This is a normal part of puberty. For most males, the breast enlargement is rather small and may be limited to a lump that others can't see but the individual can feel. It may even be tender.

Rarely, boys will have rather large breasts; this is called gynecomastia. Generally, this condition goes away without intervention; occasionally surgery is performed to remove the excessive breast tissue. Some boys who are significantly obese appear to have increased breast tissue, but it's actually fat.

Why aren't my testicles the same size?

It's normal for testes to vary in size, with the left testicle hanging lower than the right. Young men, starting in the teen years, should do testicular self-exams to look for any new or unusual lumps or bumps. This screens for testicular cancer. If you feel new lumps or something that doesn't seem right, let your parents know so you can be seen by a physician.

What is a condom?

A condom is a temporary cover for an erect penis and is usually made out of latex (rubber). The purpose of the condom is to collect ejaculated sperm so that they don't go into the vagina and potentially start a pregnancy.

A condom may also be used in an attempt to reduce the chance of transmission of a sexually transmitted infection. In no case does a condom eliminate the risk of pregnancy or totally protect you from catching an STI, even if used correctly every single time (see Appendix B in the back of this book).

What is a douche for?

A douche is a solution used to rinse the vagina. In nearly all cases, douching is unnecessary because the vagina cleanses itself. Frequent douching can change the pH balance of the vagina and cause problems. For this reason, douching is almost never recommended by physicians.

What is birth control?

Birth control is a method to eliminate or reduce the risk of pregnancy.

Abstinence is the only 100 percent effective form of birth control. Other kinds of birth control include oral contraceptive pills, patches, condoms, spermicides, diaphragms, cervical caps along with a spermicide, periodic injections of hormones, and IUDs (intrauterine devices).

Natural family planning is attempting to avoid pregnancy without using chemicals, birth control pills, condoms, or IUDs. It's based on the woman's menstrual cycle and avoiding sexual intercourse during times when a pregnancy could occur. This form of birth control can be very successful with highly motivated married couples.

While birth control may reduce the risk of getting pregnant or, in some cases, reduce the likelihood of acquiring an STI, it can't address the moral and spiritual problems associated with sex outside of marriage. Nor can it protect teens from the emotional and relational damage they may experience from sexual intimacy before marriage.

What is circumcision? What's the difference between a circumcised and an uncircumcised penis?

Circumcision is a procedure in which the loose foreskin around the tip of the penis is removed. In most cases, this is done in infancy. Circumcision is rarely medically necessary, but it's frequently performed on boys for cultural or religious reasons (see Genesis 17; Romans 2:25–29). There's some evidence that being circumcised may reduce a person's chance of acquiring certain sexually transmitted infections, particularly HIV.

In a circumcised male, the tip (called the glans) of the penis is visible. You don't see the tip of the uncircumcised penis because it's covered by the foreskin. The tip can be seen if the foreskin is retracted or if the penis is erect and the foreskin retracts on its own.

Why is my body developing slower than my friends' bodies?

The pace of your physical development is something that's genetically programmed. You have no control over it. Just because you're developing slower than your friends doesn't mean you're abnormal. If you have concerns in this area, discuss your level or rate of development with your physician.

Sometimes I feel attracted to people of my own gender. What does that mean?

Many people have had romantic or sexual feelings about someone of their own gender. It's normal for kids to go through times when they deeply admire and want to connect with someone of the same sex. Most teens have had concerns or questions about their sexuality, particularly as their bodies change during adolescence.

Confusion about sexuality probably has increased with the growing number of people who openly identify as gay, lesbian, or bisexual. Talk about homosexuality is much more common, and there's been an explosion of books, movies, and television programs with gay or lesbian-identified characters and homosexual scenes. Confusion is multiplied when many kids have seen pornography or other graphic sexual material, have engaged in sexual play with other kids, or have been sexually abused.

Homosexuality is the consistent feeling of sexual or romantic attraction to people of the same sex while feeling little or no attraction to the opposite sex. God designed us as complementary sexual beings, and His intention was that boys would grow into a healthy sense of masculinity and be attracted to women. His intention was that girls would grow into a healthy feminine identity and be attracted to men. There are a number of factors involved in the origins of homosexual feelings, and it's different for each person. But we know that sometimes the process of growing into a healthy gender identity and naturally developing opposite-sex attraction gets derailed.

What should I do if I think I'm homosexual?

It's really only been in the last one hundred years or so that people have talked about "being gay" or "being homosexual"—as if that was their true identity or the core of their being. If you feel same-sex attraction, it's important not to label yourself or let other people label you according to those attractions. Sexual attraction doesn't define who you are; God defines you. So don't take on homosexuality as an identity.

The question really is this: What should I do if I'm attracted to someone of the same sex?

Most people don't choose who they're attracted to, but we all choose what to do with our attractions. We can pretend they don't exist. We can dwell on or act on our sexual attractions through fantasy, lust, pornography, masturbation, or sexual activity with another person. Or we can follow God's design for sexual expression—a husband and wife in a marriage relationship. With God's help and the help of others, you can take a biblical approach to your sexuality. You didn't choose same-sex attraction, but you can make choices about your identity and what to do with your feelings.

If you're wrestling with unwanted same-sex attractions, it's important to share this with a safe, trusted adult who can help you think and talk through the many thoughts and emotions you have. A safe adult believes in God's design for sexuality, won't take advantage of you, listens, provides support and encouragement, and tells you the truth. Sexual behavior has consequences, and when those behaviors occur outside of God's design, the consequences are always damaging. Homosexual sexual behavior can have severe physical, spiritual, and psychological consequences.

You'll also need to learn how to develop healthy, non-sexual relationships with members of the same sex. We all need these relationships, but there's a special need for this in most people with same-sex attractions. You need people who accept you as you are—who demonstrate God's love and grace but who will also help you to grow spiritually. Pastoral or professional counseling may be helpful—not with someone who pushes a gay identity onto you, but with someone who will help you live biblically. Counseling and prayer are even more necessary if you experienced sexual abuse or early exposure to sex or pornography.

Finally, please remember you're not alone. Many people with same-sex attraction have learned how to manage their behavior in a biblical way, resisting temptation with effective tools. Some find that their same-sex attractions diminish; some develop opposite-sex attractions. Whether or not those changes ever happen, you can still choose to follow God's design for your sexuality.

12

UNFINISHED BUSINESS

Sixteen- to Eighteen-Year-Olds

S ome would like you to believe that your work with your teen is finished, that you're no longer an influential factor in his life. Nothing
could be further from the truth. Your teen needs you more than ever.
He may not want you to make his decisions, but he does need you to listen
as he processes them.

Even though your teen may be heading off to college or career shortly,
your parenting responsibilities aren't finished, especially when it comes to
sexuality. If he's involved in a serious relationship, make an effort to get
to know his girlfriend (even if you think she's not the girl for him). Now's
the time to engage him in discussions about his dreams and desires for the
future. Talk with him about the importance of his relationship with God,
and of keeping that relationship vibrant. It's also the time to remind him
how casual sexual relationships can affect his dreams of having a family.

Don't make the mistake of thinking your teen doesn't care what you
think; he does. Just remember that he desperately wants to be heard. Make
an effort to listen and understand the world from his perspective, because
it's tremendously different from the one you grew up in. Finally, get involved

in his life. And if you haven't done so already, make your home a place where he and his friends want to hang out.

Parents' Questions

Should I be concerned if my teen's involved in a long-term relationship?

It's important for parents to have a realistic sense of what the relationship is about. You can do this by getting to know your teen's boyfriend (or girlfriend). Invite him to your home and include him in family activities so that you can see how he treats your teen and how she responds to him. If they have a healthy relationship, treat each other with respect, and seem to have a genuine friendship beneath the romance, the two may certainly be in love.

This can be a good experience, especially if both have a relationship with God and share a commitment to honor Him. But long-term dating relationships can also pose problems. Research indicates that teens in long-term relationships are strongly tempted to be sexually active; this is especially true for girls dating boys two or more years older.[1] Even for teens who share a Christian faith, sexual temptations abound. Parents need to be involved and help their teens avoid sexual activity because of the negative consequences associated with nonmarital sexual activity—including broken hearts, broken relationships, future marital difficulties, sexually transmitted infections, pregnancy, emotional distress, and the danger of distancing oneself from God.

Unfortunately, some teens treat a long-term relationship as a pseudomarriage, wrongly appropriating the intimacies reserved by God for marriage. Others fall into the trap of thinking that their dating partner must be "the one"—the person they'll eventually marry. Given this assumption, many young people reason that if they're going to get married anyway, it wouldn't hurt anyone if they started getting physically intimate a little early. Teens who think this are getting the cart before the horse. It's common for teens in dating relationships to end up not marrying the person they felt certain would be their marriage partner. Besides, even if the guy and girl eventually got married, being in a long-term relationship never negates God's plans for people to remain sexually abstinent before marriage.

Some teens stay in unhealthy long-term relationships because they don't see how bad the relationship is. That's why they need parents to help them out of it. How do you know if a relationship is unhealthy? Here are some questions to help you decide:

- What's your teen like around her boyfriend? Is she irritable, or does she act more immature than usual?
- Does the boyfriend allow her space and free time, or is he possessive and domineering?
- Has your teen ever tried to break up with him, and the boyfriend refused to let her go?

Often teens stay in long-term relationships simply because they can't get out. While some parents might fear that injecting themselves into a child's relationship could be met with protests or even hostility, now is not the time to shrink. Stay engaged and pray for her. Help her evaluate the health of her relationship. Keep the lines of communication open by asking questions and staying quiet long enough to hear the answers. If you're sincere in your quest to help your teen negotiate intense relationships, she'll respond to you. If you simply preach and fail to listen, she'll shut you out.

How do I protect my child from sexually tempting situations?

You can't prevent every possibility, but you can think ahead. Long before he gets into a tempting situation, talk to your teen about what it means to be into something over his head. Help him develop a game plan to remain abstinent until he's married. Here are some ideas to help you get started:

- Think through possible scenarios in which a teen would be drawn into temptation that might be overwhelming. Long periods of time alone together shouldn't be an option; neither should baby-sitting other children together, particularly when the kids are asleep and the house is quiet. Encourage your teen to list times when he might find himself wanting to do something he's committed to not doing. Don't proceed without his input, simply laying down the rules about time alone with a girlfriend.

195

- Help him choose to spend time with his girlfriend while others are present. Make sure they date in public places—restaurants, malls, movie theaters, and so on.

- Encourage your teen to have a close friend or two commit to helping him abstain. They can confide in each other about their struggles, which will lend him tremendous support.

- Encourage your teen to carry a visible symbol as a reminder of his commitment. Some teens wear a ring, bracelet, or necklace to remind them of their pledge to remain abstinent until they're married.

- Address the issue of trust up front. Many teens complain to parents that the reason parents don't want them alone with a girlfriend is because the parents don't trust them. Clarify for your teen that helping him avoid periods of being alone with a girlfriend isn't an issue of trust. It's about helping him avoid situations where he's tempted to do something he may regret.

Should I give my child condoms or birth control, since she may have sex anyway?

No! Never assume that your child will "have sex anyway." In fact, most healthy teens take cues about sexual behavior from their parents. If your teen feels you think she's going to be sexually active, she probably will be.

If you think your teen is (or is going to be) sexually active, sit down with her at a time when the two of you are relaxed, rested, and not in the midst of a fight. It's important to listen first and then respond in love; resist the temptation to lose your cool or raise your voice if she says something you disagree with.

At the appropriate time, ask her questions like, "Why do you want to be sexually active? Do you understand the risk? Do you think sex will make you feel better?"

If she claims to have a relationship with God, ask her if she knows what the Bible says about sexual purity. If she doesn't seem to have a good grasp of the concept, explain it clearly.

This would be a good time to talk about the social, emotional, and spiritual aspects of sex outside of marriage. The truth is, most kids will respond well if you take time to listen and talk patiently with them and give them good reasons to stay away from sex until they find the person with whom they want to spend the rest of their life. This would also be a great time to discuss how beautiful and wonderful sex is at the right time in your teen's life—marriage—when she won't have to worry about having a baby outside of marriage or getting a sexually transmitted infection.

Explain that no method of contraception is perfect. When it comes to preventing pregnancy, the condom has an approximately 15 percent failure rate during the first year of use. Even the pill has around an 8 percent failure rate during the first year, in part because many users don't take it consistently and correctly.[2] Furthermore, other drugs, including various antibiotics, may reduce the effectiveness of the pill, making it even less reliable in preventing pregnancy.

In addition, condoms never eliminate the risk of any STI. At best, they reduce the risk if they're used every single time; but even then the chance of infection for most STIs is about 50 percent if you have sexual intercourse with an infected partner over time. The chance of HIV infection with 100 percent condom use is less, but HIV can lead to death—so any risk is a concern. Consistent and correct use of condoms over time is uncommon.[3]

Other forms of birth control such as the pill do nothing to reduce the risk of STIs. And no form of contraception can protect against the heartbreak and ruined relationships that arise from sex outside of marriage.

How do I stay involved in my child's life when he wants me out?

Remind yourself frequently that while your teen appears to want you out, inwardly he needs you very much. He's simply uncomfortable with the fact that he still needs you but in a very different way.

He's like a toddler—confused, wanting independence, but struggling to get it. Know that no matter what you see, he desperately needs your approval, love, and commitment to stick by him no matter what. This doesn't give you a license to micromanage his life. But continued engagement will give him the confidence and ability to avoid risky behaviors such as sex before marriage.

Find areas of common interest on which you and your teen can spend time together. This should be fun "connecting" time when the two of you

---

Losing Control without Losing Influence

Some high schoolers are having sex—but not all of them! Engage in ongoing discussions with your teen about the importance of waiting for sex until marriage. Believe it or not, this will influence her decision on whether to wait to have sex.

- Model healthy, moral relationships with appropriate public affection in your own life.
- Talk about how waiting until marriage for sexual intercourse will lead to the happiest sex life in the future. If you find out that your teen has already lost her virginity, encourage her to start over as a secondary virgin. Let her know it's never too late to start over.
- If your teen is in a serious relationship, spend a lot of time with both parties. Make sure they aren't alone together at either house, where teen sex happens the most. Talk with the other parents about whether they might make the same commitment.
- Use media examples familiar to your teen as discussion starters about shallow sexual relationships that misrepresent true love and long-term commitment.
- Fathers, continue to "date" your daughters. Take them out and spend meaningful one-to-one time over dinner or coffee. If you meet resistance, do some probing to find out why; don't just give up on them. Mothers, "date" your sons. This lets them know you care about them and want to stay connected.

---

just try to enjoy each other. Going out to lunch or dinner by yourselves is a great place to start. Spending brief periods of time together helps smooth tough conversations that need to take place and builds the groundwork for the beginnings of your adult relationship.

What do I do if I find birth control pills in my daughter's room?

First, allow yourself some reaction time before you talk to your daughter. If you're angry, sad, or disappointed, call a close friend, pastor, or Christian counselor and work through your feelings. You might feel like a failure or consider yourself a terrible parent. Don't get lost in those emotions. Remember, teens are growing up in a culture that's seducing them to be sexually active; all good parents have a lot working against them, and your family is no exception. Get over the guilt and move ahead.

Tell your daughter that the two of you need to make time to talk about some important things. Agree on a time, then wait until then to tell her what you found. She'll accuse you of having no right to get into her belongings, but don't get into that argument. If you've discovered birth control pills, you'd be negligent as a parent if you didn't confront your daughter.

Ask when she got the pills, where, and who gave them to her. Ask whether she's been sexually active; if she says yes, ask how long this has been going on. Then listen.

Ask *why* she's sexually active—and listen. Ask with whom she's been sexually active. Watch her response closely, even if she's silent. Remind her that you love and care about her and don't want her to get hurt.

When she's finished talking, let her know that while everyone around her may feel that sex isn't a "big deal," it is. Emotionally, psychologically, physically, and spiritually, sex can have very painful consequences at her age; your job is to help her avoid getting hurt. Explain that sex is an incredible gift—and if she continues to be sexually active, she risks ruining this gift for the rest of her life.

You don't want that for her. You want her to have a great sex life, and the best way to ensure this is to wait until marriage. If she's already been sexually active, the best thing is deciding to remain abstinent from now until marriage.

If she listens, keep going. If she balks and storms off, reopen the issue in a day or two. But don't let up. Pray for her and keep praying. If you don't fight for her, who will?

Find a physician who agrees that it's unhealthy for unmarried teens to be sexually active, and will do everything possible to keep your daughter as safe and healthy as she can. Remember, however, that even if her physician feels as strongly as you do about sexual activity at this age, it takes time to encourage adolescents toward abstinence. Call the doctor in advance, tell her what's up, and ask if you can schedule an appointment for your daughter. If your daughter is already sexually experienced, she'll need to be examined for pregnancy and sexually transmitted infections.

Outside support—such as family, friends, your pastor or church youth leader, your congregation, or a qualified Christian counselor—can make a world of difference for both of you. Most teenagers will make a wrong choice at one time or another, and premarital sexual activity is an unhealthy choice. When that happens, it's your job to continue loving your teen even though you disapprove of her action or lifestyle. Over time, if you continue to love and support your daughter and keep open the lines of communication, you're likely to influence powerfully her future choices.

I found condoms in my son's jeans. What should I do?

First, see the previous question. Then be prepared to talk about his friends, what they're doing, and why. Acknowledge that he has very strong physiological urges and that the urges are mostly good and normal. But encourage him to see that, contrary to what his friends might tell him, he has the ability to control his actions; self-discipline is a very masculine trait.

Without pelting him with Bible verses, ask whether he understands God's design for sexuality and the importance of sexual purity. Be prepared to explain these ideas lovingly if he's foggy on the concepts.

Ask him what he knows about condoms (see Appendix B for more information). What can he expect from condoms and under what circumstances? Does he know how to use one correctly? Does he know condoms at best only reduce the chance of infection, but never totally eliminate risk?

Realistically, condoms don't have much chance of helping reduce the risk of sexually transmitted infection unless they're used perfectly every time—which seldom happens. With typical condom use, roughly one out of six girls will become pregnant over the course of a year—odds that shouldn't inspire great confidence. Explaining this may help your son see that condoms aren't the answer. At best they may reduce certain physical risks, but they can never protect against the emotional pain, damaged relationships, and distorted view of sexuality that come with sexual activity outside marriage.

If my teen is drinking or smoking, is she more likely to be sexually active?

Yes. Studies show that teens involved in alcohol and drugs are more likely to be sexually active.[4] This stands to reason; whenever a teen is drunk or high, her inhibitions lower, and she's more likely to lose self-control. It's also been shown that teens who engage in damaging behaviors such as smoking are more likely to be involved in risky activities such as premarital sex.

So if your teen smokes or drinks, ask about her sexual activity. Remind your son that if he drinks and is sexually active with his date, he could be accused of rape. And remind your daughter that drinking places her at a higher risk for being raped.

My child wants to attend an all-night party with friends at school; is that okay?

These parties have become very popular. They originated from concerns that teens would drink and drive. Parents and teachers offered all-night parties as a way to keep teens off the roads. While the idea is well intentioned, the parties also carry risks.

First, many teens still drink, but within the confines of the party. Second, many teens still have sex, but at the party instead of somewhere else. The parties may reduce drunk driving, but not necessarily anything else. Some parties have adult chaperones, but usually this is nothing more than a parent asleep upstairs somewhere.

The best advice: Know where the party is, who's chaperoning, and who will be there. If you don't like any of the above or you don't know the parents—don't let your teen go. Even if they're "good" kids and "good" parents, too much of a good thing can turn bad.

My daughter has told me she's a lesbian; what should I do?

It may be hard, but try not to overreact. This is important because you want to keep communication open with her. If she senses you're very upset, she's likely to shut down and not trust you. So if you feel angry, confused, or hurt, try not to show it to her at first. Talk to a trusted friend who can help you.

It's important to ask your daughter why she feels this way and how long she's felt it. Depending on her age, you may find that she thinks she's a lesbian because she has strong emotional attachments to some of her girlfriends. For instance, some girls in their early teen years feel comfortable around other girls and not around boys. A young girl may think that since she doesn't like being around boys, she must be a lesbian. This, of course, isn't true.

Many girls in early adolescence experiment with homosexual play; some boys do this as well. But fondling another girl's genitalia or breasts or being the recipient of such behavior doesn't make a girl a lesbian, even though she may think she is.

A girl's sexual identity is still being formed during the early adolescent and teen years. During this time, a girl may assume she's a lesbian because she has emotional or sexual feelings toward another girl. Understanding that these feelings occur and can be confusing may help your daughter see that she's really a heterosexual experiencing mixed feelings common at her stage of development. Same-sex relationships also are very trendy in some communities, and your daughter may just want to fit in.

If, on the other hand, your daughter comes to you when she's an older teen and tells you she's a lesbian, you'll face different issues. Again, you want to be sure not to overreact. Calmly ask why she believes this. She may tell you that she's only attracted to women and has never had romantic feelings for a man. She'll probably be very defensive when talking with you and may be waiting for you to be critical, angry, and disappointed. Rather than react to her with any of these feelings, show that you're concerned about her and her emotional health.

God's Word has a lot to say regarding homosexuality, but it's not necessary to use the Bible as a sledgehammer—especially at this moment. Remind her that God loves her unconditionally and without reserve. Continue to reach out to her in love and acceptance. In time, after her defensiveness softens, ask if she'd be willing to talk with a counselor about her feelings.

Many teens who identify themselves as homosexual struggle with emotional turmoil, depression, and even a history of sexual abuse. Your daughter needs help untangling a web of complex feelings. If you genuinely show her that first and foremost you're concerned about her emotional health, not her sexual orientation, and that you want to help her toward feeling good about herself and life, she'll be more willing to consider your advice.

If she accepts the idea of counseling, do some research. Find a licensed Christian counselor who'll help your daughter with her identity and depression issues—and who's willing to offer assistance if she wants to leave her current lifestyle.

The decision to change must come from within. It's possible, however, if the individual truly desires to change. It's not easy and may take years of counseling.

The success rate of leaving the gay lifestyle is similar to that of overcoming alcoholism. Neither is easy, but both are possible. Your role at this point is to unconditionally love and support your daughter, pray for her, and help arrange and finance counseling if this offer is accepted.

My daughter wants to date a college boy; should I let her?

It depends on how old your daughter is. If she's a senior in high school, he's a freshman in college, and the two are about one year apart in age, dating might be okay—though if she wants to visit him at college for the weekend, that should be off-limits. If your daughter is sixteen and wants to date a student who's in his twenties, this is *not* appropriate.

A good rule of thumb is to allow girls to date boys the same age, or at most one year apart. Girls often want to date older boys because most boys lag behind girls in their physical and emotional development in high school.

When a girl dates a much older boy, she places herself in a situation where she can be physically, intellectually, or emotionally outmaneuvered. He has an immediate psychological advantage because she looks up to him and considers him (usually subconsciously) as more experienced, wiser, cooler, and stronger. She'll defer to him in many ways, which can be dangerous when it comes to sexual issues.

Keep your daughter on level ground when it comes to dating. In general, college boys and high school girls don't mix.

My son has gotten his girlfriend pregnant. What should I do?

When you first find out about this situation, you're likely to feel angry, disappointed, hurt, and like a failure as a parent. To make matters worse, you'll feel this in the presence of a son who, depending on his age, may feel scared to death. So take a deep breath, give yourself and your son some breathing space, and then try to sort things out and help him make the best decisions possible.

First, encourage him to be responsible. While neither of you can control what his girlfriend does with the pregnancy, you can urge your son to help her. He can assist his girlfriend in getting prompt medical care to ensure the health of the baby. Help find a good physician, and offer to take her to appointments if her parents are unwilling or unable.

This is a good time to talk with your son about the value of each human life. Some boyfriends respond to an unplanned pregnancy by suggesting or demanding that their girlfriend get an abortion. Even if you're confident that your son is not abortion-minded, initiate the discussion and get a sense of where he stands on the issue. Does he fully understand that this pregnancy involves a child, a distinct human life made in the image of God, and not just a mass of cells? Let him know that this baby is important to you, and that you're prepared to provide or find whatever help is needed for this baby to be given a chance at life.

You might want to encourage your son and his girlfriend to visit a pregnancy resource center for help with decisions about whether to keep the baby or offer it for adoption. If his girlfriend decides to keep the baby, your son will be financially responsible for the child even if they don't decide to marry.

My daughter is pregnant. What should I do?

Your first and most important reaction must be to unconditionally love your daughter. Resist the temptation to say, "How could you do this?" or, "I'm so disappointed." Initially, your daughter needs to be held and loved and told that you'll stand with her as decisions are made in the coming days about her baby's future. Thank her for coming to you for advice.

After a period of time, perhaps after a good night's sleep, you'll need to sit down with her and help her work through her options. None of the options your daughter must consider are easy, and all will involve a measure of pain and heartache. Offer your best advice in a nonjudgmental way, knowing that ultimately she may make a decision that's contrary to what you think is best. Since this is such an emotional issue, consider writing your thoughts in a letter to your daughter. Here is a sample letter.

Dear Daughter:

Thank you for letting us help you during this difficult time in your life. Your mother and I would be less than honest if we didn't tell you that, like yourself, we are hurting. Know that our love for you has not diminished because of your pregnancy.

There are many options available to you. The first option is presenting the baby for adoption. Releasing your baby for adoption will bring great joy to a married couple unable to have children of their own. There will be pain, however, in carrying your baby nine months and then having to hand over your baby to the adopting parents. The joy, however, will be knowing that a loving, married couple will rear your baby in a two-parent home.

The next option is keeping the baby as a single parent. It's difficult at times for a stable, two-parent family, much less a single teenager. Your mother and I aren't saying it's impossible but only that it will be extremely difficult.

Another option is marrying the father of your child, but many teen marriages end in early divorce. If you choose to marry, you and your husband will have to work hard to create a lasting marriage.

The last option is abortion. You know that for your mother and me it isn't an option. God loves each and every person immeasurably, and the baby growing inside you is a person made in the image of God. We believe that life begins when the sperm from a male fertilizes the egg of a female. The new life has inherited twenty-three chromosomes from each parent, forty-six in all. This one cell contains the complex genetic blueprint for every detail of human development—the child's sex, hair and eye color, athletic ability, musical ability, and personality.

Then only food and oxygen are needed for the baby to grow from one cell to a seven-pound baby nine months later.

The baby's heart begins to beat on day twenty-one. By day twenty-two, the foundation for every organ system is established and developing. At nine weeks, the baby is unmistakably recognizable as a human being.

While the pregnancy can be terminated by an abortion, the memory of the pregnancy will last a lifetime. Some women will experience post-abortion syndrome. Abortion isn't without risks, and complications can and do occur. Some women are never able to get pregnant in the future, and then you must live with the fact that you ended your one and only pregnancy.

I would encourage you to see your physician and let her be a resource to help answer your questions. I would also urge you to visit our local pregnancy resource center. Your mother and I will be praying for your decision, but also know that we love you no matter what happens and we will always be here for you.

Love, Dad

My son wants to stay at a hotel on prom night; how should I respond?

First, ask him why he wants to spend the night at a hotel. Who'll be there, and why does he think this would be a good idea? Then explain that the only "benefit" to staying at a hotel would be to continue partying with friends after the prom or to keep from driving if he's been drinking. These are common reasons teens use to defend wanting to stay at a hotel after a party or prom.

Concerning the first answer, tell him that all fun must end sometime, and two o'clock in the morning is a better time than eight o'clock. This isn't a trust issue; you want to help him stay away from situations where he'll be tempted to do things he'll regret later. He must avoid those situations in the same way that you as an adult would. Healthy maturation requires him to develop this skill; tell him that he needs to start making those tough decisions now.

Second, if he says he wants to stay at a hotel to avoid driving drunk, don't ignore the fact that he wants to drink. In no way should you encourage him to drink alcohol even in a "safe" place. Besides, he may be breaking the law.

My daughter, a high school senior, has been invited to go on a graduation trip to Cancún without adults. Should I allow her to go?

No! First of all, teens can drink whenever they want in Cancún, and alcohol and teens are a bad mix. Second, it's not uncommon for alcoholic drinks to be laced with illegal drugs in countries like Mexico, and teens can get into a lot of trouble even if they have their guard up.

If your daughter wants to go to Cancún and you can afford it, you could do one of the following: Go with her or have another trustworthy parent go with her and her friends. Or don't let her go. If she says she doesn't want adults along, that alone should raise a red flag.

Should I allow my teen to attend the school's sex education program?

Before your teen attends the class, do your homework. Ask the teacher if you can review the curriculum. Ask to look at books, and if a video is shown, ask to see it ahead of time. It's ideal if you can do this long before your teen has the class; if you ask to review the material right before it's presented, he'll probably be embarrassed.

If you find the material completely offensive when you review it, tell the principal of your school. Even if the curriculum is good, consider the fact that teachers may present it with their own bias. Ask the teacher what he intends to communicate to the class regarding abstinence, condoms and other birth control, and so on.

If the material isn't offensive to you, let your teen attend the class—and be sure the two of you discuss what was taught. He may hesitate to discuss it, but you must be bold enough to talk about it anyway. If there was material that you liked, say so. If there was some that bothered you or that you disagreed with from an ethical or spiritual vantage point, tell your teen how you feel. But before you state your feelings, ask him to tell you his. This helps keep the channels of communication open.

If you have your teen opt out of the class, share good alternative information with him. This may include your own research and guidance, appropriate books or videos, or a different class.

If peer pressure is such a problem when it comes to teens and sex, what can I do about it?

You can pay attention to who your teen's friends are. Adolescents are highly impressionable, and while they may want to be "different," they usually gravitate toward imitating their friends' behaviors. In general, whatever your teen's friends are doing, she's liable to do as well. You may want to believe she's strong enough to resist temptation to engage in bad behaviors, but the truth is that most average, healthy kids don't seem able to do so—at least consistently.

There are sound psychological reasons why this is so, but suffice it to say that most teens emulate their friends' behaviors because they desperately want to be accepted. If the kids are responsible and respect one another, that's what your teen will do. But if they engage in high-risk behaviors including sexual experimentation, that, too, is probably what she'll do.

Why is teen sex so risky?

There are several reasons. For teen girls, sex is much riskier than for older women because of anatomical differences. The cervix of a seventeen-year-old girl, for instance, has a lining that's different from that of a forty-five-year-old woman.[5] The cells in the lining covering the teen cervix are more vulnerable to bacteria and viruses that come in contact with it during sexual intercourse.[6]

Teen sex is risky because of the ways in which teens behave sexually. For instance, the popularity of oral sex has increased among teens in recent years for two reasons: Many believe they can engage in oral sex, stay disease-free, and remain virgins. Teens need to understand that almost any sexually transmitted infection they can acquire through vaginal intercourse can be acquired through oral sex. And while physically teens may be virgins after oral sex, emotionally they are not. Other sexual behaviors that place teens at higher risk include an increased number of partners, drinking alcohol or using drugs before sex, and mistakenly believing they can't contract an STI by engaging in anal sex.

A teen who begins sexual activity at an early age—say at thirteen—is more likely to have a greater number of lifetime partners; the more partners, the greater the risk of infection. If you can help a teen postpone the initiation of sexual activity, he's more likely to have fewer sexual partners and therefore will be less likely to contract an STI.

If you look at teens' mental and emotional development, it makes sense that they would be at higher risk for developing STIs. Most people's abstract-thinking skills aren't fully developed until they're close to twenty-five years old.[7] Abstract thinking allows them to grasp the future in a meaningful way—the understanding that action A today leads to consequence B tomorrow or in ten years. Until this form of thought is developed, teens

Another Risk of Early Sexual Activity

Suicide is the third leading cause of death in teens in the United States. There is growing evidence to support a connection between early sexual activity in teenagers, depression, and suicide.

A Heritage Foundation report found that sexually active teenage girls were three times as likely and sexually active teenage boys twice as likely to experience depression as their counterparts who weren't sexually active. Furthermore, the study reported that sexually active teenage girls are almost three times as likely and sexually active teenage boys almost eight times as likely to attempt suicide as teens who remained abstinent. The majority of the teens questioned wished they hadn't become sexually active (72 percent of females, 55 percent of males).[8]

It's difficult to determine whether depressed teenagers are more likely to become sexually active, or whether sexually active teenagers become depressed because of their behavior. The study seems to suggest that both may be true.

Early sexual activity often leads to psychological stress from empty relationships and feelings of self-contempt and worthlessness. Teens may become involved in sexual activity to soothe feelings of emptiness and loneliness, but sexual activity itself appears to increase the risk of depression and even suicide. Clearly, the evidence suggests that sexual activity in teenagers poses significant mental-health risks.

are limited in their beliefs about what can happen to them. They're not stupid, but are living out what psychologists refer to as the personal fable. This thinking leads them to believe they'll never become pregnant, contract an STI, or experience any other serious consequences of sexual activity.

One other reason teen sex is risky is that young people are, in general, more susceptible to becoming addicted to sexual behaviors than are older individuals.

Should my teen have a regular checkup at the doctor?

Ideally, all teens should have a physical exam once a year with an established family doctor, pediatrician, or internist. Many teens (and their parents) feel it's unnecessary to go this frequently to the doctor's office, but adolescents face many serious health threats.

Girls who are or have been sexually active—even once—should have a pelvic examination and be screened for sexually transmitted infections. Regardless of whether she has been sexually active or not, a woman should get a Pap smear at age twenty-one and then have one every three years.

Teen boys should be encouraged to see their physician yearly as well. They need to be frank with their doctor about their sexual activity so that they can be checked for any STIs. Many STIs have no symptoms; simply because a teen feels fine, this doesn't mean that he doesn't have an STI.

How do I prepare my adolescent for the sexually saturated environment on college campuses today?

There's no way around it—sex and alcohol seem to be permanent fixtures on most college campuses in our culture. It doesn't matter whether your young adult is involved in the Greek system or just hanging out in the dorm; reckless abandon is often the attitude that rules, especially during the first two years.

To help your child succeed in this environment, it's important to develop a healthy rapport with him during high school. If he knows you're willing to listen, he'll be open and honest about the peer pressure he's facing. If he fears you, the opportunity for openness will evaporate, and you won't know whether he's prepared to resist the temptations he'll encounter.

Find some young adults who've experienced negative consequences from the party scene, and have them talk with your teen. If you've made mistakes, it may be beneficial to share a bit about your experiences.

Instead of controlling your child during the last two years of high school, slowly begin to pass decision-making responsibilities to him so that he can have experience making choices in the face of peer pressure before getting to college. Better for him to make a few minor mistakes while you're there to help him navigate the consequences than to make life-altering errors when he's away from home.

Finally, let your child see you seeking and serving God and living a life that honors Him. If he shares your faith this will encourage him in his convictions; if he doesn't have the same faith commitment you have, you'll serve as great example. While it's best for your child to see from an early age that you model a godly lifestyle, don't be discouraged if this represents a relatively new set of attitudes and behaviors for you. Your sincere relationship with God, lived out in a way that your child can see, can bolster your child's faith and give him the strength to make right but difficult choices.

How involved should I be in my teen's life in order to discourage sexual activity?

Research shows that a young adult's brain isn't fully mature in terms of judgment and impulse control until the midtwenties.[9] Parents and other trusted adults, therefore, are important as supervising mentors, giving advice and direction to young people.

Consider yourself a consultant. Seek outside help if your teen is involved in activities dangerous to her physical and mental health—like alcohol, drugs, and sexual activity. Encourage the influence of trustworthy adult mentors in your child's life. As she grows, control will be rejected—but wisdom will be sought.

How can I help my child find an adult mentor?

Set the example. Each of us needs advisors and mentors. Admit that you don't have all the answers but that experience is a valuable teacher. Find mentors of your own and let your teen know who they are.

Abstinence: Attainable

Encouraging your teen to wait until marriage to have sex gives her the best chance for a happy marriage and for the most satisfying sex. Let her know at every available opportunity how you feel about saving sex for marriage, because it will influence her decision. Here's how:

- Model fidelity in your marriage; if you're single and in a romantic relationship, practice abstinence.

- Talk with your teen about your expectations for her physical boundaries if she finds herself alone and in private with the opposite sex.

- Don't let your teen be home alone with the opposite sex—after school or anytime!

- Remind your daughter that the way she dresses will communicate to guys the type of girl she is. Teach modesty by example, and set guidelines on what's appropriate to wear out of the house.

- Have a trusted and trustworthy man (dad, uncle, grandpa) whom your daughter is comfortable with talk with her about avoiding provocative clothing and actions that "turn on" guys.

- Model how one treats and shows respect to the opposite sex. Dads, "date" your daughter. Moms, "date" your son.

- Set dating rules early so your teen knows when she can start group dating and couple dating. Clarify curfew rules and the consequences when broken.

- Be generous with physical affection for your teen, making sure she feels comfortable with it. Read *The Five Love Languages of Teenagers* by Gary Chapman.[10]

Point your adolescent to trusted youth leaders, pastors, teachers, physicians, coaches, employers, or family friends. Identify people with a value system similar to yours—though they don't have to be carbon copies of you. Emphasize to your child the wisdom and strength found in advisors; then let him cultivate a relationship with a mentor without fear that you'll feel incompetent or replaced.

Questions Teens Ask

I've been dating this boy for four months. He wants to have sex, but I'm not sure. What should I do? Do I owe it to him?

If you haven't worked this through already in your heart and mind, now's the time to decide *not* to become sexually active.

First of all, you never owe sex to anyone. God designed sexuality as a gift to us, one that we have the privilege of offering back to Him to be used for His purposes. You don't owe sex to any boy, no matter how long you've been dating or how much money he's spent on dates. It's your choice, not his. Having sex with someone is such an intimate act that it should occur only in a long-term, committed relationship where you feel guilt-free and safe—that is, marriage.

The risks of early sexual involvement without the commitment of marriage include sexually transmitted infections, pregnancy, and emotional disappointment—to name just a few. If you tell your boyfriend you won't be sexually active until you're married and he breaks up with you, all he wanted was sex. If he truly loves you, he'll respect you and support your commitment.

And here's one more thing to think about: Sexual feelings and real love are two very different things.

If I'm careful about using condoms and other birth control, what's wrong with having sex?

First of all, God has a plan for sex—and that plan isn't cancelled just because you use condoms or anything else to reduce the risk of getting an STI or becoming pregnant. He created sex as a wonderful thing to be enjoyed only between a husband and a wife. Birth control doesn't change that.

Choosing to have sex before marriage is a life-changing decision. While it may bring some pleasure in the short term, ultimately it won't make your life richer or better.

You only get one first-time sexual experience, and it's kind of like getting a beautiful birthday present. If you open it before your birthday, it

The Freedoms of Dating

You're free . . .

- to refuse a date offer.
- to suggest activities on a date.
- to say what you think.
- to have your own feelings and express them.
- to tell someone when he or she is being impolite.
- to tell someone you're uncomfortable.
- to have your limits and values respected.
- to refuse affection.
- to be heard.
- to refuse to lend money.
- to refuse sex with anyone just because some money was spent on you.
- to refuse sex at any time for any reason.
- to have friends and space apart from your boyfriend or girlfriend.
- to communicate clearly and honestly.
- to determine your limits and values.
- to ask for help when you need it.
- to be considerate.
- to set high expectations for yourself and others you choose to be with.
- to avoid situations that would lead to something you might regret.

may already be broken and worn out when your big day comes around. The same thing can happen if you start having sex before you're married.

This decision also can place you at risk for contracting sexually transmitted infections, getting pregnant, and experiencing emotional distress. It can affect every area of your life. Waiting to have sex until marriage is one decision you'll never regret.

How do you know if sex is right for you?

Are you married? If you're not, sex isn't right for you—yet. God's design for sex is that it be between one man and one woman in the relationship of marriage.

Some people don't find this answer very satisfying. Others, especially if they don't have a committed Christian faith, don't find it convincing. People in these categories who are trying to decide if sex is "right" for them need to ask themselves a few other questions:

- Am I ready to handle the complex emotional and relational changes that accompany the decision to have sex?
- Am I willing to seek medical treatment if I develop genital warts or contract chlamydia?
- Am I prepared to care for a child who's "accidentally" conceived during the heat of the moment?
- Am I ready for the pain that comes with a broken heart?

These are just a few of the possible outcomes of having sex outside of marriage. Sex is fabulous when it takes place in a healthy marriage. Outside of that, it loses its power to fulfill because it lacks commitment.

How do you stop from going too far if you're really in love?

It's important to realize that love and sex aren't the same thing. For sex to really be an expression of love, it needs to be in a committed relationship—marriage. True love seeks what's best for the other person and isn't self-serving. It's considerate and doesn't demand control. These qualities take time to develop in a relationship.

Many teenagers who are dating think they're in love, but the relationship hasn't had time to grow to the deeper levels of commitment. The deepest level of commitment in a relationship is marriage. Once a couple is married, sex can be one of the most beautiful expressions of love a person can offer his or her spouse.

To slow down the physical progression of your relationship, set your boundaries before you find yourself in a situation where it's too difficult to turn back. It's a good idea to group-date with other friends committed to not going too far and avoid being home alone together for long periods of time. Try volunteering together, too. Serving others will not only develop your character, but will develop a new depth in your relationship.

If I can't show love by having sex, how can I show it?

It depends on the other person's "love language." The book *The Five Love Languages* by Gary Chapman talks about the ways in which people feel loved.[11] There are five primary love languages through which each person receives the message that he or she is loved:

1. Quality time—just spending time together.
2. Words of affirmation—telling someone that he or she is valued.
3. Acts of service—helping with a project or doing something for him or her.
4. Gifts—saying, "I'm thinking of you."
5. Physical touch—nonsexual hugs, squeezes, backrubs, or pats on the back.

In your relationship, try to figure out what the other person's love language is. Use it to communicate with him or her. Understanding this key communication tool will go a long way in helping you develop a long-lasting and emotionally fulfilling relationship.

What is love, anyway? Why would they call sex "making love" if it isn't?

After watching the latest romantic comedies from Hollywood, it's easy to assume that having sex equals love. In real life, sex and love can be two very different things.

A lot of sex takes place without love. Any teen or adult can have sex for the pure physical enjoyment of it, then get up and move on to another relationship. But the best sex occurs in a committed, caring, long-term relationship—marriage. Sex is an important communication tool for married people who love each other. Outside of marriage, sex is generally used as entertainment rather than an expression of intimate emotions.

True love is much more than a crush. It causes you to care and give to another person in a sacrificial way. It's seeking his or her best interest over yours. Love grows deeper over time and isn't something that happens overnight. As a young person, you may have intense feelings that mimic love, but only time will tell whether it's the real thing.

Can pregnancy occur without having vaginal sex?

Yes. Sperm are capable of swimming long distances. If two people have genital contact but don't have penetrative sex, it's possible to become pregnant because sperm can leak from the penis and travel to the vaginal cavity.

Can sperm swim through clothing?

Some teens try to gratify their intense sexual desires by simulating sex with their clothes on. In this instance, sperm can't swim through clothing. But if you stimulate one another with your clothes on, it's only a matter of time before the clothes come off.

Protect yourself and your heart; don't let your physical relationship progress to this point. Instead, focus on getting to know each other emotionally. Engaging in a physical relationship can ruin what might have been a fulfilling emotional one.

Can a girl get pregnant if she has sex standing up?

In whatever position you have sex, if sperm are ejaculated into a woman's vagina, pregnancy can occur.

Do males need sex more than females do?

Most people assume this, but it isn't always true. There are times, especially when women are older, that they want sex more than their husbands do.

The reality is that nobody "needs" to have sex to stay alive, be happy,

Ten Commandments of Dating

1. *Get grounded.* Get into God's Word and commit to growing in your faith.

2. *Use your brain.* Balance romance with common sense, reason, judgment, and discernment. Balance the head and heart. Refrain from physical intimacy. Go on group dates, especially at first and especially if dating at a young age. Analyze your past relationships; include others in the process. Never neglect opportunities to evaluate along the way. Set goals for your life and determine whether the relationships and dating situations you're considering will help you reach those goals or set you back.

3. *Seek similarities.* Healthy relationships and marriages have a strong foundation of similarities in background, temperament, goals, dreams, values, and the way in which individuals manage and order their physical and mental lives.

4. *Take it slow.* You don't get to know a person in a short time. You need experiences in different settings to know what a person is truly like. Protect yourself from getting attached too quickly.

5. *Set clear boundaries.* Draw definitive lines in the sexual area of your relationship. You—and only you—have the right to control your body. Communicate to your date how you feel. "Own" your feelings and separate them from your date. Take ownership of your thoughts; keep them pure. Take responsibility for your own actions; don't try to change someone.

6. *Save sex for marriage.* Practice the healthy steps of intimacy. Reserve fondling, mouth-to-breast contact, and oral and vaginal intercourse for marriage.

have a productive life, or be loved and cared for. Even married couples go through periods when they aren't having regular sex—during late pregnancy, travel, illness, or emotional distancing, for example.

The urge to have sex isn't all-powerful either, for one gender or the other. Controlling your sexual urges takes self-control and discipline, the same traits required to be an excellent athlete or student.

7. *Remember that living together before the wedding doesn't promote a healthier marriage.* Research shows that couples who live together first have a far greater chance of getting a divorce than those who don't. Women who cohabitate are more likely to experience domestic violence than married women.[12]

8. *Respond to conflict in a healthy way.* Deal with problems as they arise, and avoid defensiveness. Recognize that your feelings are valid. Fight fair; take a time-out to consider what you really need to express. Be respectful of the person you're dating. Be quiet and listen; seek to understand, then to be understood. Use "I" statements. Negotiate and compromise. Reevaluate your solution at a later time.

9. Notice danger signs and end the relationship if needed. Here are some of those signs:

   • any form of abuse: physical, verbal, emotional, or sexual.
   • addictions.
   • untruthfulness in the relationship.
   • irresponsibility and immaturity.
   • no physical/sexual attraction.
   • emotional baggage.
   • denial, or not being able to admit that this relationship isn't healthy for you.

10. *Choose your dating and marriage partner wisely.* If you date and then marry the wrong person, you'll live with significant, negative, lasting consequences of that decision for the rest of your life. Discern his or her character; character is who you are when no one's looking. Look back at prior relationships to determine patterns of behavior; crisis reveals someone's true character. Give your relationship lots of time. And ask yourself whether you feel encouraged, affirmed, inspired, and challenged to grow and be a better person when you are with him or her.

How many days a month can you get pregnant?

An egg that's been released from a woman's ovary lives for about twenty-four hours before it breaks up and can't be fertilized. This means that a woman can become pregnant for three to four days in each menstrual cycle, since sperm live between one and three days.

How many sperm cells does a man release when he ejaculates?

Anywhere from 150 to 600 million. Only fifty to two hundred sperm may actually make the journey to where the egg has been released.

How much physical contact is okay when I'm dating someone?

When you're first getting to know someone, it's impossible to know what type of relationship you'll have or how long it will last. So keeping your hands to yourself is an excellent policy.

Many young people feel obligated to hold hands and kiss on the first date. But when developing a relationship, starting slow is always beneficial for your future, especially where physical action is concerned. If your date wants to become physical, you can say you'd like to get to know him rather than taking things in that direction. If your date doesn't respect your boundaries, then he or she doesn't care about you.

Many have said it's best to be friends with someone before you start dating. This is the healthiest way to begin a relationship, because the focus isn't on the physical but on getting to know each other's personality, character, and values. If you've both decided that you have romantic feelings for each other, discuss your boundaries for physical affection and agree to respect those boundaries. Remember that holding hands leads to kissing, deep kissing leads to fondling, and fondling can lead straight to sexual intercourse in moments of passion.

If you both have decided to wait until marriage to have sex, you need to limit your physical contact. You shouldn't engage in any activity that might encourage you to lose self-control.

How often do married people have sex?

Researchers have posed this question to married couples, and the range could be once a year to every night! The average is around one to three times a week.[13]

The more important question isn't the frequency of sex, but whether husband and wife both enjoy it. Studies show that married couples enjoy sex more and feel more secure in their relationships than unmarried couples who are having sex.[14] In other words, the best sex is in marriage.

When do married couples stop having sex?

There's no time in life when married couples *must* stop having sex. If they do stop it's typically because they're physically unable to continue. That means there are people in their nineties who can still enjoy sex.

I have a flat chest; is there any way to make my breasts grow?

Women come in all shapes and sizes. Some have breasts that are too large for their comfort. Others have very little fat on their body, which includes breast tissue.

If your breasts are small and you've started your period, you may not increase your breast size much. This doesn't mean you can't please your husband once you're married or breast-feed later on, though.

Some women have undergone breast augmentation to enlarge their breasts, but this has several major medical complications associated with it. It's important to remember that while you may want people to like how you look, it's more important for them to know and like the person you are inside.

What causes infertility?

Infertility, or the inability to get pregnant, has become a significant problem. About a third of women who visit infertility clinics and undergo IVF (in vitro fertilization) treatments have a blockage of a fallopian tube, usually caused by a sexually transmitted infection. Other medical conditions also can cause a couple to be infertile, such as endometriosis or a low sperm count.

What is endometriosis?

Endometriosis is the presence of normal uterine tissue in the wrong place. When endometrial tissue, which lines the uterus, is found anywhere else in the body, it's called endometriosis.

Female hormones circulate through a woman's body, stimulating endometrial tissue growth, no matter where the tissue is, during the month. When the hormone levels drop to produce menstrual bleeding, the endometrial tissue—wherever it is in the body—will bleed, too.

Normal endometrial tissue lining the uterus bleeds into the vagina, but in other parts of the body the blood can't escape. Pockets of blood form in the tissue containing it. These pockets are irritating and cause the tissues around them to develop scarring.

Endometriosis can appear on the outside surface of a woman's uterus, fallopian tubes, ovaries, bladder, or intestines. It can cause a great deal of pain in the pelvis; the scarring, along with other changes, can cause infertility. Medicines are often effective in treating this problem, but sometimes surgery is necessary.

What is in vitro fertilization (IVF)?

IVF is a method of assisted reproduction in which the man's sperm and the woman's egg are combined in a laboratory dish, where fertilization occurs. The resulting embryo is transferred to the uterus to develop naturally. Usually two to four embryos are transferred with each cycle.

Infertility, a disease of the reproductive system, affects males and females with almost equal frequency. Fewer than 5 percent of infertile couples in treatment actually use IVF. It's usually the treatment of choice for a woman with blocked, severely damaged, or absent fallopian tubes, or with endometriosis—or when male infertility is preventing pregnancy. It's also used to treat couples with unexplained, long-standing infertility that hasn't responded to other treatments.

The success rate for IVF is 29 percent per egg retrieval. This is similar to the 20 percent chance that a healthy, reproductively normal couple has in any given month of achieving a pregnancy that results in a live baby.[15]

Sometimes during IVF procedures fertility specialists create more embryos than will be transferred to the uterus, and the excess embryos are "frozen away." When you consider the fact that these embryos are human lives, you can begin to see that this practice has some moral and ethical problems—especially in cases where embryos are frozen away and are never transferred to the mother's uterus. In other words, these embryos may never be given a chance to be born. Other moral questions are posed by the use of IVF in unmarried couples, the use of donor eggs or sperm, having a surrogate carry the pregnancy, and the high cost of the procedure.

While some Christians object to IVF and all other kinds of assisted reproduction, some ethical problems may be limited if IVF is used only in a married couple, if the doctor only creates the number of embryos that will be transferred to the uterus at a given time and none are frozen away, and no third parties (sperm or egg donors, or surrogates) are involved.

Infertility is a heartbreaking condition, and couples who experience it need the love, compassion, and support of those around them. It can be difficult to treat, and the decisions made are often very complex. Couples should pray about every decision regarding their treatment, and seek information concerning all the pros, cons, risks, and benefits.

What does "secondary virginity" mean?

Secondary virginity is a term for a person who's been sexually active in the past but makes the decision to not have sex again until marriage.

Anyone, at any time, can decide to stop having sex and wait for marriage. This decision will eliminate your chances of getting a new sexually transmitted infection (assuming you don't already have one), becoming pregnant, or experiencing additional emotional pain. It can also allow believers in Christ to begin or resume the process of spiritual growth that may have been interrupted by choosing a way of life that conflicts with God's standards.

What does abstinence mean?

Abstinence is willingly doing without sexual intercourse. If you want to be technical, sexual intercourse occurs when a man's penis enters a woman's vagina. But if you broaden the definition beyond the physical and include the emotional, spiritual, and relational, then any time your sexual organs (penis, clitoris, and breasts) are sexually stimulated by the touch of another person, you're involved in a form of sexual activity. Abstinence includes doing without that, too.

Abstinence isn't going without sex forever—just until you're in a lifelong, committed marriage relationship. Even in marriage, there are periods of

Does Faith Boost Abstinence?

Teenagers, especially girls, with strong religious views are less likely to engage in sexual activity than teens who aren't religious. Data gleaned from a recent study of adolescent health shows that religious commitment reduces the likelihood of adolescents engaging in early sex by shaping their attitudes and beliefs about sex.

This report analyzed data from the National Longitudinal Study of Adolescent Health by ADD Health, the largest comprehensive survey of seventh through twelfth grades ever conducted.[16] The survey measured the effect of family, peer group, school, neighborhood, and religious institutions on behaviors that promote good health in young people.

The teens were interviewed twice with a one-year interval between the interviews. Researchers asked teens about their commitment to religious activities, the importance of religion in their lives, and their beliefs about how having sex would affect them and people close to them. In addition to finding a direct relationship between religious commitment and sexual restraint, the ADD Health Study found that teens who made a personal commitment (usually based on religious values) to purity, primarily shown by signing a pledge card, were much more likely to remain abstinent during the adolescent years.

The results of this study are reassuring: Beliefs do affect behavior. This also reminds parents that a family atmosphere encouraging spiritual development and affirming religious participation helps teens confront and resist the values of contemporary society.

abstinence. Regardless of age or circumstances, people can control their sexual behavior and practice abstinence.

What does it mean to be bisexual?

A bisexual is a person who prefers to have sex with both men and women.

What is nymphomania?

It refers to uncontrollable sexual desire in women. In men this used to be called satyriasis. Both terms are considered outdated, and neither is used by mental health professionals today.

What is exhibitionism?

It's a perverse act marked by a compulsive need to expose the genitals in public.

What is a pedophile?

A pedophile is an adult who is sexually attracted to children—and acts on the attraction. It's psychologically very damaging to children to be exploited sexually by an adult.

What is voyeurism?

It's a preoccupation with seeing the sex acts or sex organs of others, especially from a secret vantage point.

What is a pelvic exam?

This is an internal examination of a woman's vagina, cervix, uterus, and ovaries. The doctor or nurse uses a speculum, an instrument inserted into the vagina that spreads open the walls of the vagina so that the cervix can be inspected for signs of infection. A Pap smear, which is often but not always performed in conjunction with a pelvic exam, is done to detect any kind of precancer or cancer caused by a sexually transmitted infection called human papillomavirus (HPV). Cultures for STIs can also be taken from the cervix or vagina.

A bimanual exam is also done as part of a pelvic exam. The examiner puts two gloved fingers inside the woman's vagina and feels with the other hand on the abdomen for her uterus and ovaries. The examiner is checking for enlargement or tenderness of these organs that could mean pregnancy or pelvic inflammatory disease (infection in the fallopian tubes).

Pelvic exams are usually done yearly once a woman has become sexually active, or beginning in a virginal young woman between ages eighteen and twenty-one. According to current guidelines, a woman should have a Pap smear at age twenty-one and every three years afterward, regardless of whether she's been sexually active. Women should see their health care professional for a regular wellness checkup each year.

What is mutual masturbation?

This occurs when two people stimulate each other's genitals to reach orgasm without having sexual intercourse. During mutual masturbation, sexually transmitted infections can be passed through bodily secretions on the hands of your partner.

What should I do if I've had sex?

If you've already had sex, stop and ask yourself a few questions:

- Why did I start having sex?
- Was I pressured into it?
- Was I hungry for love and thought this would fulfill that need?
- Was I lonely or depressed, thinking this would fill a vacuum?
- Was I curious and just wanted to see what "everyone" was talking about?
- Was I drunk or high on drugs and couldn't say no?

By digging deeper you may be able to address some of the needs or wants that led you to become sexually active, or identify problems that kept you from saying no to sex. You can then find healthy, appropriate ways to meet those needs and bolster your ability to resist temptation or pressure.

Consider the fact that God created sex. He knows all about it and knows when it's most satisfying: within marriage. Shouldn't you trust the Creator of sex to know how to best experience it? While sex outside of marriage is against God's plan and design, He's eager to forgive and help you to start fresh.

Think about the good reasons not to have sex again until you're married. Sex isn't worth the risks of contracting a sexually transmitted infection, experiencing a pregnancy, feeling emotional disappointment, and jeopardizing your future marriage. Think about your long-term goals and how being sexually active may interfere with them. No matter how you look at it, sex before marriage is not worth the risk and the heartache.

If you've been sexually active, even once, see your doctor to be sure you aren't pregnant and get tested for STIs. The safest and healthiest choice is to wait until marriage to have sex again.

Why does my doctor want to know if I've been sexually active?

He needs that information in order to rule out possible medical conditions. You need to tell him if you've had any type of sexual contact—whether you've had oral sex, genital contact without penetrative sex, anal sex, or penetrative vaginal sex. This information is confidential, and it's important to be honest because it will help you receive the best health care you can get.

If you've had any form of sexual contact, your physician needs to make sure you don't have a sexually transmitted infection. Since so many STIs don't have any symptoms, it's important to find them before they cause permanent damage.

Why is it so important to be married before I have sex?

By abstaining from sex before marriage, you honor God and cooperate with His plans. Having sex before you're married contradicts His intent.

It's also risky. Sex with more than one partner increases your chance of getting a sexually transmitted infection like chlamydia, human papillomavirus, or genital herpes. You might think, *I'll just use a condom and be safe*. Unfortunately, condoms don't eliminate the risk of contracting an STI.

Sex before marriage can result in pregnancy if you're a girl or financial responsibility for a baby if you're a boy. One out of five sexually active girls becomes pregnant by the time she's twenty.

People who have sex before marriage tend to ignore the emotional and spiritual aspects of a growing relationship. They also end up bringing a lot of emotional baggage with them into their marriage, which may decrease the quality of sex in the marriage and increase the chance of divorce.

Am I weird if I'm not dating or never had a boyfriend?

No. Having a boyfriend or dating has some benefits. You feel special, get attention and presents, and have someone to talk to and hang out with.

Yet there are so many benefits to being "unattached." You have more time to spend with family and friends. You can focus on your relationship with God, you have time to think about your future, and you have the freedom to explore your goals. And later you won't have the baggage of being emotionally tied up in failed relationships.

The majority of boy-girl relationships in high school are relatively shallow and not based on friendship first. It's always best to get to know people for who they are before you let yourself develop romantic feelings for them.

How will I know who I'm supposed to marry?

This is one of the most important questions to ask yourself if you want a happy, healthy marriage. But success in marriage is not primarily a result of *finding the right spouse*. It's about *being the right person*.

At the same time, it's crucial to be wise and discerning in your choice of a marriage partner. First, avoid some of the pitfalls that jeopardize a marriage from the start:

- *Getting married too quickly.* Relationships do the best over several seasons of "weathering," or seeing how you overcome some hurdles together. If you don't give it time, you really don't know the person you're marrying.
- *Marrying too young.* Your personality is still evolving through the teen years, and you're in for too many surprises if you marry too young.
- *Not being on the same page when it comes to your faith.* The Bible is clear that believers in Christ are not to be "yoked"—or linked—together with those who don't share that faith (2 Corinthians 6:14). Ignoring this instruction can lead to a lot of conflict and heartache.
- *Failing to work out problems from your family of origin.* Resolving these before marriage would be ideal, but in reality most people have to keep working on them after tying the knot. Unfortunately, most of us come from families that are dysfunctional to some degree, and this

can poison our future marriage. Figure out what your issues are, and work on them before you damage your marriage with them.

Write down on paper what's important to you in a person you want to be with for life. What personality type do you enjoy being with? How important are intelligence and looks to you? What values and character should that person have? What are your family and parenting goals? (If you want five kids and he doesn't want any, that will be a problem and has broken up marriages!)

What Does "Unequally Yoked" Mean?

The Bible is pretty clear about relationships between believers and nonbelievers. While there's no verse that says, "Thou shalt not date a person who isn't a Christian," it specifically states that believers in Christ should not be "yoked together with unbelievers" (2 Corinthians 6:14).

That image is meant to describe two oxen of different strengths or dispositions bound together to pull a plow. In such a mismatched team, the wandering or weaker ox would cause the other to veer off course and plow a crooked furrow—a sure recipe for frustration and failure for the farmer.

In a similar way, when a person sincerely follows Christ she has goals for her life that include obeying God and honoring His plans and purposes—including His plan for sex. If two people in a dating relationship don't share these goals the results, in the best of cases, will be disagreement and a parting of ways. In the worst case—which occurs all too often—the non-Christian will influence the Christian to compromise or jettison her convictions altogether.

Many Christian teens who find themselves attracted to a nonbeliever adopt a fig-leaf strategy sometimes called "missionary dating." The stated goal is to evangelize the non-Christian (while allowing the Christian to enjoy dating a person he wants to be with). Unfortunately, in many cases the believer ends up being negatively influenced by the nonbeliever, while the nonbeliever is moved no closer to Christ.

Don't try to use dating as a tool for evangelism. In fact, given the spiritual dangers and potential heartache, believers should avoid dating anyone who doesn't share their faith.

You may have heard that opposites attract, but the fact is similarities make for the happiest relationships over the long haul. You'll want to find a person a lot like you with shared interests, values, beliefs, and background. Otherwise your differences can end up causing lots of conflict.

As you spend time together, you'll see how caring or how self-centered the person is. Everyone's on his best behavior when he wants to impress someone, but over time and with some hurdles, the real person inside should show his true colors.

Be open to close family members' and friends' opinions about your relationship, too. They're more objective and may see red flags that you don't. Sometimes love really *is* blind!

What should I do if my girlfriend is after me to have sex?

In our society, many girls are the aggressors instead of the boys. This attitude is picked up from TV, movies, and ads where the woman is always enticing the man. In those cases, it's usually about having power over him.

Some girls have underlying issues of pain from sexual abuse and the need to feel love—which she thinks is connected to sex.

Asking your girlfriend good questions about her feelings might reveal other ways for her to be affirmed. But the "No, I'm not interested!" statement should speak for itself. If she doesn't respect that boundary, she doesn't care about you—and it's time to move on.

Why shouldn't I have sex if I'm in love?

Wanting sex and each other isn't the same as really loving each other. Real love is the kind that cares more about the other person than yourself. Real love wants what's best for the other person and is willing to sacrifice for him or her.

God created sex with a plan and purpose in mind. He knows what's best for us, and that includes abstaining from sex before marriage. If one person really loves another he'll honor God's plan for sex and not engage in sexual intimacy, even if the other person wants to get more physical.

Besides, is giving the other person a sexually transmitted infection (because you've had sex with someone who had one) a loving thing? Is getting her pregnant what's best for her at this point in her life? If you really loved your partner, you wouldn't want these things to happen to her. One of the best gifts of true love is waiting for marriage, where these risks aren't present.

Saying *no* now makes saying *yes* when you're married the "I love you for always" that it's meant to be. If your relationship has the right foundation, your feelings can grow and last without sex; in fact, just knowing that you're saving sex for marriage can make your relationship even more special. And abstaining from sex before marriage is good practice for abstaining in marriage during times of illness, pregnancy, or separation from your spouse.

How can my boyfriend and I be close without having sex?

Developing intimacy without sex is a skill that will serve you for life. As married couples can attest, sexual activity doesn't always equal emotional intimacy.

The best things you can do are communicate with your boyfriend about your dreams and desires and keep yourselves out of compromising situations. Talk about your goals and make a plan to reach them.

Spend time meeting the needs of others. Whether it's volunteering at a retirement center or helping to build someone a home, developing common interests through outside activities develops closeness. And be creative in the way you spend time on dates.

Challenge each other to build memories; create photo journals of your time together. If this boyfriend turns out to be your mate, you'll have created a treasure chest of memories for your future.

I want to save sex until marriage. How can I succeed when all my peers are having sex?

First things first: Not all your peers are having sex. Many are, but it's not uncommon for teens to exaggerate what they have or haven't done.

The best thing you can do to save sex for marriage is not allowing yourself to get into a tempting situation (like being home alone with a boyfriend or girlfriend and no adult supervision). Sex is progressive; kissing can lead to fondling, and fondling can lead to sex.

Talk about the goals each of you has for your physical relationship. You need a plan ahead of time to avoid moments of passion that can cloud your judgment.

Make it a policy to go on group dates. If you do date individually, spend time with each other's family. Young couples who spend time with each other's parents generally develop a respect that can protect them from pushing physical boundaries.

Keep yourself busy. Stay involved in after-school programs, volunteer in your community, and plan your dates. Don't push your curfew. Avoid seeing sexually explicit movies. And don't spend time lingering with your girlfriend or boyfriend; it's during these moments of boredom that many young people slip over the sexual line.

Always keep in mind that not having sex today is one of the greatest gifts you can give yourself and your future mate.

What are "date rape" drugs? How do I protect myself against them?

These are drugs used to take advantage of a person sexually. One example is Rohypnol. It's a derivative of Valium, but ten times more potent. It's also called "roofies" or "roaches." Rapists use it to take control of their victim and eliminate any memory of the abuse. Under its influence, a person can't move or yell.

Rohypnol can be taken orally and dissolves in liquid. To protect yourself from it, don't go to parties where alcohol or drugs are being used. At other parties, drink only beverages when you've seen them poured into a glass directly from the bottle or can. Avoid punch bowls. Keep your glass in your hand at all times; never set it down where someone can slip a drug into it without your knowledge.

Why shouldn't I drink alcohol?

For one thing, at your age it's illegal. That alone is reason enough.

There are several other good reasons, though. Alcohol is a depressant and lowers a person's inhibitions. It weakens resolve and judgment. You might be convinced you'd never have sex before marriage, but after a few beers you might think, *Why not?*

Research shows that if you drink alcohol, you're more likely to have sex. Teens who drink are more likely to have more than one partner, which increases the risk of sexually transmitted infections and pregnancy.[17]

Many teens also participate in binge drinking (having five or more drinks for a man, or four or more drinks for a woman, within about two hours).[18] Binge drinking is dangerous and can kill you. Consuming alcohol this quickly causes your blood alcohol level to rise and become toxic to your brain. Research indicates that the teen brain is more susceptible to the toxic affects of alcohol.

A majority of first-time sexual encounters between teenagers involve alcohol.[19] And it's easier for a girl to be raped when she's too drunk to say no or to know what's happening to her.

Paying attention to the Bible's warning against getting drunk (Ephesians 5:18) honors God. It also pays off, especially when it comes to making good choices about sex.

13

MOVING OUT

College and Beyond

Let's face it: An adolescent's quest for independence can be more exhausting than keeping your ten-month-old away from the electrical outlets.

If you're like most parents, you've been working your way to this stage of life for eighteen years. Some days you may feel exhilaration at the thought of having your teenager move out. Other days you may worry about whether or not she's ready for the world. But ready or not, she's going to have her chance to meet the world head-on. It's time for you to switch roles from hands-on parent to key advisor.

The relationship you've developed with your child will determine how broad a role you'll play in her life from this point forward. At this stage many teens flee from home to the reckless abandon of a college campus in order to find themselves. That may not happen if, during the last few years, you've given your child just enough rope to find herself *before* heading off to college.

As your child journeys down the road to independence, the questions or concerns you have—or the questions your young adult may be asking—might be too difficult to articulate in person. Consider handling these delicate interactions with letters, especially since many young adults aren't living at home. If you're one of those rare parents who is articulate and still has his or her teen's attention, you're more than welcome to handle these questions face-to-face. Otherwise, the letters in this chapter may help you develop the messages you want to communicate to your young adult.

You'll note that some of the following letters come from "your mother and I" or "your father and I." You can use the content to craft a message that's appropriate for you, whether you're married, divorced, or never married.

Parents' Questions

What do I tell my young adult daughter who wants to come home for the holidays with her unmarried, cohabiting partner?

The following sample letter assumes that your grown child knows your objections to cohabitation. However you word your message, love must prevail. Your child needs to know she can always find unconditional love in your home.

> *My dearest daughter,*
>
> *Thank you for wanting to come home for the holidays and for being sensitive to our beliefs and values. Your father and I look forward to your visit and meeting your new boyfriend. As parents of a grown adult, we of course have long ago released you to follow your own path.*
>
> *We would make one condition of your visit, and that is that you and your boyfriend sleep in separate bedrooms while you're staying in our home. For our part, we resolve to resist the temptation to offer you parental advice or express our concern in regard to your current lifestyle. While your father and I are concerned for your future, we love you very much, and we look forward to having you home for the holidays.*
>
> *Love,*
> *Mom*

Why Marriage?

Live longer! Get married!

This isn't a bumper sticker you're likely to see while driving down the highway. To say that our society views marriage differently from the way it did two or three generations ago is an understatement.

Since 1970, the average age at first marriage has increased substantially, along with rates of nonmarital births. Divorce, while currently occurring at rates that are down from their peak in the early 1980s, continues to devastate families and children. At the same time, rates of cohabitation (people living together outside of marriage) have increased as well.[1]

The response of many in our culture to such statistics is a resounding, "So what?" Family scholars and social science researchers have identified a number of reasons why marriage matters.[2] Here are just six of them:

1. Cohabitation is not the same as marriage. Cohabiting couples on average are less committed, less faithful, and more likely to break up than married couples.

2. In almost every known human society, marriage exists as a way of regulating the reproduction of children, families, and society.

3. Married couples seem to build more wealth on average than singles or cohabiting couples.

4. Children who live with their own two married parents enjoy better physical health than do children in other family forms.

5. Married people, especially married men, have longer life expectancies than do otherwise similar singles.

6. Marriage is associated with better health and lower rates of injury, illness, and disability for both men and women.

My daughter's getting married soon. What do I tell her about sex in marriage?

This is an easy question to avoid, especially if your own emotional baggage makes it hard to approach the subject.

There's no one answer to this question, since so many factors are involved. Is the father or mother asking the question? Is the daughter entering marriage as a virgin or is she sexually experienced, especially with her fiancé? Is the daughter's fiancé a virgin or sexually experienced, even from a previous marriage? Is the parent who's speaking married or divorced? Do the daughter and her fiancé have a personal faith in Christ?

The following letter is written by a father to his daughter, who is a virgin. It includes information that's technical in places and rather frank. Feel free to modify it for your circumstances. Some may wish to echo its spirit, if not its details.

My dearest daughter,

Your mother and I are looking forward to your marriage. You were wise to get premarital counseling, and I know you'll be committed to your vows of "'til death do us part." Your counseling may have discussed a few basic male/female differences, but I doubt it addressed some of the tougher issues.

I've written my thoughts down because, quite frankly, I might forget or stumble over some points. Besides, in your excitement of getting married, you probably wouldn't hear half of what I say, so maybe in the months to come you can reread this letter and hopefully share it with your husband.

I hope I have conveyed to you in our previous talks how beautiful and wonderful sex can be in a committed marriage. I commend you for waiting for sex until your wedding night. For some, especially for a woman, it can be difficult to say yes to sex after saying no for so many years. Perhaps the best advice I can give you is just to be patient. I can also guarantee you that sex will be better ten years into your marriage than even on your wedding night.

I hope your wedding night and honeymoon are all bells and whistles with fireworks like a Fourth of July in Washington, DC, but if they aren't, don't despair.

One thing that might cause some problems would be getting honeymoon cystitis (a bladder infection that occurs during the first few days of marriage due to frequent intercourse). If you develop painful urination, call your doctor for medication. You might want your physician to give you a written prescription, which you can fill if it's needed, for a urinary tract antibiotic and for Pyridium to control the pain. (Pyridium will change the color of your urine.) Hopefully, you won't get an infection, but if you do, take your medication and realize that it won't be a recurring problem.

Even if your sex life is incredibly fulfilling on your honeymoon, I must tell you that it won't always be like that. Both men and women go through seasons of sex. Poor health may put a damper on sex for a while for either spouse. A business failure or problems at work may seriously affect your husband. Two children in diapers and the "baby blues" may make sex difficult for a while for you. I guess what I'm trying to say is that sex within a marriage will vary from time to time; don't be discouraged. You have before you a whole lifetime and different seasons of life to find out how to please each other. Simply put—be patient, but at the same time be a student of what pleases your husband.

No two couples are exactly alike, but most likely there will be differences in how the two of you view sex. In general, men want more sex more often than women, but this will vary with seasons of life, and as you get older, this could reverse. There's no right or wrong answer about the frequency of sex, and it will change with age, children, and external circumstances. The main thing is to learn to communicate with each other your desires, needs, frustrations, and expectations.

Men in general feel rejected if their wife doesn't want to have sex. Wives, on the other hand, generally feel no rejection if their husband is too tired for sex. My advice is to make sure your husband knows that you aren't rejecting him, you love him, and you're willing to give him a rain check to look forward to.

At other times, you might sense your husband really needs sexual release, and basically you give him the freedom to satisfy himself without attempting to satisfy you or bring you to a climax. To your husband, this unselfishness on your part is going the extra mile.

In regard to simultaneous climaxes, it's wonderful when it happens, but it's also okay when it doesn't. Allow each other the freedom from having to perform perfectly every time you have sex.

Sex is such an intricate part of marriage that if you're having problems, you should get professional help. Be careful talking about sex, the most intimate part of your marriage, especially to anyone of the opposite sex. I'd suggest you get help from a counselor who's not only qualified, but who also shares your faith and values.

I believe your entire bodies belong to each other, but with this one caveat—every aspect of your sex life must be mutually satisfying. Trouble abounds if one of you forces some touch or sex act and it isn't mutually satisfying. Oral sex tends to be a guy thing, but it's something the two of you will have to decide for yourselves. From a medical standpoint, however, you must know that if you or your husband has "fever blisters," genital herpes can result from oral sex. I would also caution you with regard to anal sex, for health and physical reasons. The rectum simply wasn't designed for penile intercourse.

Sex during a menstrual period is another controversial area. Sex during this time in a woman's cycle is usually not as pleasurable, especially for the female. It's in these areas and other areas of your marriage that communication between husband and wife is so critical. Again, if you're reaching an impasse—seek counseling.

There may be times in your marriage when for medical reasons the two of you can't have sexual intercourse for a period of time. Late pregnancy is just one example. I'd encourage you to consider your husband's needs at this time. If it's agreeable to your husband, you could manually stimulate him to release his sexual tensions. You may prefer for it to be mutual stimulation in times when sexual intercourse isn't possible for periods of time due to illness, during late pregnancy, or after delivery, if it's mutually satisfying. Again, you must communicate at a very deep level. With time, it will become easier to talk about this and any other issue in your marriage.

There's one more important matter I wanted to address. I trust you've talked with your husband-to-be about whether you'll use birth control and, if so, what type. The issue of contraception isn't one that all Christians agree on. Some say it's okay to use in marriage, while others say it has no place at all. This is the type of thing that you should consider with great prayer, and you should both be in sex. I'd suggest that you get help from a counselor who's not only qualified, but who shares your faith and values.

I believe your entire bodies belong to each other, but with this one caveat—every aspect of your sex life must be mutually satisfying. Trouble abounds if one of you forces some touch or sex act and it's not mutually satisfying. Oral sex tends to be a guy thing, but it's something the two of you will have to decide for yourselves. I believe, however, that it must be a mutual decision and no one spouse should force it upon the other spouse. From a medical standpoint, however, you must know that if you or your wife has "fever blisters," genital herpes can result from oral sex. On the other hand, I'd caution you in regard to anal intercourse, but for health and physical reasons. The rectum simply wasn't designed for penile intercourse.

Sex during a menstrual period is another controversial area. First of all, sex during this time in a woman's cycle is usually not as pleasurable, especially for the female. It's in this area and other areas of your marriage that communication between husband and wife is so critical. In this area of sex during a menstrual period, it's always wise for a husband to yield to his wife. Again, if you're reaching an impasse, seek counseling.

There may be times in your marriage when for medical reasons the two of you can't have intercourse for a while. A period of time during pregnancy is just one example. I'd encourage you to express your needs to your wife. Perhaps she's willing to manually relieve your sexual tension. In my opinion, this is highly preferable to masturbation by yourself. Your wife may prefer mutual stimulation in times when sexual intercourse isn't possible due to illness, for periods of time during late pregnancy, or after delivery, if it's mutually satisfying to both partners. Again, you must communicate at a very deep level that at first may be very difficult for one or both of you. With time it will become easier to talk about this and any other issue in your marriage and to seek to truly satisfy and please each other. This is the meaning of true intimacy, where you can take your mask off and be yourself with no fear of rejection.

agreement on it. I would ask you to seek God's counsel on how many children you ought to have. I know many couples who, later in life, wished they'd had more children. They wonder now if they limited God's blessing in their life. I'm not trying to tell you that you need to have a large family, but please, just be listening to God.

In closing, I just know you're going to have a good marriage, which includes a great sex life. The great thing about sex within a committed marriage determined to go the distance is that you're not on stage and you don't have to perform perfectly every time. Allow each other the freedom to fall flat on occasion. Learn to laugh at yourself and to laugh together as a couple.

Have a great marriage.

> *We love you,*
> *Dad*

What do I tell my son, who's getting married, about sex in marriage?

It depends on your son's situation, but here's a letter written to a son who hasn't been sexually active. As with the previous letter, this one is very candid. You can modify it for your circumstances; feel free to replicate its spirit even if you might not feel comfortable exploring some of the sexual issues in this much detail.

Dear son,

Your mother and I are so looking forward to your marriage. You were wise to get premarital counseling, and I know you'll be committed to your vows of "'til death do us part." Your counseling probably discussed a few basic male-female differences, but in this letter I'll address some of the tough issues.

I hope I've conveyed to you in our previous talks how beautiful and wonderful sex can be in a committed marriage. I commend you for waiting for sex until your wedding night. You can go into marriage with no fear of giving a sexually transmitted infection to your wife and no [troublesome] memories from the past.

The media unfortunately have given many people the wrong impression of what sex is like in a good, vibrant marriage. It's special and wonderful, but TV and movies only show the peaks and the highs, not the lows that every good, married sex life transitions through. So let's begin.

I'm sure that your counselor discussed the differences in sexual arousal between males and females, but let me give you my take on the issue. Males are visual, and women are relational and emotional. A man can have a fight with his wife, but when he sees her in a sexy nightgown, he's ready to have sex immediately. Women, however, don't easily forget the fight from two hours ago or perhaps two days ago. Women are turned on by romance and kind words.

I trust you've talked with your bride-to-be about whether you'll use birth control and, if so, what type. The issue of contraception isn't one that all Christians agree on. Some say it's okay to use in marriage, while others say it has no place at all. This is the type of thing that you should consider with great prayer, and you should both be in agreement on it. I would ask you to seek God's counsel on how many children you ought to have. I know many couples who, later in life, wished they'd had more children. They wonder now if they limited God's blessing in their life. I'm not trying to tell you that you need to have a large family, but please, just be listening to God.

Also, I imagine your fiancée has been seen by her doctor by now. Her physician can usually spot any potential major problem, but sex for a woman the first few times can be a little bit painful, so please be patient with your wife. Having patience and understanding for your wife in the beginning of your sex life together will pay huge dividends for you in the future.

Taking time and getting to know each other's bodies is especially important for your wife, as this will provide the lubrication she needs to make sex really enjoyable for both of you but especially for her. In the beginning, she might need some extra lubrication, so I'd suggest you take along a tube of water-soluble lubricant that any pharmacist can provide for you. Also, something that men don't often hear about is premature ejaculation. Don't be embarrassed if this happens; it

can be normal given the stress of the day and also the anticipatio of something you've undoubtedly longed for.

If your honeymoon is fabulous and your sex life is great, I mus tell you that it won't always be like that. Both males and females go through seasons of sex within marriage. Poor health may put a damper on sex for a while for either spouse. A business failure or problems at work may seriously affect your sexual drive. Two children in diapers and the "baby blues" may make sex difficult for a while for your wife. You have before you a whole lifetime and different seasons of life to find out how to please each other. Simply put—be patient, but at the same time be a student of what turns your wife on and how to please her.

No two couples are exactly alike, but most likely there will be differences in how the two of you view sex. Males in general want more sex more often than females, but this will vary with seasons of life, and as you get older, this could reverse. There's no right or wrong answer about the frequency of sex, and it will change with age, children, and external circumstances. The main thing is to learn to communicate with each other your desires, needs, frustrations, and expectations. If both of you are satisfied, it really doesn't matter how often you're having sex.

Men in general feel rejected if their wife doesn't want to have sex. Wives, on the other hand, generally feel no rejection if their husband is too tired for sex. If you feel you're getting shorted on sex, then take the time to prime the pump. Bring home some flowers, go out for a romantic dinner or a weekend getaway, and at the right time, convey your frustrations to your wife. Timing is everything in life and in marriage.

In regard to simultaneous climaxes, it's wonderful when it happens, but it's also okay when it doesn't. Allow each other freedom from having to perform perfectly every time you have sex.

Sex is such an intricate part of marriage that if you're having problems, get professional help. Be careful talking about sex, the most intimate part of your marriage, especially to anyone of the opposite

In closing, I just know you're going to have a good marriage, which includes a great sex life. The great thing about sex within a committed marriage determined to go the distance is that you're not on stage and you don't have to perform perfectly every time. Allow each other the freedom to fall flat on occasion; that's okay. Learn to laugh at yourself and to laugh together as a couple.

Love,
Dad

My daughter has found "the love of her life" and wants to get married, but she hasn't finished college. What should I do?

There's no easy answer to this question, and ultimately it's your daughter's decision; but as a parent you can provide guidance and direction.

The first questions to ask are these:

- Do you think your daughter has made a wise choice?
- What do her friends think of this match?
- If you have older sons or daughters, what do they think of their sister's choice?

If you believe your daughter is mature enough for marriage and that she and her boyfriend are a good match—and, if you're a Christian, that they share a commitment to Christ—consider giving your blessing to the marriage. If possible, be willing to help them out financially until she finishes college. If you were planning to help with college anyway, you'd be using funds that were already committed—though additional money might be required. Perhaps the offer to help them financially would be conditioned on their having premarital counseling. If they're planning to get married in a church, that church may require that a couple undergo counseling before the wedding can take place.

If you aren't sure about the person your daughter has chosen, counseling is even more important. It would be best for your daughter and her boyfriend to discover with the aid of a counselor that perhaps they'd be wise to call off the marriage or at least delay it.

What are the possible repercussions for not giving your blessing and financial help? Your daughter and her boyfriend could just decide to cohabit, and due to lack of funds and commitment, the relationship could blow up before marriage. Your daughter could be left pregnant or a single parent with a child in tow. Or they could get married without your blessing, and in part due to financial struggles and lack of counseling and preparation for marriage, their marriage could self-destruct and end in divorce.

Even if you think your daughter's choice is wrong, the marriage could work if she and her boyfriend get premarital counseling. They need to clearly see and accept their differences, understanding that their marriage will take a lot of work. They must be committed to making it succeed, no matter what.

The key to this discussion and many others is the resolve to stay cool, calm, and objective without raising your voice or saying words you'll later regret. You can't control your children at this age; you need to provide godly advice and options that in time they may accept as their own.

What can you tell your young adult who's told you she intends to be sexually active?

This question, like the others, can be difficult to answer—and there are a number of ways to approach it from a biblical standpoint. One constant that should be part of any version of the following letter, however, is unconditional love for your child even if you disapprove of the decision she's making. This letter is frank and at times technical, so feel free to adapt it to your own style.

Dear daughter,

Thank you for your willingness to share with me your decision about being sexually active. I know that it was probably a very difficult thing to share.

Let me first say that even though you must know I was disappointed by your decision, I hope it was clear that my love for you remains no matter what choices you make now or in the future. If you hear nothing else, please know that I love you. There's nothing you could do or say that could ever cause me to stop loving you. Your father and I will always open the door for you to come home, even though we may have to put restrictions on what takes place under our roof. I hope you understand that.

I couldn't tell for certain whether your decision is totally made or whether you were asking me to give you permission to become sexually active. It should have been no surprise, based on our previous discussions about sex, that I couldn't give you my approval.

My response, in large part, was based on an understanding of God's plan for sex, but some of that also came from my feelings as a mom. No mother wants to see her child, regardless of her age, get hurt or even enter into situations where she might get hurt. I believe your having sex outside of marriage will result in some pain at some point in your life, sooner or later.

If your decision is final, then you must make some hard and fast decisions. If he's had sex before, he needs to be checked for STIs, because most STIs show no symptoms, and there's no way to know if you have them except by being tested. Some can be treated, but if he has a viral STI (such as herpes or HIV), then you must understand that the odds are good that eventually you will become infected. HIV and herpes are incurable. You could pass them on to future partners or to your children. Can you accept that? While consistent and correct use of condoms may reduce the risk of transmission for most but not all STIs, your risk of acquiring an STI, especially a viral STI, from your partner is greater over time with multiple acts of sex even with the correct use of a condom. It also needs to be said that less than 100 percent correct use may not even help in reducing the risk.

Assuming that you don't want children now, you'll need to talk to your physician about the best choice of birth control for you. While the pill is close to 100 percent effective if taken perfectly, you must know that the overall first-year failure rate even for the pill is about 8 percent. Why? Because we're humans, and sometimes we just forget to take our medications. Also, the pill offers no protection against STIs.

Marriage is a great stabilizer for men, and most men in marriage will be faithful to their wives. A man is much more likely to be unfaithful to a nonmarried partner. If your partner has sex with somebody else and contracts an STI, it's likely he'll pass it on to you, especially if you aren't using condoms correctly 100 percent of the time.

Have you thought about what will happen if you become pregnant? You know, of course, my feeling about abortion. God loves and values each human life from the moment it starts at fertilization. But have you thought about what you would do? Would your partner marry you, and is this someone you want to spend the rest of your life with? If he wouldn't marry you, would you try to rear the baby by yourself? Would you release your baby for adoption? I pray that you would not choose to have an abortion, but I hope you'll talk to me or speak with someone at a pregnancy resource center before you'd ever pursue that option. There are no easy answers to having a child outside of marriage.

There's a good chance you won't marry the first person you have sex with. Even if you don't get an STI or get pregnant, how will the sexual experience affect your future marriage relationship? Will the excitement of sex with multiple partners put a damper on sex in a future marriage relationship because of past memories, scars, or expectations? I can't tell you this will happen, but there's a likelihood of it, and no parent wants to see their child get hurt or have a marriage that's less than it could be. I'm also not saying that hurts and scars can't be healed through time and counseling, but that in itself can be costly in terms of finances and personal pain.

Know that I love you and I'm ready to give you a hug or talk to you at anytime in the future, even though I may disapprove of the path you've chosen. It will be difficult, but for my part I have spoken what's on my heart, and I promise not to bring up the subject with you in the future unless it's a discussion you initiate.

I love you.
Mom

What do I say to my grown son who's just told me he's a homosexual?

Your answer will depend in part on previous discussions you've had with your son about homosexuality, and whether he understands the biblical injunctions against homosexual activity. The following answer is from a mother and father who love their son very much, but disagree with his embracing a gay identity and engaging in gay relationships.

Dear son:

First things first: We love you, and we always will. There's nothing you can ever do that would cause us to stop loving you. You're our son and we love you.

We hope we've raised you to know that people who love each other deeply can disagree about serious issues. And it's in that context, loving you deeply but disagreeing, that we want to talk to you about homosexuality. It's been a while since we've talked about this, and we're still figuring out our own thoughts and feelings. We've had lots of questions and felt guilt, pain, and fear. Did I (Mom) hold you too close or use you as my confidant? Was I (Dad) too hard on you or was I away at work too much? Was there any sexual abuse in your childhood or adolescence?

We are not perfect parents; far from it. If we've wronged you, please come talk to us about it. Maintaining and developing our relationship with you is so important to us. Honesty and forgiveness are part of developing our relationship.

You want us to accept and embrace you as gay. That's one of the things we disagree about and where we hope you'll allow us to be in relationship even though we disagree. Allow us to believe what we believe and be where we are in this whole process. You see "being gay" as an identity, as who you are. We see you as our boy, our son, a man—and same-sex attractions as just one aspect of your life.

We believe strongly in God's design for sexuality: Sexual expression is reserved exclusively for a husband and wife. Anything outside of that is sin. That's what we believe from God's Word; it's a big part of our faith. Being sexually attracted to men isn't the real issue; it's what people do with those attractions. Homosexual lust and sexual activity are sins, and sin damages people—body, soul, and spirit.

Because we love you, we don't want to see you damaged. One of our fears has to do with your physical safety; men who engage in sexual activity with other men have a risk of contracting HIV/AIDS. There are other risks, too, and we plead with you to please talk to your doctor about this part of your life and seek the best medical advice possible.

We're also grieving. Most parents hope and pray that one day their child will grow up and find a spouse to marry and that grandchildren will soon follow. Having children is the hope and dream of most married couples. Perhaps it's also the wish of us as human beings who know that one day we will die but our children and grandchildren may be our legacy. So we are sad about the loss of that dream. We're telling you this not to place guilt on you, just to explain what we're feeling.

God is powerful and transforms people. That doesn't mean we expect Him to "turn you straight," but there are people with same-sex attractions who choose not to identify as gay and not to engage in same-sex relationships. With professional help and with loving support, some people leave homosexuality. This area is controversial, but we have met and visited with individuals who have successfully left homosexuality. Some of these people are single; some are married. We are not saying that change is easy or even 100 percent, but that it's possible. We won't dwell on this possibility, but merely lay it out on the table along with the offer of financial help for counseling if that's a path you choose to follow in the future.

In closing, let us say again that we love you so very much. You're always welcome home, but we would need to talk about how to handle the situation if you wanted to bring a male friend with you. We hope you understand.

We love you.
Mom and Dad

How do I respond to my grown child when he asks why it's wrong to have sex before marriage if the people involved are mature and care for each other?

First, resist the temptation to lecture or get defensive. No matter how worried or concerned you are, you can't control your grown child. It's best to acknowledge that this is his decision and your love for him will continue no matter what he decides—but to tell him your thoughts and the reasons you hope he'll consider before making his final decision.

The following letter is written to a grown child who's at least been exposed to his father's beliefs and a biblical understanding of sex and sexuality.

Dear son:

You know that God's Word is clear that sex is meant to occur only between a husband and wife in the context of a lifelong, mutually faithful relationship called marriage. You know that I believe sex within the context of marriage is wonderful and beautiful. Sure, sex can be pleasurable outside of marriage, but it's the best (safest, healthiest, and most fulfilling) within marriage.

In marriage, where the couple has committed to stay together for a lifetime and work through any difficulties they may have, spouses have the freedom to be intimate not only in the sexual act but in every aspect of their life and marriage. With the true intimacy that's found in a committed marriage, the wife and the husband have the ability to take off their masks and share their innermost dreams and feelings without the fear of failure, ridicule, rejection, or even abandonment.

Sexual intercourse between two people who care for each other is powerful and wonderful. What happens when the relationship breaks up for whatever reason? There's usually pain and rejection for at least one party, perhaps both. It can be like taking off a bandage when the bandage is stuck to the skin and flesh is literally ripped apart. It hurts and often leaves a scar—and the individual remembers that hurt and pain. The human body is resilient to pain and usually recovers, but scars remain that can interfere with a future relationship—especially in marriage.

Deep intimacy in future relationships can be hindered because of the memory of being hurt last time. There can be hurt and pain even in relationships that haven't experienced sexual intercourse, but sex is so powerful that the scars and hurts are likely to be more severe and more prone to interfere with deep intimacy in a later marriage.

A child can also result when sexual intercourse occurs, and then you're faced with difficult decisions. While some choices are better than others, none is easy and without pain. Also, the more partners you have before marriage, the greater the likelihood of acquiring a sexually transmitted infection and potential lifelong complications. Since most STIs are asymptomatic, if either you or your partner has had sex in the past, it's possible to acquire or transmit an STI to each other without knowing it unless you've been screened and treated as necessary. While bacterial STIs can be treated, viral STIs can't be cured, although your body may clear some (like HPV) over time. Some, such as herpes and HIV, persist for a lifetime.

Another possible problem with having sex before marriage is that you may end up marrying someone you ultimately wish you hadn't. Sex may mask your differences and blind you to a person's true personality, thereby making a future marriage difficult or possibly causing it to end in divorce. It's good to marry someone you're attracted to, but over time, passion may fade a bit as a more stable and deeper love develops. A marriage built only on passion will likely not last for a lifetime.

As a parent, I don't want to see you get hurt. I know that sex outside of marriage is likely to cause pain and suffering sooner or later. I hope you'll reconsider your decision. If you think you've found the person you want to spend the rest of your life with, then get to know each other without sex possibly blinding your eyes to each other's faults and blemishes. Get counseling, and if both of you decide you truly want to stay together for a lifetime, get married. Then enjoy sex in the context of marriage, where it's not only the best sex, but also the healthiest sex.

Regardless of your decision, I will always love you.

Dad

Questions Young Adults Ask

What's wrong with casual sex?

Aside from the fact that it dishonors God and ignores His plan for sex, it can ruin your opportunity to enjoy a pleasurable and fulfilling sex life in the future.

The problems associated with casual sex include sexually transmitted infections, emotional distress, the possibility of pregnancy, and an inability to develop close relationships in the future. Sex produces neurochemical changes in the brain that cause emotional bonding between two people. This bonding makes it harder to see the other person's faults, produces an automatic trust of the other person, and makes it painful to end the relationship.

In terms of exposure to sexually transmitted infections, when you have sex you're not only having sex with that individual but with all of his previous partners and his partners' partners. If a person is willing to have casual sex with you, chances are very good that he's had many sexual partners before you and could easily have one or more STIs. Since most STIs have no symptoms, it's almost impossible to know if your potential partner has such an infection.

There's also the risk of a nonmarital pregnancy. If a pregnancy occurs without a committed marital relationship, most people make decisions they'll someday regret. The bottom line is that sex was created to be a special bond in a permanent marital relationship.

Do men need sex more often than women?

What does "need" actually mean? Food, water, and oxygen are what we need to live. While sex is certainly a fantastic part of living, a person can have a long, happy, fulfilled life without it.

Most men desire sex more than women do, though sexual desire varies from one person to the next. Men and women desire sex in different amounts during various phases of life.

If I've been infected with an STI, will it affect my ability to have sex in marriage or my chances of having children?

That depends on whether a male or female is asking the question, and whether the STI is no longer present.

Bacterial and parasitic STIs (gonorrhea, chlamydia, syphilis, bacterial vaginosis, and Trichomonas infections) can be treated, and most go away over the course of months and in some cases years, even if not treated. The scars or damage that may result, however, are likely to be permanent.

Viral STIs (HIV, herpes simplex virus [HSV], and human papillomavirus [HPV]), can't be treated completely and may last a lifetime. HIV and HSV are lifelong. With HPV, the body usually clears most infections after a number of months; some infections persist and may lead to cancer. Both males and females with a history of an STI (and even those who are sexually experienced but have no history of an STI) who are getting married should be seen and tested as needed by a physician to make sure they aren't still carrying an STI from the past. An STI may have no symptoms and could be passed on to their marriage partner.

STIs are sexist. Men generally don't experience the problems females have with initial pain as well as complications such as infertility and inability to experience pleasurable sex in marriage. Men may have temporary infertility due to chlamydia or gonorrhea infection, but this is usually reversed by treatment or passage of time. With some STIs, like genital herpes, the male may think he's cured since he hasn't had any blisters or symptoms for years. The virus, however, may still be present and could be passed on to his spouse in the future. If that happens, the male's frequency of sex within the marriage may be altered by the wife's recurrent outbreaks of herpes that can last for years. A man may face possible resentment by his wife because he transmitted this very painful infection to her.

Around a third of couples undergoing in vitro fertilization are dealing with the blockage of a fallopian tube, which is often the result of scarring from previous STIs (chlamydia and gonorrhea). Most women with chlamydia and gonorrhea have no symptoms, and even though the infection is eventually treated, irreversible damage that may cause infertility may have already happened.

A history of an STI may or may not cause problems in a future marriage. Anyone getting married who's had sex with a previous partner should be evaluated and treated, if necessary, for STIs. If an STI is found that can't be treated and cured, the couple needs to be counseled and the uninfected partner needs to understand and accept the potential risk of being sexually active. The best way to avoid this situation is for both partners to be abstinent before marriage and faithful within marriage.

I used to be sexually active, but now I want to abstain. Is it okay? How do I do it?

Returning to an abstinent lifestyle is not only okay, it's the best choice you can make for your future health, hope, and happiness. You can't change the past, but you can make changes that affect your future.

How? Make it known at the beginning of any new relationship that you've decided not to have sex again until you're married. This could end some relationships before they get started, but it's the best way to keep from being sexually involved outside of marriage. Enlist the help and support of friends who can pray for you and provide accountability. Finally, don't forget that God offers His children the strength to resist temptation. He wants you to succeed even more than you do.

Once you've decided to remain abstinent, talk with your physician about it. He or she will likely test for any sexually transmitted infections you may have that aren't causing symptoms. Regardless of sexual history, a woman should have a Pap smear at age twenty-one, and one every three years thereafter. She should also have an annual wellness checkup (at which she can receive preventive care, regular screenings, and health counseling) each year. Bacterial STIs can be treated; unfortunately, viral STIs can't be cured and some can last for a lifetime.

Is there any danger in having sex while I'm engaged?

God's plan is for sexual activity to occur within the relationship of marriage, not in the relationship leading *up* to marriage. Ignoring God's purpose is fraught with spiritual dangers, among them clouded judgment and a damaged relationship with Him.

Engagement is a time when couples can get professional counseling to uncover any basic problems that are likely to lead to divorce. Once problems are discovered, the couple can either choose to continue toward marriage—hopefully with a plan to work on these issues—or cancel the engagement. Sexual intercourse during this time may mask some basic personality differences that might lead to divorce.

Even if contraception is used, there's always a chance of pregnancy that will leave you and your partner with tough decisions to make. A pregnancy may cause you to marry even though counseling indicates that your future marriage is heading for trouble. Even if counseling indicates a perfect match, you may be faced with the problem of walking down the aisle visibly pregnant or having your teenager do the math and find out that she was born seven months after the wedding date. An abortion would not only destroy a human life, but might terminate the life of the only child you as a couple ever conceive. If the engagement is called off, you'll face tough decisions, some better than others but none without pain. To keep the baby as a single mom, to release the baby for adoption, or to terminate the pregnancy all have major consequences.

If either of you has had previous sexual experience, there's a possibility of acquiring or transmitting a sexually transmitted infection that had no symptoms. For this reason, regardless of whether sex takes place before or after the wedding, screening for the possibility of asymptomatic STIs should be done prior to sexual intercourse. Some STIs can be cured, some cannot; the uninfected partner must understand and accept those risks prior to initiating sex.

If the uninfected partner accepts those risks and becomes infected before the wedding and the wedding is called off, he or she will face the possibility of transmitting that STI to any future partner, including a spouse.

When should I get married?

The simple answer: When you're ready financially and emotionally to support yourself and another person.

Several generations ago, individuals typically married in their teens—but it's a rare teenager today who's emotionally and financially ready to support a marriage and any children who may follow. Teenage marriages today, unlike those several generations ago, are rarely successful.

Starting in your early twenties, you should have the freedom to be open to the possibility of marriage if you find someone who fits your criteria for a spouse. In preparation for marriage, it's a good idea to start thinking of the characteristics, goals, and qualities you want in a future spouse. While you're unlikely to find a spouse who completely fulfills your wish list, it's a beginning.

There are some characteristics, such as sharing the same faith, that you shouldn't compromise on. The Bible is clear that followers of Christ are not to be bonded that closely with unbelievers. When a Christian marries someone who doesn't have the same faith, heartache and disappointment can ensue. Marrying someone with the simple hope that he'll eventually develop a relationship with Christ generally doesn't work; in fact, the nonbeliever frequently has a negative influence on the believer, weakening the latter's faith.

There's been a gradual increase in the average age of marriage in recent years, but many are questioning the wisdom of this trend. A female's fertility and ease of childbearing is the greatest in the early- to mid-twenties. This doesn't mean a woman can't conceive and bear children in her thirties and forties, but fertility does decrease yearly in the late twenties and into the thirties. Starting a family at a younger age is more critical for those desiring a large family, especially if one wants a little spacing between children. There's also an increased risk of certain genetic disorders, such as Down syndrome, with increasing maternal age, especially in the late thirties and early forties. While couples in their twenties may be more immature and less financially established than couples in their thirties, they tend to be more adaptable to change and may have more energy and stamina to cope with an active toddler.

This doesn't mean that individuals should get married at an early age for the sake of being married. It just means to be open to marriage starting in your twenties if you find somebody who fits your standards for a spouse. Regardless of your age, it's always wise to receive premarital counseling and even better to get counseling prior to a formal wedding announcement. If a counselor, friends, and family have reservations about the person you're planning to marry, consider this to be a very large red flag. If this happens, you should proceed very slowly or even put the marriage on hold until the problems can be resolved.

What's wrong with living together?

God designed marriage to be the only relationship in which sexual intimacy is to be expressed. Cohabitation dishonors God and degrades sex by placing it in the wrong context.

Some couples live together as a sort of trial for marriage compatibility, but it seldom works. Others cohabit for sex, for convenience, to save money, or in hopes of avoiding divorce; most children of divorce desperately want to avoid the mistakes of their parents.

Since a marriage begun today has about a 40 percent chance of dissolving, it's natural for single young adults to want to avoid divorce. But look at the facts. The problem with cohabiting as a form of trial marriage is that about 60 percent of cohabiting couples don't end up marrying. Of the remaining 40 percent who do, the divorce rate is close to 75 percent—higher than for couples who don't cohabit prior to marriage. This means that approximately 10 percent of cohabiting couples will marry and stay married for a lifetime.[3] Rather than paving the way for marital success, cohabitation actually reduces the likelihood of a stable and enduring marriage.

What's missing in cohabitation? Commitment—the kind expressed through marriage certificates and vows made to each other in front of witnesses to stay together "till death us do part." That's crucial to the success and longevity of a relationship. With cohabitation, either party can leave anytime for any or no reason. This lack of commitment undermines the relationship. Rather than cohabiting, it would be more beneficial to get counseling and uncover potential differences, which allows you to decide whether to proceed with marriage or not.

Every couple living together, married or not, will have differences and conflict. The big question is whether or not there's the will to work out differences and work through conflicts. Commitment means you'll take the time and effort to make a marriage work no matter what. Commitment is needed for any relationship to endure. Marriage provides commitment; cohabitation rarely does.

Why Not Live Together?

Many young adults feel living together is a great alternative to marriage. Most have experienced the pain of never seeing a marriage work. They don't realize that by cohabiting, they could actually be sabotaging their chances at experiencing a fabulous marriage in the future. Here are some facts about cohabiting:

- Cohabiters who later married experienced significantly more difficulty in their marriages with adultery, alcohol, drugs, and independence than couples who hadn't lived together.[4]

- Compared to married couples, cohabiting couples have less healthy relationships. They have lower relationship quality, lower stability, and a higher level of disagreements.[5]

- Cohabiters are much more violent than marrieds. The overall rate of violence for cohabiting couples is twice as high as for married couples, and the overall rate for "severe" violence is nearly five times as high.[6]

- One of the most respected studies in the field of psychiatry, conducted by the National Institutes of Mental Health, found that women in cohabiting relationships had rates of depression nearly five times higher than those of married women, second only to those of women who were divorced.[7]

- The National Sex Survey reports that cohabiting men are nearly four times more likely than husbands to have cheated on their partner in the past year. While women are generally more faithful than men, cohabiting women are eight times more likely than wives to cheat.[8]

- Research strongly and consistently indicates that marriage is a wealth-building institution. Married people typically earn and save more than their unmarried counterparts.[9]

In other words, the very thing many young couples think can enhance their future relationships in fact can serve to undermine them.

Can a person never marry and be happy?

Yes! You can read the stories of those who've lived in singleness for a lifetime and have had happy, productive lives. Some are called to singleness because of faith (Catholic priests, monks, nuns); some are single because their profession was their passion and they chose not to marry. Some wanted marriage but just never found the right person or the right person at the time in life when marriage was considered an option.

A single person needs to find, through alternative sources, the companionship and emotional strength that a husband and wife provide for each other. A single person needs a healthy base of friends who can help share his or her burdens, hopes, and dreams. A singles ministry at a church might supply a base of support as well as a social outlet. It might even lead to marriage at some point.

Many of these principles apply to the never married as well as the person who's single due to death or divorce. Regardless of whether we're single lifelong or single due to death or divorce, we all need companionship and love. While sex between a husband and wife who are committed to each other is wonderful and beautiful, we can live without sexual intercourse if we have family and friends and a purpose in life, and know we are loved.

SEXUALLY TRANSMITTED INFECTIONS

S ex, drugs, and rock 'n' roll!" It was the liberating mantra of a previous generation of young people. Unfortunately, kids today don't
understand why the sixties were such a big deal. After all, they've
grown up in a society bombarded by sexuality.

Sex is no longer a secret. Song lyrics, TV shows, Hollywood, and the
Internet seem to celebrate it all day, every day. The social scene surround-
ing sexually transmitted infections has vastly changed from the days of
Woodstock. Casual sex is as common for youth as going to the movies.
In fact, to some adolescents, sex is just a game—something to do when
they're bored.

The difference between now and then is that forty years ago there were
only two sexually transmitted infections (STIs, then known as venereal
diseases) of significant prevalence: syphilis and gonorrhea. Both were easily
treated with antibiotics. Today there are more than twenty-five STIs that
paint the sexual landscape, and some, like HIV (human immunodeficiency
virus) can have deadly consequences. In addition, teens today are having
sex with more partners—thus putting themselves and others at significant
risk of contracting viral infections that can't be cured.

This section will help you tell your children and others around you about the impact of STIs—and why condoms often fail to prevent the spread of these infections.

What is a sexually transmitted disease (STD) or sexually transmitted infection (STI)?

These are terms for what used to be called venereal disease (VD). STDs are the result of an infection with various types of "germs" (bacteria and viruses) and parasites. Examples of bacteria are chlamydia, gonorrhea, and syphilis. Examples of viruses are HIV, genital herpes, hepatitis B, and human papillomavirus. Trichomoniasis is caused by a protozoan parasite called *Trichomonas vaginalis*.

When an individual is first infected, it's called an STI. If part of the body malfunctions because of the STI, the infection is then considered a disease (STD). For example, when an individual is infected with HIV, the person would be considered as having an STI. However, when the person develops full-blown AIDS, which can be years later, it would be called an STD.

One way in which STIs differ from each other is how they're spread. Some STIs (gonorrhea, chlamydia, trichomoniasis, and HIV) are spread through body fluids such as semen, vaginal secretions, and blood. Others (genital herpes, syphilis, and HPV) are spread by direct skin-to-skin contact.

Most STIs are spread almost exclusively by intimate sexual contact and usually infect the genital area, mouth, or rectum. The delicate lining of these areas and their warmth and moisture allow the growth of the STIs. Some STIs, such as HIV or hepatitis B, can also be transmitted by exposure to another person's blood (contaminated blood or needles). STIs aren't spread from toilet seats, shaking hands, and other nonsexual contact. Due to better screening of blood and blood products, it's now exceedingly rare to acquire HIV or hepatitis B or C through a blood transfusion.

Why are sexually transmitted infections and diseases important?

They can produce lifelong consequences for anyone who becomes infected—problems that destroy future hopes and opportunities and make life difficult.

STIs can permanently damage and infect a person's body and even cause death. These infections and the diseases they lead to are much more common than most people realize. It's estimated that there are approximately 18.9 million new cases of STIs yearly in the United States alone.[1]

Since some of these infections are viruses, they have no cure and can infect a person for his or her entire life. Some infections, such as chlamydia and gonorrhea, can damage a woman's fallopian tubes so severely that pregnancy may not be possible without undergoing in vitro fertilization. HIV/AIDS is life-threatening, HPV may be, and hepatitis B and C may result in chronic illness. Human papillomavirus (HPV) can cause a woman to develop precancerous and cancerous growths on her cervix; more than 99 percent of all cases of cervical cancer are linked to HPV.[2]

One of the biggest risk factors for becoming infected with an STI is having multiple sexual partners. Having sex with only one faithful, uninfected partner for a lifetime is the best way to avoid STIs. This scenario is seldom found outside of marriage.

What is chlamydia?

Chlamydia is a very common sexually transmitted infection. It's an STI men carry and can pass on but rarely experience any long-term consequences from.

Women, however, often suffer many long-term consequences from contracting it. Chlamydia can cause infertility when the infection moves through a woman's cervix and uterus into her fallopian tubes. If a woman who's had pelvic inflammatory disease or PID (an infection of the fallopian tubes) becomes pregnant, she has an increased risk of experiencing a tubal or ectopic pregnancy. An ectopic pregnancy places the mother's life at risk and requires a woman to either have surgery or take medication for treatment. Babies almost never survive an ectopic pregnancy.

The disturbing thing is that up to three out of four women who are infected with chlamydia experience no symptoms and don't know they're infected—and all the while, the infection can be permanently damaging their fallopian tubes. Even when chlamydia is diagnosed and treated with appropriate antibiotics, the tubes may be irreparably damaged, resulting in infertility. Approximately 5 to 10 percent of all sexually active teenagers are infected with chlamydia and are at risk of becoming infertile.

What are the signs and symptoms of chlamydia?

Generally men experience no symptoms at all. Occasionally they may have some discharge from their penis or pain with urination. Even though they may not experience any symptoms, if they're infected, they can pass on this infection to a woman during sexual intercourse (vaginal, anal, or oral) or through genital contact without penile insertion.

If a woman becomes infected, she usually won't experience any symptoms but could develop pelvic inflammatory disease (PID). PID can be silent or present with high temperature and severe pelvic and abdominal pain. Infertility may result from PID whether or not symptoms are present. She may also have vaginal discharge that's different from her normal vaginal secretions. The discharge can smell foul and look discolored.

If a woman has had sexual intercourse with a new partner (or her partner has had a new sexual partner) and she starts having a fever and pelvic pain, she should see a physician immediately. If the physician finds she has PID, antibiotics will be started to minimize the scarring of her reproductive organs. Since the majority of women with chlamydia have no symptoms, it's recommended that all single, sexually active adolescent women be screened for this STI at least annually.[3]

How can I avoid getting chlamydia?

The only way to totally avoid becoming infected with chlamydia is to not have sexual intercourse (vaginal, oral, or anal) or to have intercourse only within the context of a lifelong, mutually faithful, monogamous relationship with an uninfected partner. This scenario seldom occurs outside of marriage.

If you've had sexual intercourse in the past and are under twenty-five and single, you should be evaluated and screened. If you're a carrier of chlamydia, you should be treated with antibiotics even if you have no symptoms.

Condoms, if used 100 percent of the time, may reduce the risk of infection by approximately 50 percent or less.[4] However, they'll never totally eliminate the risk of transmission.

What is gonorrhea?

Gonorrhea is an infection of the genital organs of a man or woman caused by a germ called *Neisseria gonorrhea*. This germ is easily passed from man to woman or woman to man during sexual intercourse. It's also easily passed during oral and anal sex.

In men, the infection can cause scarring of the urethra (the tube for urinating). If a woman is infected, she'll often develop scarring in her fallopian tubes or around her ovaries. This scarring may render her infertile and can cause her to experience severe pelvic pain for many years. This pain may be so severe that a hysterectomy may be needed to eliminate it. Though gonorrhea isn't as common as chlamydia in the United States, it's still a very dangerous infection.

What are the signs and symptoms of gonorrhea?

If a man is infected with gonorrhea, he'll often have a discharge from his penis and burning with urination when he first becomes infected. Then, after a period of time without symptoms, the germs could cause scarring of his genital organs, or he could pass the infection on to a sexual partner.

Many women don't experience symptoms from gonorrhea infection. If they do have symptoms, the most common are fever and pelvic pain resulting from pelvic inflammatory disease (PID). If a woman has had sexual intercourse and has never been tested for gonorrhea, she needs to see a physician—especially if she starts developing a fever and pelvic pain. Antibiotics can kill the bacteria, but it's possible the fallopian tubes may already be damaged.

Individuals who suspect they are infected with gonorrhea should be tested and treated immediately if gonorrhea is present. Anyone who has sexual intercourse with a new partner or whose partner has had sex with someone else should be evaluated for gonorrhea as well as for other STIs.

How can I keep from being infected with gonorrhea?

The only way to totally avoid becoming infected with gonorrhea is to not have sexual intercourse (vaginal, oral, or anal) or to have intercourse only within the context of a lifelong, mutually faithful, monogamous relationship with an uninfected partner. This scenario seldom occurs outside of marriage.

Condoms, if used 100 percent of the time, may reduce the risk of infection by approximately 50 percent or less.[5] Condoms will never totally eliminate the risk of transmission.

What is syphilis?

Syphilis is an STI caused by an organism called *Treponema pallidum*. This germ is easily transmitted during sexual intercourse (vaginal, anal, or oral). It can be a dangerous infection.

When a person is first infected, he or she will usually have a painless sore at the place where the syphilis germ penetrated the body. For a man, this can be on the penis. For a woman, it can be on the labia or farther up in her vagina where she would have no symptoms and therefore not know she was infected. If a person doesn't see a physician for diagnosis and treatment, the sore will heal and the infected individual will believe he or she is well. But the infection has only gone underground in the person's body, and a few weeks later, secondary syphilis will develop.

Symptoms of secondary syphilis are many and varied, including fatigue, fever, hair loss, skin rash, and other problems. If an individual isn't diagnosed and treated at that point, the process can go underground again and is now called tertiary syphilis (third-stage syphilis). This late stage can cause several serious health problems later in life.

What are the signs and symptoms of syphilis?

The first sign of syphilis is a painless sore that's usually a quarter inch to one inch in size. This sore is called a chancre (pronounced *shanker*). When the sore heals after about two weeks, a person may think he or she is well.

Within a few weeks, however, signs of secondary syphilis develop, which include fatigue, fever, hair loss, skin rash, warty-looking growths (*condyloma latum*) around the vulva and anus, and enlarged lymph nodes in various parts of the body. Secondary syphilis can also cause inflammation of the liver and kidney, changes in the bones, and eye infections.

Unless antibiotics are used to fight the infection, tertiary (third-stage) syphilis will develop in about a third of people infected with syphilis and can result in damage to the large arteries of the body, the heart valves, and the brain.[6] At the end stage, syphilis can cause dementia.

How can I keep from getting syphilis?

The only way to totally avoid becoming infected with syphilis is to not have sexual intercourse (vaginal, oral, or anal) or to have intercourse only within the context of a lifelong, mutually faithful, monogamous relationship with an uninfected partner. This scenario seldom occurs outside of marriage.

Condoms, if used 100 percent of the time, may reduce the risk of infection by approximately 50 percent or less.[7] Condoms will never eliminate the risk of transmission. If you think you might have had sex with someone who could be infected with syphilis or any other STIs, or if you have any rash or sore in the genital area, you need to see a health-care provider and be evaluated and tested.

Since syphilis and other STIs don't always have obvious symptoms, it's important to tell your physician if you or your partner have had sex with other individuals so that screening for syphilis and other STIs can be considered. This is especially true for pregnant women because untreated syphilis can be passed from mother to child with devastating results.

What is HIV/AIDS?

HIV (human immunodeficiency virus) invades the immune system of the body and destroys it over time. A person is infected with HIV by exposure to infected blood, semen, or vaginal secretions during any type of sexual encounter. The use of shared needles when taking illegal injectable drugs and getting a tattoo with instruments that haven't been appropriately cleaned can also expose a person to HIV. The risk of HIV exposure through medical and dental procedures and accidents is very small. Safeguards in place at blood banks in North America and much of Europe make it almost impossible to become infected with HIV from a transfusion in these places, although elsewhere in the world the risks from transfusion are higher.

Once people are HIV-infected, they're infected for life; we have no cure for any virus, including HIV. With modern drugs and early diagnosis, however, we can keep many individuals from progressing to full-blown AIDS.

The destruction of the immune system over time reduces a person's ability to fight off infections and some cancers, at which time the HIV-infected individual is said to have AIDS (acquired immunodeficiency syndrome), which is treatable but not curable. Advances in the treatment of AIDS have turned this disease into a chronic illness that can be controlled for years. Because of modern drug therapies, some individuals have no evidence of infection while being treated, and most people with HIV who are undergoing treatment will die from other causes. Some, however, will die from infections that can't be controlled due to their HIV infection.

What are the signs and symptoms of HIV?

Infected individuals may initially experience flulike symptoms (fatigue, fever, aches, and sometimes a rash) for a limited period of time. After the initial infection, most individuals have no recognizable symptoms for years, even though they're capable of infecting their sexual partner during this period of time. Typically after about ten years, the body's immune system is weakened enough to cause symptoms, and the individual is said to have AIDS (acquired immunodeficiency syndrome).[8] Early diagnosis of HIV infection and new therapies may further delay the onset of full-blown AIDS as well as allow the infected person to alert any potential sexual partners of the risk of acquiring HIV.

How can I prevent becoming infected with HIV?

Avoiding drug use and tattoos or body piercings from a place that doesn't have a current inspection certificate from your local health department is one way to avoid infection. If you're single, abstain from sexual activity. If you get married, be faithful. If you haven't had sex (vaginal, oral, or anal) and don't shoot drugs, your chances of getting HIV/AIDS are extremely low.

While consistent and correct use of a condom can reduce your risk of getting HIV, it doesn't totally prevent you from contracting HIV. If a condom is used 100 percent of the time, your chance of infection is reduced by about 85 percent, but that still leaves a 15 percent risk of becoming infected with a potentially fatal disease.[9] Inconsistent condom use, which is more common, offers significantly less risk reduction, if any.

If you've already had sex, get checked out and decide to abstain in order to avoid putting yourself at risk for acquiring HIV.

What is genital herpes?

Genital herpes is an STI caused by the herpes simplex virus (HSV). Genital herpes most commonly infects a man's penis and, less commonly, the skin around the genital area. It commonly infects a woman's vulva, vagina, or cervix and the skin adjacent to her genitalia. If individuals have oral or anal sex, herpes can spread to those areas as well.

Once people contract genital herpes, they may be infected for life. Approximately 70 percent of individuals infected with genital herpes will have recurrences.[10] The frequency of these recurrences usually decreases over time, but it's possible for some individuals to have outbreaks throughout their lives. These outbreaks can happen as often as every few weeks or as seldom as every few years. It's also possible to pass this infection on even when there's no obvious outbreak.

While painful, genital herpes is generally not life-threatening in adults. But occasionally it may spread to the central nervous system and cause meningitis or encephalitis.

What are the signs and symptoms of herpes?

Burning sores in the genital area are usually the first sign of a herpes infection. For a woman, this burning may be so severe that she can't urinate because it makes the burning worse. This initial infection usually heals within a couple of weeks.

After the initial infection, there may be outbreaks of new sores in the same area as the original infection every few weeks or months. Subsequent infections tend to last only a few days and generally aren't as painful. The sensation a person gets just before a recurrence is called a *prodrome* and may include fever, chills, tingling, burning, or pain. While there's no cure for genital herpes, antiviral medications can reduce the severity of symptoms and shorten the duration of the lesions.

A devastating aspect of herpes infection for a woman is that if she breaks out with herpes at the time she's delivering a baby, her baby could become infected. The presence of herpes lesions at the time of delivery will almost always necessitate a C-section in an attempt to minimize the risk of a mother transmitting herpes to her child. For the initial episode of genital herpes, the risk of transmission when a baby is delivered vaginally is about 50 percent. If it's a recurrent episode, the risk decreases to under 3 percent.[11]

How can I keep from becoming infected with herpes?

The only way to totally avoid becoming infected with genital herpes is to not have sexual intercourse (vaginal, oral, or anal) or have intercourse only within the context of a lifelong, mutually faithful, monogamous relationship with an uninfected partner. This scenario seldom occurs outside of marriage.

Condoms may reduce the chance of becoming infected with genital herpes, but they never eliminate risk. Part of the reason is that herpes can be anywhere on the genitals and surrounding areas of skin, and condoms don't cover the entire genital area. Because HSV can be spread so readily even when a person has no symptoms, some researchers suggest that anyone with the virus should receive medication daily to suppress viral reproduction and transmission.

Genital herpes is extremely common. About one in five Americans over the age of eleven test positive for the herpes simplex virus. While approximately one million Americans get infected with HSV yearly (called incidence), a total of about forty-five million Americans have antibodies for the genital herpes virus (called prevalence)—because once a person is infected, the antibodies persist for a lifetime.[12]

If you have sexual intercourse with more than one person and your sexual partners have had intercourse with other people, it's possible that you'll be infected with this virus.

What is human papillomavirus?

Of the nearly nineteen million new STIs that Americans acquire yearly, HPV is the most common with an estimated 5.5 million new cases yearly in the United States.[13] Of all Americans living, however, more are infected with genital herpes than HPV, since in most individuals the body clears itself of the HPV virus over the course of a year or two.

Unfortunately, some people don't spontaneously clear HPV from their body; about 10 percent of women with HPV will have persistent infection. It's these persistent infections from certain strains of HPV in women that can lead to precancer (cervical dysplasia) or cancer if not diagnosed and treated. (It is worth noting, however, that not all dysplasias will become cancerous.)

Since HPV is so common and infectious, if you have sexual intercourse with more than one person, or your partner has had sex with other people, you may become infected with this virus. Approximately 45 to 60 percent of sexually active adolescents do become infected, regardless of whether they use condoms. About one in five women infected with HPV will experience an abnormal Pap smear, genital warts, precancer, or cancer of the cervix.[14]

One of the more dangerous aspects of HPV infection is that 99 percent of women infected with the virus don't know it because there are no symptoms. Thus a woman can develop precancer or cancer of her cervix and never know she has a problem until she has an abnormal Pap smear. For this reason, it's recommended that all women, regardless of their sexual history, get a Pap smear at age twenty-one. Current guidelines call for Pap smears to be repeated every three years.

What are the signs and symptoms of HPV infection?

Most people who are infected with HPV don't know it, except for about 1 percent who have genital warts. The warts can vary from a small bump which is hardly noticed on the man's penis or the woman's vulva, to large warts that are easily seen.

Most genital warts are caused by strains of HPV that don't turn into cancer. However, a physician should still evaluate them; in women, a Pap smear is needed to identify cancer-causing strains of HPV. In addition, physicians will probably screen for the presence of other STIs.

The most common problem linked to HPV in women is that specific strains of the virus may cause precancer or cancer of the cervix. Over 99 percent of all precancer and cancer of the cervix is caused by HPV.[15] There are approximately 3.5 million cases of atypical cells (dysplasia) in the United States each year and about twelve thousand cases of cervical cancer, which result in just over four thousand deaths.[16] In addition to cervical cancer, HPV infection has been linked to cancer of the anus, vulva, vagina, and penis, as well as oropharyngeal (mouth and throat) cancers, and head and neck cancers.

What can I do to prevent becoming infected with HPV?

The only way to totally avoid becoming infected with HPV is to not have sexual intercourse (vaginal, oral, or anal) or to have intercourse only within the context of a lifelong, mutually faithful, monogamous relationship with an uninfected partner. This scenario seldom occurs outside of marriage.

Condoms may reduce the chance of becoming infected with HPV but they never eliminate risk. In addition, there are two vaccines on the market that are designed to offer some protection against certain types of HPV. One of the vaccines targets two of the HPV types responsible for a large percentage of cervical cancers and is approved only for use in women. The other vaccine provides immunity for the same two types of HPV that cause cervical cancer, but also for two HPV types that are common causes of genital warts. This vaccine is approved for use in males as well as females.

While these vaccines can provide some reduction of risk against some types of HPV, there are some important points to consider:

- No vaccine is 100 percent effective against disease;
- There are more than one hundred types of HPV and the existing vaccines are effective against, at most, four of these;
- The types of the virus that these vaccines protect against are the cause of most *but not all* cases of cervical cancer;
- The HPV vaccines do not protect against other STIs or prevent pregnancy.

The HPV vaccines do not, in any circumstance, negate or provide a substitute for the best health message—sexual abstinence until marriage and sexual faithfulness during marriage.

There is no cure for HPV. The warts caused by HPV can be treated, but this treatment is uncomfortable and the warts can recur and require treatment again. Although cervical dysplasia and cancer of the cervix usually can be successfully treated, treatment can damage the cervix and interfere with future fertility and pregnancy.

What is viral hepatitis?

Viral hepatitis is the inflammation of the liver as a result of infection by a virus that selectively chooses the liver to infect and inflame. One group of viruses causing hepatitis is classified as hepatitis viruses. Hepatitis B virus is commonly spread through sexual contact. Hepatitis C is another virus that can sometimes be sexually transmitted. While the primary method for the spread of hepatitis B and C is nonsexual contact with another person's blood (blood transfusion, contaminated needle, razor, knife), these viruses (especially hepatitis B) can be transmitted through sexual intercourse.

The problem with hepatitis is not only that a person can become a carrier of the virus and infect others, but that occasionally the infection will damage the liver and even lead to liver cancer over a period of months or years. With improved methods for screening the blood supply in the United

States, it's now extremely rare for a person to contract hepatitis B or C through a blood transfusion or use of other blood products. Hepatitis A isn't transmitted by vaginal intercourse but can be transmitted by oral sex and men having sex with men.

What are the signs and symptoms of hepatitis?

When people first become infected with viral hepatitis, they may develop flulike symptoms. These can include fatigue, mild fever, nausea, vomiting, and a general feeling of discomfort in the abdomen. A loss of appetite and weight may also result. Because of the infection to the liver, infected individuals may develop dark-colored urine, and their skin may become yellow (jaundiced). If they develop chronic hepatitis and then cirrhosis or liver cancer, they can have symptoms related to these diseases. Both of these diseases can lead to death.

How can I keep from being infected with hepatitis?

In the United States, the most common types of hepatitis are A, B, and C. Hepatitis A is usually acquired by consuming food and beverages contaminated with fecal matter, although it can occasionally be in a person's blood for a short period of time. Hepatitis B and C are often found in an infected person's blood. Any exposure of nonintact skin to infected blood can result in infection.

The only way to avoid being infected with hepatitis B and C (and occasionally A) is to avoid exposure to blood contaminated with any of these viruses. Vaccines for hepatitis A and B, which are about 90 to 95 percent protective, greatly reduce the risk of infection.[17] No vaccine exists for hepatitis C. Because blood is now carefully screened for hepatitis, transfusions rarely contribute to transmission.

Avoiding exposure to contaminated blood is the first step you can take to protect yourself; this includes not using injectable drugs, not sharing household items such as razors or toothbrushes with infected persons, and staying away from tattooing and body piercing establishments that aren't routinely inspected for sanitary practices by a health department.

Hepatitis B and C can also be spread through a variety of sexual practices, and hepatitis A can be spread through oral sex. Therefore, the second thing you can do to protect yourself from the hepatitis viruses is to abstain from intercourse or to have intercourse only within the context of a lifelong, mutually faithful, monogamous relationship (marriage) with an uninfected partner.

What is trichomoniasis?

Trichomoniasis is an STI caused by a parasite called *Trichomonas vaginalis*. New studies suggest that trichomoniasis is almost always transmitted by sexual contact. Most men who are infected have no symptoms, and trichomoniasis doesn't damage a man's body. An infected woman will often experience irritating discharge that's profuse and greenish.

Trichomoniasis has recently been found to be occasionally associated with pelvic inflammatory disease in women. If a woman thinks she might be infected with trichomoniasis, it's important that she be tested and treated as soon as possible. In addition, having trichomoniasis can increase a person's risk of contracting HIV if exposed to the virus.[18]

What are the symptoms of trichomoniasis?

Most people who are infected, particularly men, have no symptoms. Women will often have a very heavy, frothy, greenish vaginal discharge that's very irritating. If a woman has abnormal discharge or begins having a fever and pelvic pain, she needs to be seen by a physician as soon as possible.

How can I keep from becoming infected with trichomoniasis?

Currently there is no conclusive data to show whether condoms offer any significant risk reduction. The only way to totally avoid becoming infected with trichomoniasis is to not have sexual intercourse (vaginal, oral, or anal) or to have intercourse only within the context of a lifelong, mutually faithful, monogamous relationship with an uninfected partner. This scenario seldom occurs outside of marriage.

If you think you might have been exposed to someone who has a tricho-moniasis infection or any other STI, you should see a physician to be evaluated and treated if necessary.

How can I tell if a person has a sexually transmitted infection?

Unless a person has sores, blisters, or warts on his or her genitals, you can't tell by looking whether he or she is infected with an STI. More than half the people who are infected with STIs have no symptoms and don't know they're carrying such an infection.

STIs can be transmitted to another person through sexual intercourse in the absence of symptoms. We now know that most people who become infected with an STI are infected by a sexual partner who doesn't have sores, discharge, or obvious symptoms at the time.

In addition, many people don't tell the truth even if they know they're infected with an STI. They may fail to do this because many fear that if they reveal their infection to a potential sexual partner, the partner will refuse to have sex with them. Surprising as it may seem, a significant number of people infected with HIV/AIDS don't share this information with potential partners, even though they may be passing on a deadly disease.

Will having a sexually transmitted infection hurt my sex life?

People who become infected with STIs often feel dirty, sexually unattract-ive, and depressed. This is particularly true with infections such as genital herpes. Herpes can cause pain during intercourse and is a constant reminder to individuals that they have an STI. In addition to the emotional turmoil caused by an STI, most people who know they have a chronic infection worry about passing the infection to someone they care about.

Can a pregnant mother pass her STI to her baby?

Many STIs can be transmitted during pregnancy, at the time of childbirth, or even later when the mother is nursing her baby. Because of this, it's terribly important that a woman who might be at risk for or has become infected with an STI see a physician early in pregnancy to be tested and then treated if possible. Some diseases that can be transmitted from mother to child include the following:

- Hepatitis B can be transmitted to the baby during pregnancy; it can cause the infant to have hepatitis B and become a chronic carrier and transmitter of that disease. In addition, infants who acquire hepatitis B are at high risk for chronic disease and cancer of the liver.[19]

- Hepatitis C can be passed from a mother to her baby during childbirth; these infants are at risk of developing severe chronic liver disease.[20]

- Human papillomavirus (HPV) can be transmitted to a baby at delivery, and the infant could develop polyps on its vocal cords that could require surgery.[21]

- Chlamydia can be transmitted to the baby and cause an eye infection; one type of eye infection can even lead to blindness if left untreated. Chlamydia can also cause viral pneumonias in the infant during the first few months of life.[22]

- Gonorrhea can be transmitted to an infant during childbirth, and can result in potentially serious eye infections in the newborn.[23]

- Herpes simplex virus can be transmitted to an infant at the time of delivery. HSV can cause fever, sores on the baby's mouth, tongue, and gums, and lesions in the genital area. It can also result in encephalitis, neurologic impairment, and death.[24]

- HIV can be transmitted to a baby during delivery or when the mother nurses her newborn baby.

Can you get sexually transmitted infections from oral sex?

Yes! Most STIs can be transmitted during oral sex. It isn't possible to become pregnant through oral sex, but STIs are still a real danger. Some, including syphilis, gonorrhea, genital herpes, and chlamydia, are easily transmitted during oral sex. Even HIV can be transmitted through oral sex.[25]

Can I get an STI if I use a condom?

Yes! While consistent and correct condom use can reduce the risk of most STIs, condoms never totally eliminate risk. Even if you use condoms perfectly 100 percent of the time, you still can become infected with any number of STIs.

If condoms are used 100 percent of the time, they appear to reduce the risk of HIV transmission by approximately 85 percent. For other STIs such as chlamydia, gonorrhea, genital herpes, and syphilis, transmission is reduced by 50 percent or less.[26] With the possible exception of genital herpes and HIV/AIDS, we have no reliable scientific studies that show any risk reduction from inconsistent condom use.[27] Even if condoms are used perfectly every time, there are still risks due to slippage or breakage. For some STIs, there are risks because the condom doesn't always cover all of the infected areas of the genitalia and surrounding skin. Unfortunately, the vast majority of individuals are unable to use condoms both consistently and correctly.

It's also important to understand that risk is cumulative. For example, in the situation of a woman having sex with a male partner with gonorrhea, the estimated risk per one act of sex without a condom is believed to be approximately 50 percent.[28] If a condom is used perfectly 100 percent of the time and the slippage and breakage is 3 percent, then the estimated risk for the female to acquire gonorrhea from her infected male partner is 1.5 percent. The calculated cumulative risk of condom failure in the scenario above is 14 percent for ten acts of sex with an infected individual, 26 percent for twenty acts of sex, and 37 percent for thirty acts.[29] Incorrect and inconsistent condom use dramatically accelerates the cumulative risk.[30]

Will a dental dam prevent STIs?

A dental dam is a square piece of latex used for hygienic reasons during dental procedures. Scientists have never checked to see whether using a dental dam during oral sex reduces a person's chance of catching a sexually transmitted infection. Recommendations to use dental dams during oral sex are based on urban legends.

Can I get a sexually transmitted infection with my first act of sex?

Yes. If your sexual partner has had sex with previous partners, you can contract an STI if your partner is currently infected. If your partner has ever been infected with herpes, hepatitis B, hepatitis C, or HIV, he or she may well still be infected—since these infections generally last a lifetime.

Can I get an STI if I only have sex with one person—my spouse—and we were both virgins when we married?

It's highly unlikely. STIs are transmitted from one infected person to another person through sexual activity—oral, vaginal, or anal intercourse (or through genital contact without penile insertion). If neither you nor your spouse has ever been sexually active with anyone else and you're faithful to each other, you'll almost never get a sexually transmitted infection or disease.

Possible exceptions would be STIs transmitted through blood that could be passed through lab accidents, accidental needle sticks, and through contaminated blood or blood products. But infections by these means are very rare.

How are sexually transmitted infections treated?

Some can be treated and cured with antibiotics. These include syphilis, gonorrhea, chlamydia, and trichomoniasis. This statement, though, can be too reassuring. For example, if chlamydia and gonorrhea are present and not detected, they can damage a woman's fallopian tubes and cause her to become sterile even though she doesn't know she's infected. Yes, once her infection is found, she can be treated—but by then it may be too late for her fertility. Syphilis can be treated with antibiotics, but that must be done early in the course of the disease to minimize its potential irreversible impact.

Viral infections such as genital herpes and HIV have no cure. Though drugs may control HIV/AIDS, once someone becomes infected, it's usually for a lifetime. Suppressive antibiotics and antifungal medication may also be necessary when treating a patient with HIV/AIDS. In addition, even if a person is taking drugs to control these infections, he or she can still transmit the infection to a sexual partner.

Genital warts caused by HPV can be treated, but often this is a prolonged and uncomfortable process. In addition, HPV can cause precancerous or cancerous changes to the cervix that must be treated with either minor or major surgery or even radiation.

Should I be tested for STIs?

If you've had sexual intercourse with a person who's had intercourse with other partners, you should mention this to your physician; he'll decide if you need to be screened for STIs. It's currently recommended that all single, sexually active females under the age of twenty-five be screened for gonorrhea and chlamydia at least annually. Single, sexually active males should be evaluated and tested as necessary. High-risk individuals, including those with a past history of an STI, are usually tested more often.

Any ulcerative lesion should be screened for genital herpes (HSV) and syphilis. Most individuals should probably also get tested for HIV.

It's important to tell your physician your sexual history, as some people may need to be screened for other STIs as well. Each time you change sex partners or your partner gets a new partner, your risk for catching an STI increases; check with your doctor about whether you should be tested again. Remember, most STIs don't cause any symptoms—at first.

Choosing to remain sexually abstinent until marriage, marrying an uninfected individual, and then remaining faithful in the marital relationship will ensure a much healthier and happier sexual experience.

What should I do if I think I have an STI?

Anyone who thinks he might have an STI or is notified that his partner is infected needs to be evaluated by a physician or nurse practitioner as soon as possible. It's vital to be totally honest with your doctor so he can perform the necessary screening tests. That might be a blood test, a urine test, or a swab of the cervix or urethra.

Since most infected individuals don't know it, it's important to tell your physician at any visit, especially the yearly checkup, of any sexual exposure (vaginal, rectal, or oral).

APPENDIX B

WHAT YOU NEED TO KNOW ABOUT CONTRACEPTIVES

Do oral contraceptives protect against sexually transmitted infections?

No, they're only effective in reducing the risk of becoming pregnant. They provide absolutely no protection against STIs.

What are oral contraceptives, and how do they work?

Oral contraceptives (OCPs), or birth control pills, contain synthetic estrogen and progesterone—two natural hormones for the human female body. These synthetic hormones work by "putting the ovaries to sleep." In this condition, the ovaries don't release an egg monthly. If the ovaries don't release an egg, a woman can't become pregnant. OCPs also alter cervical mucus to interfere with sperm penetration, and they change the endometrial lining.

While a woman is using the pill, her ovaries don't produce as much estrogen and progesterone. The estrogen and progesterone for her body come from the pills she's taking by mouth.

If birth control pills are taken perfectly, they're very effective. Less than 1 percent of women who take the pills properly will become pregnant each year. The primary problem with OCPs is that many women forget to take their pills or take them incorrectly. Using the pill incorrectly may result in a pregnancy. Surprisingly, the failure rate for the pill during the first year of use is 8 percent, due primarily to inconsistent use.[1] In addition, other drugs, including various antibiotics, may reduce the effectiveness of the pill, making it less reliable in preventing pregnancy.

OCPs, in addition to preventing pregnancy, may decrease abnormal and painful bleeding and decrease the risk of ovarian cyst formation.

What is the contraceptive patch?

This is a way of delivering continuous levels of hormones through the skin. The contraceptive patch contains hormones similar to those in birth control pills.

Hormonal contraceptives aren't for everybody. Side effects may make you sick, moody, tired, bloated, irritable, and easily annoyed. Most side effects of the contraceptive patch aren't serious, and those that are occur infrequently.

As with oral contraceptives, the contraceptive patch offers no protection against STIs.

What is the vaginal ring?

This is a flexible ring, about two inches in diameter, that contains hormones similar to those in birth control pills. Once inserted into the vagina it releases these hormones, which are intended to prevent ovulation. After the ring is inserted, it remains in the vagina for three weeks; then it is removed and a new ring is inserted one week later.

The most common side effects of using the vaginal ring include vaginal infections and irritation, vaginal secretion, headaches, weight gain, and nausea. Most side effects aren't serious, and those that are occur infrequently.

As with oral contraceptives, the vaginal ring offers no protection against STIs.

What is Implanon?

This is a flexible plastic rod about the size of a matchstick; it contains progesterone, a synthetic hormone. The rod is inserted under the skin of a woman's upper arm, where it releases progesterone for up to three years. The insertion (and removal) are accomplished through a small incision. Implanon acts as birth control by inhibiting ovulation, by changing the cervical mucus to help prevent sperm from getting into the uterus, and possibly by changing the uterine lining to prevent the implantation of a fertilized egg if a woman were to ovulate and the sperm reached and fertilized the egg. If this third mechanism were to occur, it would result in the loss of the new human life.

Common side effects of Implanon include changes in menstrual periods, weight gain, headaches, acne, and mood changes. Most side effects aren't serious, and those that are occur infrequently.

As with oral contraceptives, Implanon offers no protection against STIs.

What is "emergency contraception" or the "morning-after" pill, and how does it work?

The emergency contraceptive/morning-after pill contains a synthetic hormone (progesterone) that is intended to prevent pregnancy when taken *after* sexual intercourse. It can be taken up to seventy-two hours after intercourse and can work in three possible ways:

- Ovulation is inhibited, meaning the egg won't be released.
- The normal menstrual cycle is altered, delaying ovulation.
- The pill can alter the lining of the uterus so that if the first and second actions fail, the tiny baby will die because it cannot attach to the lining of the uterus.

What are condoms, and how do they work?

Condoms are devices usually made of latex rubber. They are made to fit over a man's erect penis. To be effective, the condom must be tight enough to stay in place during sexual intercourse.

Condoms can be used for two purposes. First, they catch a man's semen when he ejaculates so the sperm in the semen don't get into a woman's reproductive tract. Second, the condom can prevent part of the genitalia of one person from touching part of the genitals of another during sexual intercourse.

A major problem with condoms is that people often don't use them correctly or don't use them every single time. Both correct and consistent condom use are necessary to reduce transmission of sexually transmitted infections.

It's important to understand that some STIs are highly infectious. For example, a woman has an estimated 50 percent chance of getting gonorrhea from an infected male partner each time she has sex with him if no condom is used. It's obvious why inconsistent or incorrect use (such as genital contact prior to putting on a condom) can easily lead to infection. Another problem is that condoms don't cover or protect the entire genitalia of either the man or the woman, and an STI that's transmitted skin to skin (such as HPV or HSV) can still be transmitted if there's any genital contact.

In addition to these problems, semen can leak out when the condom is removed, and condoms can break or slip off, allowing leakage of fluid that can have both sperm and germs present. In fact, about fifteen out of one hundred women who rely on condoms to prevent pregnancy become pregnant during the first year of use.[2]

If a condom is used correctly 100 percent of the time, the risk of acquiring HIV is reduced by approximately 85 percent. For more contagious STIs such as gonorrhea, chlamydia, genital herpes, and syphilis, a person's chance of infection is reduced by approximately 50 percent or less if the condom is used for every act of sex.[3] While studies are limited, there appears to be little or no risk reduction for bacterial vaginosis and Trichomonas infection. With the possible exception of HIV and genital herpes, there appears to be no risk reduction from inconsistent condom use. Unfortunately, very few individuals are able to use a condom consistently and correctly over many months of use.

For those allergic to latex, there are polyurethane male condoms. They appear to have higher slippage and breakage rates than latex condoms.

What is a female condom?

It's a contraceptive method used by women to prevent pregnancy and sexually transmitted infections. It's a soft, plastic (polyurethane), tubelike device that a woman can insert into her vagina to collect sperm and secretions. The female condom's typical-use, first-year failure rate for preventing pregnancy is estimated to be 21 percent.[4]

What is an IUD, and how does it work?

An intrauterine contraceptive device (IUD) is a small, plastic object that can be inserted by a physician through a woman's cervix and into her uterus to prevent pregnancy. This procedure is done in a physician's office, usually during or immediately after a menstrual period so that a woman can be sure she isn't pregnant.

No one knows exactly how an IUD works, but it seems fairly certain that the contraceptive effect is produced in several ways. For the most part, IUDs appear to either kill sperm or keep them from swimming through the uterus into the fallopian tubes, so IUDs generally prevent conception. IUDs also appear to sometimes interfere with implantation after fertilization has already occurred. Some people consider this to be a very early abortion.

The estimated typical-use, first-year failure rate for an IUD is less than 1 percent.[5]

What is a diaphragm?

A diaphragm is a dome-shaped rubber cap with a flexible spring rim. Actually, a diaphragm should be called the diaphragm-plus-jelly contraceptive, because the diaphragm itself doesn't produce any significant contraceptive effect. The diaphragm merely holds the contraceptive jelly against the cervix; it's the jelly that kills the sperm. If the contraceptive jelly is put into the vagina without a diaphragm, the jelly will "glob up" into one corner of the vagina, making it relatively ineffective as a contraceptive.

Since the diaphragm doesn't completely seal off the upper vagina, sperm can swim around the edges of it. When they do this, they're killed by the contraceptive jelly. Even if you have a small hole in your diaphragm, any sperm that swim through the hole are usually killed by the jelly held in position by the diaphragm. This form of birth control isn't usually used by teenagers. The estimated typical-use, first-year failure rate for a diaphragm is 16 percent.[6]

What is Depo-Provera, and how does it work?

Depo-Provera is a synthetic hormone (progesterone) that's injected by a health-care professional into a woman's buttocks or arm muscle every three months. Depo-Provera is very effective in preventing pregnancy. It does so by inhibiting ovulation (the monthly release of a mature egg from the ovary), by changing the cervical mucus to help prevent sperm from going into the uterus, and by changing the uterine lining to prevent the implantation of a fertilized egg if a woman were to ovulate and the sperm did reach and fertilize the egg. It's rare for this third event to happen because it's very uncommon for a woman to ovulate if she receives her Depo-Provera regularly.

Though Depo-Provera is effective in preventing pregnancy (typical-use, first-year failure rate is 3 percent[7]), it can be dangerous for an unmarried adolescent to use. The danger is that she can feel it's safe to have intercourse. She's not safe from any sexually transmitted infection and is potentially exposing herself to great risk. In addition, Depo-Provera can cause loss of hair, acne, weight gain, feelings of constant premenstrual tension, and irritability. Anyone contemplating the use of Depo-Provera needs to consider all of these issues.

What is natural family planning (NFP), and how does it work?

This is a technique requiring a woman and her husband to predict when she's going to ovulate and to avoid sexual intercourse from a few days before to a few days after ovulation. With proper training, most couples are able to forecast when ovulation will occur, and with self-control, the couple can avoid sexual intercourse at that time of the month and prevent pregnancy.

Used by a motivated couple who adhere to NFP techniques, this method has a first-year failure rate of 3 to 5 percent. With typical use, however, it has a first-year failure rate of about 25 percent.[8]

If a woman has extremely irregular menstrual cycles, it's difficult to predict when ovulation might occur; it's unlikely that natural family planning will be successful in this situation. Obviously there's no protection against sexually transmitted infections, so this isn't a good technique for a single woman who might be having intercourse with STI-infected individuals.

What is spermicide, and how does it work?

Spermicides are creams, jellies, or foams that contain a chemical that kills sperm. Only one chemical has been approved for this purpose: nonoxynol-9.

Spermicides must be inserted into the woman's vagina before intercourse, and the typical-use, first-year failure rate for spermicides is estimated to be 29 percent.[9]

It has been shown that spermicides can irritate the woman's vaginal tissues. This could make her more susceptible to HIV infection. Because of this, it's now recommended that women not use spermicides for pregnancy prevention if there's any chance that a sexual partner might be HIV-infected.

Notes

Chapter 1: Where's the Party? *The Need for Parental Guidance*

1. H. Weinstock, S. Berman, and W. Cates, "Sexually Transmitted Diseases among American Youth: Incidence and Prevalence Estimates, 2000," *Perspectives on Sexual Reproductive Health* 36, no. 1 (2004): 6–10.

Chapter 2: The Big Deal Is You! *Parents Do Make a Difference*

1. Linda J. Waite and Maggie Gallagher, *The Case for Marriage: Why Married People Are Happier, Healthier, and Better Off Financially* (New York: Doubleday, 2000); R. T. Michael and others, *Sex in America: A Definitive Survey* (Boston: Little, Brown, and Company, 1994), 140–41.

2. M. D. Resnick, P. S. Bearman, and R. W. Blum et al., "Protecting Adolescents from Harm: Findings from the National Longitudinal Study on Adolescent Health," *Journal of the American Medical Association* 278 (1997): 823–32.

Chapter 3: What a Girl Wants: *Attention, Affection, and Affirmation*

1. J. Harasty, K. L. Double, G. M. Halliday, J. J. Krill, and D. A. McRitchie, "Language-associated cortical regions are proportionally larger in the female brain," *Arch Neurol*, February 1997, 171–76, found at PubMed.gov, USNational Library of Medicine, National Institutes of Health (http://www.ncbi.nlm.nih.gov/pubmed/9041858).

Chapter 6: Questions, Anyone? *What Parents Need to Know*

1. J. N. Giedd, "Structural Magnetic Resonance Imaging of the Adolescent Brain," *Annals of the New York Academy of Sciences* 1021 (2004): 105–9; E. Sowell, P. Thompson, and C. Holmes et al., "In Vivo Evidence for Post-adolescent Brain Maturation in Frontal and Striatal Regions," *Nature Neuroscience* 2 (1999): 859–61.

2. Ed Schor, MD, *Caring for Your School-age Child* (New York: American Academy of Pediatrics, 1995), 47–48.

3. United States Department of Veterans Affairs, National Center for PTSD, "Child Sexual Abuse," January 1, 2007, found at http://www.ptsd.va.gov/public/pages/child-sexual-abuse.asp.

4. American Academy of Child and Adolescent Psychiatry, "Facts for Families: Child Sexual Abuse" (March 2011), found at http://aacap.org/page.ww?name=Child+Sexual+Abuse &section=Facts+for+Families.

5. T. R. Eng and W. T. Butler, eds., *The Hidden Epidemic: Confronting Sexually Transmitted Diseases* (Washington, DC: National Academy Press, 1997), 1–448. Available at www./nap.edu/openbook/0309054958/html.

6. Centers for Disease Control and Prevention, "HIV among Gay and Bisexual Men," (May 2012), http://www.cdc.gov/hiv/topics/msm/index.htm.

7. Centers for Disease Control and Prevention, "Hepatitis A Vaccination of Men Who Have Sex with Men—Atlanta, Georgia, 1996–1997," *Morbidity and Mortality Weekly Report* 47 (September 4, 1998): 34, 708–711.

8. G. M. McQuillan and others, "Prevalence of Hepatitis B Virus Infection in the United States: The National Health and Nutrition Examination Surveys, 1976–1994," *American Journal of Public Health* 89, no. 1 (1999): 14–18.

9. L. Corey and A. Wald, "Genital Herpes," in *Sexually Transmitted Diseases*, 2nd ed., ed. K. K. Holmes, P. A. Mardh, P. F. Sparling, and P. J. Wiesner (New York: McGraw Hill, 1999), 285–312.

10. M. A. Lynch and R. Ferri, "Health needs of lesbian women and gay men: Providing quality care," *Clinician Review* 7 (1997): 85–117.

11. See Centers for Disease Control and Prevention, et al., "Reporting on Suicide: Recommendations for the Media" (http://www.suicidology.org/c/document_library/get_file?folderId=231&name=DLFE-71.pdf), as referenced by Candi Cushman, "Teen Suicide Is a Complex Issue," CitizenLink (October 5, 2010), found at http://www.citizenlink.com/2010/10/05/teen-suicide-is-a-complex-issue/.

Chapter 8: First Comes Love: *Five- to Seven-Year-Olds*

1. Resnick, Bearman, and Blum et al., "Protecting Adolescents from Harm," 823–32.

2. Several dating tips in this section are taken from Joneen Krauth Mackenzie, WAIT training curriculum (Denver: Wait Training, Inc., 2003).

Chapter 9: Breaking Free: *Eight- to Ten-Year-Olds*

1. L. Escobar-Chaves and others, "Impact of the Media on Adolescent Sexual Attitudes and Behaviors" (Center for Health Promotion and Prevention Research and University of Texas Health Science Center Houston, 2004), 25–26; J. M. Dempsey and T. Reichert, "Portrayal of Married Sex in the Movies," *Journal of Sexuality and Culture* 4 no. 3 (2000): 21–36; G. M. Wingood et al., "Exposure to X-Rated Movies and Adolescents' Sexual and Contraceptive-Related Attitudes and Behaviors," *Pediatrics* 107, no. 5 (May 2001): 1116–9.

2. Joseph Nicolosi, PhD, *A Parent's Guide to Preventing Homosexuality* (Downers Grove, IL: InterVarsity Press, 2002), 162–63.

3. Ibid.

Chapter 10: Tell Me More: *Eleven- to Twelve-Year-Olds*

1. Resnick, Bearman, and Blum et al., "Protecting Adolescents from Harm," 823–32.

2. D. A. Cohen and S. N. Taylor et al., "When and Where Do Youths Have Sex? The Potential Role of Adult Supervision," *Pediatrics* 110, no. 6 (2002): E66.

3. Resnick, Bearman, and Blum et al., "Protecting Adolescents from Harm," 823–32.

4. Paul C. Reisser, MD, primary author, *Complete Guide to Baby and Child Care* (Colorado Springs: Focus on the Family; Carol Stream, IL: Tyndale House Publishers, 1997, 2007).

Chapter 11: Diving In: *Thirteen- to Fifteen-Year-Olds*

1. Teri Reisser, MFT, and Paul Reisser, MD, *A Solitary Sorrow* (Colorado Springs: WaterBrook Press, 1999).

2. R. K. Jones and M. L. Kavanaugh, "Changes in Abortion Rates Between 2000 and 2008 and Lifetime Incidence of Abortion," *Obstetrics & Gynecology*, 2011, 117(6).

3. "Spiritual State of the World's Children," a survey conducted by One Hope, referenced at http://www.citizenlink.com/2011/02/18/most-teens-want-to-be-abstinent-until-marriage.

4. Carol J. De Vita, "The United States at Mid-Decade," *Population Bulletin*, vol. 50, no. 4 (Washington, DC: Population Reference Bureau, Inc., March 1996).

5. "Youth Risk Behavior Surveillance—United States, 2011" (*Morbidity and Mortality Weekly Report*, June 8, 2012, Vol. 61, No. 4), Centers for Disease Control and Prevention, US Department of Health and Human Services, found at http://www.cdc.gov/mmwr/pdf/ss/ss6104.pdf.

6. The National Campaign to Prevent Teen Pregnancy, "With One Voice: America's Adults and Teens Sound Off About Teen Pregnancy," (April 2001), http://www.teenpregnancy.org/resources/data/pdf/chrtbook.pdf.

7. The National Campaign to Prevent Teen Pregnancy, "Not Just Another Thing to Do: Teens Talk about Sex, Regret, and the Influence of Their Parents" (2000), www.teenpregnancy.org/resources/data/pdf/teenwant.pdf.

8. Bill Albert, "With One Voice 2012: America's Adults and Teens Sound Off About Teen Pregnancy" (The National Campaign to Prevent Teen and Unplanned Pregnancy, August 2012), http://www.thenationalcampaign.org/resources/pdf/pubs/WOV_2012.pdf.

9. Weinstock, Berman, and Cates, "Sexually Transmitted Diseases among American Youth," 6–10.

10. Albert, "With One Voice 2010: America's Adults and Teens Sound Off About Teen Pregnancy."

11. D. P. Orr, M. Beiter, and G. Ingersoll, "Premature Sexual Activity as an Indicator of Psychosocial Risk," *Pediatrics* 87, no. 2 (1991): 141–47.

12. Ibid.

13. Albert, "With One Voice 2010: America's Adults and Teens Sound Off About Teen Pregnancy."

14. Resnick, Bearman, and Blum et al., "Protecting Adolescents from Harm," 823–32.

15. Kaiser Family Foundation, "Substance Use and Sexual Health among Teens and Young Adults in the US Fact Sheet," (February 2002), http://www.outproud.org/pdf/CASA-FactSheet.pdf.

Chapter 12: Unfinished Business: *Sixteen- to Eighteen-Year-Olds*

1. Resnick, Bearman, and Blum et al., "Protecting Adolescents from Harm," 823–32.

2. R. A. Hatcher, J. Trussel, A. L. Nelson, W. Cates, F. H. Stewart, and D. Kowal, *Contraceptive Technology, Twentieth Revised Edition* (Atlanta, GA: Bridging the Gap Communications, 2011). Also see previous edition's Table 9–2, page 226, found at http://www.contraceptivetechnology.com/table.html.

3. J. Fitch et al., "Condom Effectiveness: Factors That Influence Risk Reduction," *Sexually Transmitted Diseases* 29, no. 12 (2002): 811–17; J. Fitch et al., *Sex, Condoms and STDs: What*

We Now Know (Austin: Medical Institute for Sexual Health, ver. 2.0, 2003): 5–8; National Institutes of Health, "Workshop Summary: Scientific Evidence on Condom Effectiveness for Sexually Transmitted Disease Prevention," (July 20, 2001), http://www.niaid.nih.gov/about/ organization/dmid/documents/condomreport.pdf; S. Ahmed, T. Lutalo and M. Wawer et al., "HIV Incidence and Sexually Transmitted Disease Prevalence Associated with Condom Use: A Population Study in Rakai, Uganda," *AIDS* 15 (2001): 2171–79.

4. Orr, Beiter, and Ingersoll, "Premature Sexual Activity as an Indicator of Psychosocial Risk," 141–47.

5. Institute of Medicine, *The Hidden Epidemic: Confronting Sexually Transmitted Diseases* (Washington, DC: National Academy Press, 1997), 1–432.

6. Ibid.

7. Giedd, "Structural Magnetic Resonance Imaging of the Adolescent Brain," 105–9; Sowell, Thompson, and Holmes et al., "In Vivo Evidence for Post-adolescent Brain Maturation in Frontal and Striatal Regions," 859–61; J.S. McIlhaney, F.M. Bush, *Hooked: New Science on How Casual Sex Is Affecting Our Children* (Chicago: Northfield Publishing, 2008).

8. National Longitudinal Survey of Adolescent Health, Wave II, 1996. For analysis of this data, see The Heritage Foundation, "Sexually Active Teenagers Are More Likely to Be Depressed and to Attempt Suicide," *Center for Data Analysis Report* no. 03–04 (June 3, 2003).

9. Giedd; Sowell, Thompson, and Holmes et al.; J. S. McIlhaney, F.M. Bush.

10. Gary Chapman, *The Five Love Languages* (Chicago: Northfield Publishing, 1992).

11. Ibid.

12. David Popenoe and Barbara Dafoe Whitehead, *Should We Live Together? What Young Couples Need to Know about Cohabitation before Marriage: A comprehensive review of recent research* (Piscataway, NJ: National Marriage Project, 2002), 8.

13. Edward O. Laumann, John H. Gagnon, Robert T. Michael, and Stuart Michaels, National Health and Social Life Survey, 1992 [United States] [Computer file]. ICPSR version. Chicago, IL: University of Chicago and National Opinion Research Center [producer], 1995. Ann Arbor, MI: Inter-university Consortium for Political and Social Research [distributor], 1995.

14. Ibid.

15. American Society of Reproductive Medicine, http:/www.asrm.org/patients/faqs .html.

16. Resnick, Bearman, and Blum et al., "Protecting Adolescents from Harm," 823–32.

17. The National Campaign to Prevent Teen Pregnancy, "14 and Younger: The Sexual Behavior of Young Adolescents," (2003), http://www.teenpregnancy.org/resources/reading/ pdf/14summary.pdf.

18. Kaiser Family Foundation, "Substance Use and Sexual Health among Teens and Young Adults in the US Fact Sheet," (February 2002), http://www.kff.org/youthhivstds/ upload/KFF-CASAFactSheet.pdf.

19. Ibid.

Chapter 13: Moving Out: *College and Beyond*

1. Institute for American Values, http://www.americanvalues.org/pdfs/dl.php?name= wmm3es.

2. "Why Marriage Matters: 26 Conclusions from the Social Sciences," Center for Marriage and Families at the Institute for American Values, found at http://www.familyscholars. org/assets/Why-Marriage-Matters-summary.pdf.

3. Popenoe and Whitehead, *Should We Live Together?*, 8.

4. Ibid.

5. Ibid.

6. Deborah Graefe and Daniel Lichter, "Life Course Transition of American Children: Parental Cohabitation, Marriage, and Single Motherhood," *Demography* 36 (1999): 205–17.

7. Popenoe and Whitehead, *Should We Live Together?*, 8.

8. Waite and Gallagher, *The Case for Marriage*, 93.

9. Ibid., 110–23.

Appendix A: Sexually Transmitted Infections

1. Weinstock, Berman, and Cates, "Sexually Transmitted Diseases among American Youth," 6–10.

2. X. Castellsague, F. X. Bosch, and N. Munoz et al., "Male Circumcision, Penile Human Papillomavirus Infection, and Cervical Cancer in Female Partners," *New England Journal of Medicine* 346, no. 15 (2002): 1105–12.

3. Centers for Disease Control, "Sexually Transmitted Diseases Treatment Guidelines—2010," *Morbidity and Mortality Weekly Report* 59, RR12 (2010): 1–110.

4. Ahmed, Lutalo, and Wawer et al., "HIV Incidence and Sexually Transmitted Disease Prevalence Associated with Condom Use: A Population Study in Rakai, Uganda," *AIDS* 15, no. 16 (2001), 2171–79; L. Warner, K. M. Stone, and M. Macaluso, et al., "Condom use and risk of gonorrhea and Chlamydia: A systematic review of design and measurement factors assessed in epidemiologic studies," *Sexually Transmitted Diseases* 33, no. 1 (2006), 36–51; National Institutes of Health, "Workshop Summary: Scientific Evidence on Condom Effectiveness for Sexually Transmitted Disease Prevention," July 20, 2011 (http://www.niaid.nih.gov/about/organization/dmid/documents/condomreport.pdf).

5. Ibid.

6. P. F. Sparling, M. N. Swartz, D. M. Musher, and B. P. Healy, "Clinical Manifestations of Syphilis," in *Sexually Transmitted Diseases*, ed. Holmes et al., 661–688.

7. Ahmed, Lutalo, and Wawer et al., "HIV Incidence and Sexually Transmitted Disease Prevalence Associated with Condom Use: A Population Study in Rakai, Uganda."

8. S. Moir, T. Chun, F. S. Anthony, "Immunology and Pathogenesis of HIV Infection," in *Sexually Transmitted Diseases*, ed. Holmes et al., 341–58.

9. K. R. Davis and S. C. Weller, "The Effectiveness of Condoms in Reducing Heterosexual Transmission of HIV," *Family Planning Perspectives* 31, no. 6 (1999): 272–79; J. Fitch et al., *Sex, Condoms and STDs*, 5; National Institutes of Health, "Workshop Summary: Scientific Evidence on Condom Effectiveness for Sexually Transmitted Disease Prevention."

10. J. K. Benedetti, J. Zeh, and L. Corey, "Clinical Reactivation of Genital Herpes Simplex Virus Infection Decreases in Frequency over Time," *Annals of Internal Medicine* 131 (1999): 14–20.

11. D. H. Watts, Z. A. Brown, and D. Money et al., "A Double-Blind, Randomized, Placebo-Controlled Trial of Acyclovir in Late Pregnancy for the Reduction of Herpes Simplex Virus Shedding and Cesarean Delivery," *American Journal of Obstetrics and Gynecology* 183 (2003): 836–43.

12. F. Xu, M. R. Sternberg, and S. L. Gottlieb et al., "Seroprevalence of Herpes Simplex Virus Type 2 Among Persons Aged 14–49 Years—United States, 2005–2008," *Morbidity and Mortality Weekly Report* 59, RR15 (2010), 456–59; M. Fatahzadeh and R. A. Schwartz, "Human herpes simplex virus infections: epidemiology, pathogenesis, symptomatology, diagnosis, and management," *Journal of American Academy of Dermatology* 57, no. 5

(2007), 737–63; Centers for Disease Control, "Genital Herpes—Fact Sheet," September 2012 (http://www.cdc.gov/std/herpes/herpes-fact-sheet-sept-2012.pdf).

13. Weinstock, Berman, and Cates, "Sexually Transmitted Diseases among American Youth," 6–10; Centers for Disease Control, "Genital HPV Infection—Fact Sheet," August 2012 (http://www.cdc.gov/std/HPV/HPV-Factsheet-Aug-2012.pdf).

14. B. E. Sirovich and H. G. Welch, "The Frequency of Pap Smear Screening in the United States," *Journal of General Internal Medicine* 19, no. 3 (2004): 243–50.

15. Castellsague, Bosch, and Munoz et al., "Male Circumcision," 1105–12.

16. American Cancer Society, "Cancer Facts & Figures: 2012," (2012), http://www.cancer.org/acs/groups/content/@epidemiologysurveilance/documents/document/acspc-031941.pdf.

17. D. A. Baker, "Hepatitis B Infection in Pregnancy," in *Protocols for Infectious Diseases in Obstetrics and Gynecology*, ed. Mead et al., 208–14 (Malden, MA: Blackwell Science, 2000).

18. F. Sorvillo, L. Smith, and P. Krendt et al., "Trichomonas Vaginalis, HIV, and African-Americans," *Emerging Infectious Diseases* 7, no. 6 (2001): 927–32.

19. Centers for Disease Control, "Sexually Transmitted Diseases Treatment Guidelines—2010," *Morbidity and Mortality Weekly Report* 59, RR12 (2010), 1–110.

20. L. T. F. Yeung, S. M. King, and E. A. Roberts, "Mother-to-Infant Transmission of Hepatitis C Virus," *Hepatology* 34 (2001): 223–229.

21. M. J. Silverberg, L. Grant, and A. Munoz et al., "The Impact of HIV Infection and Immunodeficiency on Human Papillomavirus Type 6 or 11 Infection and on Genital Warts," *Sexually Transmitted Diseases* 29 (2002): 427.

22. S. A. Kohlhoff and M. R. Hammerschlag, "Gonococcal and Chlamydial Infections in Infants and Children," *Sexually Transmitted Diseases*, ed. Holmes et al., 1613–27.

23. US National Library of Medicine, "Neonatal Conjunctivitis," (June 2012), http://www.nlm.nih.gov/medlineplus/ency/article/001606.htm.

24. S. G. Pinninti and R. W. Tolan, "Pediatric Herpes Simplex Virus Infection Clinical Presentation," (March 2012), http://emedicine.medscape.com/article/964866-clinical

25. A. R. Lifson and P. M. O'Malley et al., "HIV Seroconversion in Two Homosexual Men after Receptive Oral Intercourse with Ejaculation: Implications for Counseling Safe Sexual Practices," *American Journal of Public Health* 81 (1991): 1509–11.

26. Ahmed, Lutalo, and Waver et al., "HIV Incidence and Sexually Transmitted Disease Prevalence Associated with Condom Use," 2171–79; J. Fitch and others, *Sex, Condoms and STDs*, 5; National Institutes of Health, "Workshop Summary: Scientific Evidence on Condom Effectiveness for Sexually Transmitted Disease Prevention"; J. Fitch et al., "Condom Effectiveness: Factors That Influence Risk Reduction," *Sexually Transmitted Diseases* 29, no. 12 (2002): 811–17.

27. National Institutes of Health, "Workshop Summary: Scientific Evidence on Condom Effectiveness for Sexually Transmitted Disease Prevention," July 20, 2001 (http://www.niaid.nih.gov/about/organization/dmid/documents/condomreport.pdf).

28. R. Platt et al., "Risk of Acquiring Gonorrhea and Prevalence of Abnormal Adnexal Findings among Women Recently Exposed to Gonorrhea," *Journal of the American Medical Association* 250, no. 23 (1983): 3205–9.

29. J. Mann, C. Stine, and J. Vessey, "The Role for Disease-Specific Infectivity and Number of Disease Exposures on Long-Term Effectiveness of the Latex Condom," *Sexually Transmitted AppendixDiseases* 29, no. 6 (2002): 344–49; Centers for Disease Control; "Sexually Transmitted Diseases Treatment Guidelines—2002," *Morbidity and Mortality Weekly Report* 51, RR06 (2002): 1–80.

30. Fitch et al, "Condom Effectiveness."

Appendix B: What You Need to Know about Contraceptives

1. R. A. Hatcher, J. Trussel, et al, *Contraceptive Technology*, Twentieth Revised Edition.

2. Ibid.

3. J. Fitch and others, Sex, Condoms and STDs, 5; Ahmed, Lutalo, and Waver et al., "HIV Incidence and Sexually Transmitted Disease Prevalence Associated with Condom Use," 2171–79.

4. Hatcher and Trussel, *Contraceptive Technology*, Twentieth Revised Edition.

5. Ibid.

6. Ibid.

7. Ibid.

8. Ibid.

9. Ibid.

INDEX